To Edd, Niki and Doil / you will read about it there in the term if there much on 1 love So / much [?] Aunt Sis

Becoming Myself

A Passage of Grace

BY SARA F. MUNDAY

RoseDog❖Books

PITTSBURGH, PENNSYLVANIA 15222

ISBN: 978-1-4349-9744-9

Printed in the United States of America

First Printing

For more information or to order additional books, please contact:
RoseDog Books
701 Smithfield Street
Pittsburgh, Pennsylvania 15222
U.S.A.
1-800-834-1803
www.rosedogbookstore.com

"The events in our lives
happen in a sequence in time,
but in their significance to ourselves
find their own order...
the continuous thread of revelation."

Eudora Welty

Dedication

I lovingly dedicate this book to:

Generations past in whom I am rooted;

Gerald, my husband, whose love, support, and inspiration
have encouraged me
to tell my story;

Our children
Lynn
Mark
Mike
who bring meaning to my life;

Our grandchildren and great-grandchildren,
who may someday read these stories
and wonder,
"Is this how it really was?"

Acknowledgments

I am deeply indebted and grateful

to Sue Wagstaff, for beginning a small group
of fledgling writers desiring to leave their life stories as a legacy
for their children;

to John Neel and Annice Webb,
for carefully reading, editing, making suggestions, and encouraging me
to bring these stories together in book form;

to Wrenn Weston, my sister,
for listening (by phone) to each story,
and remembering with me the times about which I have written;

for the nurture, love, and inspiration
of every person about whom I have written, for
they are the folk who stretched and grew me into
MYSELF.

TABLE OF CONTENTS

Preface

She was an old lady—well into her nineties. As she reflected upon her life while at the same time admitting to her rich old age, she used to say, "The older I get, the more like myself I become." With each passing day, I become more convinced that her statement reflects profound wisdom.

From the birth cry to the last breath, life is an ever-flowing metamorphosis. The stories in this book constitute a sketchy account of just such a process. They have been my transportation to times and places long since past. They have allowed me to renew precious relationships with special people. Some became so real as I wrote that I became homesick for the presence, the touch, the smiles of folks who were a part of the village that grew me.

In writing about my roots, my birth, my childhood, my school days, I have stumbled upon the stuff from which I came, and it is good. As I wrote, I remembered how painfully shy and insecure I was both as a child and as an adolescent; I relived our courtship, marriage, the birth of each of our three children; where we lived; the people who became a living, breathing part of our lives; the work we have done; the painful agony of losses, deaths, and separations. During my trips to other times and places, I have uncovered an unseen transformational process that began years ago and is taking place in me to this very moment. Many of my childish fears and insecurities have slipped away. I do not always give in now when I am pressured to conform. I have finally learned and am convinced that I am a unique creation of God, Who made the heavens and the earth, and therefore, I am a person of worth. This newly found freedom and honesty feel good.

These stories uncovered my yearnings for those dusty roads; the kerosene lamps that needed to be filled and their chimneys that needed cleaning; the pear tree in the front yard; the small basins in which we bathed; the bus rides to school; picking violets in the spring; and the creativity to know how to gracefully do without what

1

we did not have.

Love, joy, fear, disappointment, sorrow, loss, loneliness, embarrassment, respect, admiration—so many emotions overwhelmed me as I wrote. I have always been aware of the Profound Presence that directed me—on occasions propelled me—to this very moment. Telling my stories has brought me face to face with a simple (though normal) process: the process of growing up...the process of growing old...the process of *becoming myself.*

Cherished Trips

A page in my Baby Record Book is entitled "First Outing," and print-ed there is a four-line rhyme that reads as follows:

Gracious—what a world this is—
And oh—what lovely skies!
So big—and I can see it all
With just my little eyes.

In Mother's handwriting is the date "Dec. 27, 1930." On a second line, she added, "Sunday—spent at Mrs. Richardson's." That means that I was one month and seven days old when I went on my first trip, which may explain why I do not remember much about the occasion.

Mother told me that when I was about a year old, Daddy decided to take me to Emelle (pronounced "M.L."). She dressed me in a frilly white dress, and I was "adorable." Daddy had on white trousers. Upon arriving at the country store, Daddy promptly bought me a stick of peppermint candy. Both of us were a complete mess upon our return—still wearing our whites, but streaked with peppermint!

Traveling to visit with my father's family or my maternal grand-mother's family were day trips over country roads that could not be traveled when they were wet, so the weather was always the deter-mining factor in those trips. Though things and times are different now, today's children still ask the same questions that we asked over and over on every trip: "How much farther?" or "How much longer till we get there?" Distances were not that long in actual miles when I was a child, but cars were not as sleek and speedy then, and roads were not conducive to rapid travel, so day trips always seemed long.

However, there were other trips that we did not take in cars: trips about which we dreamed; trips that could bring a thrill or break a heart. They were those strolls that we took "down the drive" or "up to the top of the hill" when we played "Pleased or Displeased." The church youth enjoyed monthly "socials" that took place in different

3

homes in our community, and all the neighborhood children came. The parties were all different: maybe a hayride or a dance, or an ice cream social where there were several kinds of ice cream made in freezers cranked by hand. There were no electric freezers!

One of our favorite parties was a moonlight picnic. As the name implies, it was always planned for a moonlit night—preferably when the moon was full. Tables of picnic foods and drinks were placed outside, and chairs were arranged nearby on the lawn. There was an obvious advantage to this type of arrangement other than just being a romantic setting. None of the homes were air-conditioned, and even though it was not cool outside, it was better than having a crowd of young people inside. Preparation for a moonlit evening was a lot of work, but a committee of the youth helped the hostess with setup and cleanup details.

On those special evenings, we played a variety of games such as Gossip, Cross Questions and Crooked Answers, and others, but the game we liked best of all was Pleased or Displeased. One person was "It," and it was his or her duty to go from one person to the next, asking, "Pleased or displeased?" If the person being asked the question responded, "Pleased," then "It" passed to the next person and asked the same question. But if the answer was "Displeased," the person who was "It" would ask, "What will it take to please you?" The respondent would single out a couple who really "liked" each other, and say that he or she would like for them to walk to the mailbox (or up the hill, or to the road) holding hands. Of course the game participant expected the same kind of favor for themselves from the person they had sent for a walk. At times the crowd grew very small because almost everybody was walking…somewhere.

Those were the days when puppy love was alive and well. Hearts bursting with adoration for that special someone were "for sure and for certain" that their feelings were real love and would last forever. As a couple left the group in order to "please" the person sending them, they shyly joined hands and disappeared into the moonlit night. They shared a lot of conversation on the way and back, and most of the time a kiss or two was stolen in the light of the full moon—or better still, in the shadow cast by a large oak tree. Those summer nights were sultry and humid, and our hair, which had taken hours to curl, as well as our beautifully starched and ironed dresses, quickly drooped. Most of us left the party in love, and as we drifted off to sleep that night, it was with thoughts of our sweethearts. Those feelings of love were much too personal to share with anyone—unless it was our best friend, with whom we would trust our life.

In later years, Gerald and I have had some wonderful trips: to Maine; to Guatemala; to Colorado and Arizona; following the Lewis and Clark Trail to Oregon and the West Coast. There is, however, another trip that I enjoy. I take it often and I am always eager to start. That trip affords me the grand opportunity to travel down Memory Lane. I love to recall sitting on the front porch every night in the summer, or playing hopscotch, jacks, or Mother, May I?; looking for four-leaf clovers during lunchtime at school; climbing trees; writing love notes and having my friend deliver them to "the object of my affection"; taking my lunch to school in a brown paper bag and sometimes having "smushed" sandwiches; paper chains and angel hair on the Christmas tree; dancing close to my steady boyfriend and wearing his class ring with an inch of adhesive tape wrapped around it to make it fit my finger. It takes little to no preparation for a trip down Memory Lane, and I can stay as long as I like. I can choose my companions and change them as often as I wish. This trip costs nothing at all, and I recommend it highly to anyone seeking a pleasant distraction and hours of fun. There is, however, one requirement: Travelers must defy and slip the bonds of responsibility and reality— take a deep breath and jump smack-dab into the middle of that special time and place where with pure delight they sigh and whisper, "Yeah, I remember that!"

Pools of Water

"In the beginning God created…" and from that time, water has been accompanied by dramatically impressive moods such as peace, quiet, calm, rage, anger, playfulness—and each of those moods is capable in its own right of demanding complete and rapt attention from those who observe. From early childhood, water has had a spiritual significance for me. Many scriptural references are made to water. I often heard many of those Scriptures as a child when we came together nightly for family prayers. Mother always read a passage from the Bible, after which we knelt beside our chairs while Mother prayed, thanking God for our numerous blessings of that day and asking rest and safety throughout the night.

It is a scientific fact that man's survival is dependent upon water; however, as with other things, we have taken water for granted. We have often wasted it, never thinking about nor recognizing the value, necessity, and sanctity of it.

The area of Alabama where I grew up is known as the Black Belt. This is a strip of land that stretches from eastern Mississippi across central Alabama and into Georgia, and the term Black Belt is a reference to the black, fertile soil. The acres that made up our farm were fertile and produced good crops; however, those acres were not graced by meandering streams or springs that bubbled cool and clear from somewhere deep within the earth. Several artesian wells within the area flowed constantly, but the water usually had a heavy mineral taste accompanied by an odor.

As children we loved visiting Grannie's brothers and sister, who lived in Mississippi on the farm that had belonged to their father. A lovely creek flowed through the barnyard located just behind the house. We looked for reasons to walk out on the handmade bridge spanning that beautiful stream as it ran playfully over the rocks scattered about its sandy bottom. My uncles had piled flat stones across the creek to form a dam, carefully leaving a spillway on one side.

6

Standing on the bridge, we lowered the bucket tied to the end of the rope. With just the proper jerk, we turned the bucket on its side, allowed it to fill with water, and drew it up to the bridge. Water from the creek was used for washing dishes, laundry, bathing, and watering the flowers. Sometimes we were allowed to wade in the water below the dam—never above, because activity of that nature stirred the silt and sand and caused the water to become muddy. We carefully watched for snakes that sunned on the flat rocks or took refuge from the heat in the cool waters.

The family's drinking water was a bit harder to come by. In front of the house, across the railroad track, and about a half mile into the woods was a spring that flowed continuously, the source of wonderfully sweet, cold water. The way to the spring was across the railroad track and through the woods. A gap (actually an opening or a breach in the fence) allowed passage through the fence. A path worn smooth by many trips back and forth was easily discernable even to anyone who had not made the trip previously. Uncle Tom and Uncle Dee had cleaned around the place where water bubbled cool and clear from the ground. Carefully laying rocks around the edges and along the bottom of the spring, they formed a firm, clean place where the water pooled, making it easier to dip the water out with a cup or bucket. The nearby earth and rocks were abundantly covered with soft, verdant moss, and the dense foliage on giant trees refused to allow even one ray of sunshine to penetrate. The coolness beneath those heavy branches offered respite to all who came with buckets to fetch water for the Roberts household. Many years later, after the two brothers and their sister had died, I returned to that place and found the spring covered over with leaves. Stones that had once surrounded the spring and served as walls to collect the water were scattered and fallen away— perhaps moved by some thirsty animal's foot as it sought to drink. I used a small branch that had earlier fallen from a tree and become a part of the landscape to dig into the soft earth as I pulled the debris away from the place that I had known and loved as a child. Though in a state of disrepair and obvious neglect, water still flowed cool and sweet from the spring, providing moisture for the lush vegetation that grew in such abundance around it.

My own family's drinking water came from a cistern dug in the 1840s, when our house was built. A cistern was a big jug-shaped hole dug in the ground and lined with brick for the express purpose of holding water. There was no spring bubbling from the earth, nor was there any seepage from the water table located far below the bottom of the cistern. A system of gutters caught and directed rainwater from the roof into the cistern, and though there were periods of drought that limited the amount of water left in the cistern, we were never without. There were occasions when people who lived near us were forced to haul water, but according to my grandmother, our cistern had never gone dry.

Periodically, it was necessary to clean the cistern, and in order to drain this jug-like reservoir, tenant farmers drew the water in buckets fastened to the end of a chain and then emptied it onto the ground. It was a large amount of water, according to Grannie: "Enough to run down the hill and all the way to the road." Most likely the best description of the size and shape of the cistern came from an elderly black man who went into the depths to clean it. The neck to the cistern was fifteen to twenty feet deep, and the jug part was said to be like a room big enough "to turn a team of mules and a wagon around."

As tenant houses were built, Granddaddy Burton dug cisterns for the farmers who lived on his plantation. A number of these reservoirs dotted the farm. Today some of them still hold water. These cisterns provided water for family use; however, there was need for even more water, since there were cattle, pigs, mules, and horses that required it. Large lakes and ponds were not as common then as they are today. At that time there were no earth-moving machines that could construct dams capable of holding several acres of water behind them. Small earthen dams were built by men using handheld scrapers pulled by mules. When a pool needed to be cleaned out, it was done by the same method. It was killing labor.

Small manmade dams were strategically placed across narrow valleys bordered on both sides by small hills. This formed a basin into which rainwater and runoff were collected and held. My grandfather built many of these small cup-like pools in order to provide adequate water for the animals. Because the area surrounding the pools was moist, it was a perfect place for willow trees to grow, and since the pools were surrounded by shade, they appeared cool, even on a hot day. On the days when the heat seemed unbearable, cows made their way to the water's edge, waded in until it almost covered their backs, and then stood there. Being nearly submerged in the water also gave them protection from the flies that came in swarms during the summer.

Often on summer afternoons, children and elderly black people with cane poles fished for small minnows that resided in the waters of those little pools. Nobody knew exactly where those little fish came from; maybe eggs had been brought on the feet of birds that had visited another area pool. Water levels dropped significantly in late summer after too little rainfall. The sun's scorching rays relentlessly drew water droplets throughout the hot season, and thirsty cattle drank deeply from the pools' depths all summer. The changes occurring during drought times were obvious: dry, cracked, parched earth edged the water where earlier there had been lush green grass. When the fall rains came, the little pools filled again, becoming the oases they had been before. On the colder days of late autumn or early winter, ducks sometimes took refuge on the waters of those small pools as they rested from their long flight further south.

I never knew my grandfather. He died four years before I was born, but there are times when I get a glimpse of the person he must have been. I believe that John Wesley Burton was a good man, a gentle man, a man who knew God, and purposefully worked to protect and nurture His creation. While he came from humble beginnings, he was somehow able to amass a respectable amount of earthly wealth. He provided well for his family and saw after the welfare of his tenant farmers. He was a good neighbor, helping those in the community who were in need. He believed in justice and fair play. A licensed local preacher in the Methodist Church, he preached somewhere every Sunday—sometimes to black congregations. He never accepted any recompense for his services.

When I think of the life of my grandfather, when I walk across the fields of which he was the steward for a while, when I observe the provisions for water (pools, wells, and cisterns) that he made for man and beast, I am convinced that he was wise, frugal, and keenly sensitive to the fact that God had entrusted him to be the keeper of a portion of His great creation. I am convinced that he was a man after God's own heart, and he followed closely the admonitions of his Creator.

"Drink waters out of thine own cistern, and running water out of thine own well" (Prov. 5:15).

Verses 4 and 5 of the 84th Psalm describe this man who is my ancestor, my blood relative, this man who is my spiritual mentor even though he remains unseen:

"Blessed is the man whose strength is in thee; in whose heart are the ways of them. Who passing through the valley of tears make it a well; the rain also filleth the pools."

Rev. John Wesley and Sallie Roberts Burton,
my maternal grandparents

One of a Kind

How profoundly exquisite are the ancient words of the Psalmist who said, "When I consider thy heavens, the work of thy fingers, the moon and the stars, which thou hast ordained, what is man? A little lower than the angels, and crowned with honor and glory" (Ps. 8:3–5). The vastness, the beauty, and the mystery of man's worth and posture in the universe each call for more perception and insight than I am capable of mustering.

We learned at an early age that everything in creation has its own uniqueness. Teachers told us that every single snowflake is different—individual. One snowstorm was reason enough to cause us to scratch our heads in amazement, to make us question how it could possibly be that every flake was unique. Could it possibly be so? Mrs. Seale, who taught civics and history in high school, pushed her students to begin thinking that we were special—unique—and that "difference" was not bad. Maybe that was her effort to correct what she clearly recognized as our herd mentality, for without exception, we wanted to *do*, to *be*, to *go*—because "everybody else was."

What a grand privilege has been mine through the years to encounter so many people, and each person so different in his or her own right. Race, faith, nationalities, economic status, backgrounds, and dreams and hopes possessed and held dear by each individual are all contributing factors to the total person and who they became. Perhaps it is the differences in each of us that are the basis for our personal likes and dislikes of other individuals.

Some people have absolutely no appeal, and others must "grow on us," while there are still others who capture and keep our attention as well as our affection from the moment we meet. Sometimes years pass before we realize the worth and impact these special individuals have made upon us. My maternal grandmother was such a person. She was different, cut from a different pattern—one of a kind. Though she died in 1964, and though I am now in my mid-seventies, my sister, two brothers, and I frequently recall what Grannie said or did when we were children.

On September 25, 1875, Sallie Lillian Roberts was born to a poor Mississippi farm couple. She was the second child of seven born to John James Roberts and Sarah Elizabeth Selby Roberts. As a child, she learned how to make lye soap and how to wash clothes with water brought from the creek or the spring. She milked cows, fed chickens, gathered eggs, and worked in the garden and fields. She learned how to cook and preserve fruits and vegetables, and how to care for the five children younger than she. Since the log homestead was very small, those siblings grew up in close proximity to each other; still, Sallie was likely the most private person I have ever known, as was evidenced by her continuous shock at the lack of "modesty" in younger generations.

Entering school at the age of six, she completed all seven grades. That was all that was available to her. We never tired of her stories of how all grades learned spelling, multiplication tables, and reading from the McGuffie Reader, the Blue Back Speller, and the Bible in one room. Children stood in a line for spelling. If a child misspelled a word, he or she was sent to "the foot of the line." The schoolmaster or schoolmarm was the final authority in matters of discipline. The old proverb of "spare the rod and spoil the child" was firmly believed and practiced. Grannie never failed to add that if any one of them got a whipping at school, they knew they would expect the same from their parents upon coming home. According to her, there were no discipline problems among her siblings. They were "taught better."

Children of the 1880s, like children of all generations, looked forward to recess and dinnertime. Lunches usually consisted of a freshly baked biscuit with cane syrup poured into it. Some days there might be a piece of ham or pork sausage, or possibly even a baked sweet potato. Of course, there were no grand playgrounds with see-saws and slides. Instead, children played running games or hide-and-go-seek. We loved to hear over and over how the girls slipped into the edge of the woods at recess or lunchtime and broke grapevines from the trees and ran them inside the hems of their dresses. The stiffness from the vines caused their dresses to stand out like hoopskirts. Grannie always smiled as she told how they bumped against each other while they stood in line for spelling, causing their skirts to move gracefully back and forth.

My sister Wrenn and I were both blessed with good, thick, but very straight hair. Grannie used to roll it up for us on paper or rags, and she always managed to make the curls so tight that our scalps became sore. In the process, she recalled that she and her sisters rolled their hair by the same method, except on those occasions when they wanted their hair to be curlier or if the curl needed to stay in for a longer time; then they used sugar water to dampen their hair before they rolled it. Wrenn and I wondered if honeybees found their heads more attractive when they used sugar. Grannie had thick hair that she pulled to the back of her head into a bun. She allowed the front to be loose enough to fall into soft waves about her face. She was a very attractive lady.

Though Sallie Lillian Roberts's beginning was modest, and her education limited, her former teacher, Rev. John Wesley Burton, returned to Mississippi to claim her as his bride when she was thirty-one years of age. Rev. Burton was fifty-six years old. He had been married, and his wife had died. His lovely two-story house in Alabama was already furnished, but a woman needed to be there. Sallie left her family and home in Mississippi and moved to that large plantation in Alabama. She gave birth during the first year of their marriage to their one child, Margaret Elizabeth—my mother. Grannie almost lost her life at that time, and surgery was required later because of damage done during the birth.

This new bride already knew the fine arts of keeping house, cooking, sewing, and raising chickens, and she quickly learned the business of "Mr. Burton's" two general mercantile stores, as well as the operation of the twenty-five hundred-acre plantation. Grannie always referred to her husband as "Mr. Burton," which I suppose was a carry-over from school days when he was her schoolmaster. He likewise had a chosen name for her: he called her "Ole 'oman," southern vernacular for "Old Woman."

After the death of her husband in 1926, Grannie continued to manage the plantation for many years. She was a capable woman, highly respected by those who knew her, and spoken of as being a "dignified lady." She never thought of herself in those terms; rather, I think she considered herself to be a person of integrity, "morally upright," honest, trustworthy, and one who took advantage of each opportunity that came her way. Her brothers and sisters loved and depended upon her; and she was always generous to them with gifts of food, clothing, and money.

This child of poor Mississippi farm parents was a proud woman. Her posture was flawless, even into her old age. Her vanity sometimes conflicted with her early religious upbringing. She believed that make-up was an indication of "worldliness," although a bit of face powder was permissible. Rouge and eye shadow only tended to cheapen a lady's appearance, she said. My sister and I knew, however, that Grannie often lit a match and extinguished it, leaving one end of it charred. When the match cooled, she carefully dampened the burned wood with her tongue and darkened her eyebrows. She also had a small red wooden ball that had once been a part of a toy. It was kept on Grannie's dresser, and when licked, added a bit of color to her lips. Now mind you, this addition of color was never spoken about. We learned at an early age that there were things that must be kept secret—like the bottle of wine hidden among the quilts in the quilt closet to be used when Grannie had a "sinking spell." But the biggest secret of all was the Color Back.

Color Back was a product advertised to keep people's hair its original color, thus maintaining the coveted appearance of youth. Such results would, of course, relieve the anxiety of fading hair color that would draw attention to the onset of old age. Grannie never told her age. She became furious when asked because she considered age a personal matter. She made every effort to keep her hair "young" as long as she could, and using Color Back was a part of the process. It was quietly purchased through a local merchant who ordered it by the case. Grannie thought her transaction was completely secret. She hid the product beneath clothes in the wardrobe along with the small dish for the daily application. But to Grannie's great dismay, her secret was somehow discovered.

Oscar Richardson, known to the community folk as "Sonny Boy," was a Marine in the Pacific theater during World War II. He was a great teaser, and he especially enjoyed teasing Grannie. One year he drew Miss Sallie Burton's name for the community Christmas gift exchange, and what to her wondering eyes should appear, but a bottle of Color Back. The secret was out! Grannie was furious, and never quite recovered. She never liked Sonny Boy as much again, either!

Grannie was a fearful person. She worried that too much rain would ruin the crops, or that dry weather would burn them up. She was terrified that fire might someday destroy our home or the barns. She was afraid of people she knew and those she did not. There was also an underlying fear that someone was going to break into the house and do us harm.

On the other hand, she loved her family beyond anything, and her every waking moment was spent planning and caring for them. She was always present for recitals, school programs, and church activities when we were involved. Her support was not limited to our family's physical and financial need, for she frequently called one of the black tenant farmers as they walked past our house on the dirt road. She wanted to either feed them a meal that was eaten on the kitchen porch or give them food to take home with them. She was a generous person.

Grannie felt a bit inferior because of her lack of book learning. She sometimes was silent in crowds because she did not want people to know that she was limited educationally. In her mind, it was better to "remain silent and be thought a fool than to speak and remove all doubt." Though she was not well educated formally, she never had any difficulty making the person to whom she spoke understand exactly what she was saying.

For example, her descriptions were brilliant, always unique, and sometimes profound. She described a dreadful-looking person as being "as ugly as a mud fence daubed with misery." A person was seldom "poor"; to Grannie, he was as "poor as Job's turkey." A woman was not pregnant out of wedlock; rather, "she fell through the bridge and broke her leg." A bra was a "breast girdle." One of her most graphic phrases was what she called our paternal grandmother: "Old Sunk Rump." That name was descriptive because Grandma Fuller's posture was not good. She walked with her shoulders a bit stooped as if she were very tired, and the lower half of her body usually preceded the top half. A large person was "big as a 'skint' [skinned] mule," while a thin person was "a string bean." Someone without morals or scruples was "sorry as gully dirt." When a large meal was voraciously consumed, the one who ate had "eaten like a wage-hand." Huge or tremendous was "big as all out-of-doors." She disallowed the old saying "Ignorance is bliss" by countering with "If that were so, I would be a solid blister!" When someone made a statement that could be considered degrading, condescending, or contradictory, Grannie tossed her head, assumed a lofty air, and said, "When I hear nothing, I notice nothing!"

Remembering this wonderfully complex person, I am persuaded that she has bled into many areas of who I am. Though some things were inconsistent in her life, there were many elements that were dead center—core elements that made hers a strong and remarkable life. She was consistently attentive and sensitive to things that went unnoticed by others, and this made her unique. Her letters to me while I was away in college told me which flowers were blooming, how much rain had fallen, whether the hens were laying enough eggs for the family's use. My life today reflects much of who she was and what she taught. My prayerful hope is that somehow in the Great Beyond, she will know of my deep, deep love and appreciation for her and for her relentless insistence that I "hitch my wagon to a star!"

Can You Hear Me Now?

Cell phones burst upon the scene and broke into the market as a smashing success. Television screens continue to be generously sprinkled with ads promoting countless programs of competing providers. One company's TV salesman convincingly informs consumers of his product's efficiency under any circumstance. He quickly moves from place to place while asking, "Can you hear me now?"

It would appear to a casual observer that cell phones have reached a saturation point in today's market. They are purchased and used by diverse consumers, young and old, all races and nationalities, educated and not so educated, male and female, by those who can afford them as well as those who have no visible source of income. Users are not limited to any specific group, profession, or occupation, for each user has his or her own compelling reasons and needs that necessitate ownership and use of the cell phone.

Today's easy access and wide availability of cell phones remind me that there was no phone of any kind in my home until I went away to college. I was near seventy when I first had my own cell phone. When I think of the phones that were available in my younger years, I am quickly reminded that there was a significant evolutionary process from the phone invented by Alexander Graham Bell in 1876 to today's models with their choices of multiple features.

Though we had no phone in our home, our neighbors, Nannie and Travis Wooldridge, were fortunate enough to live at the end of the line where phones were available. They lived just a short distance from us on the hill to the west of our house. Nannie was actually related to us, and we used their phone as needed; however, we were careful never to take advantage of her kindness. Besides, Nannie loved to know what was going on, especially among the "younger set." She was actually known in the community as something of a gossip, so when we went to use the phone at her house, she listened attentively to our end of the conversation. She would then insist that we sit and talk awhile. Without fail, she questioned us extensively regarding our phone conversation, or anything else about which she was curious; consequently, her coffer was filled to the brim with new and interesting facts to be shared the next time she went to have a Coke at the country store in Emelle.

It was in the mid-1940s, and World War II was just ending. Our country was on its way to financial recovery and better times. Americans, particularly people who lived in the country, were anticipating more and better services such as indoor plumbing, electricity, and telephones, so every new convenience was anticipated with great joy. At long last, the telephone was coming to Emelle. It did not take long, however, for the folks in and around our community to become aware that they were involved in an evolutionary process through which this wonderful instrument of communication was destined to go.

The phone system when activated in our community was an experimental one. This was explained to subscribers, who paid it little mind. They were too overjoyed with the long-anticipated convenience that this service would provide. The new experimental system was designed to utilize the electric power lines that were already in place. The phone unit itself contained and operated off of a number of tubes. There actually was no way to predict the strange and interesting things that would result from this trial arrangement. Even though we had no phone in our home, we were able to tune our radio sets to a certain frequency and listen to the conversations of our neighbors. By the time it was learned that private conversations were being broadcast over the radio, it was too late: news of numerous conversations was already public. And to further complicate matters, there were eight subscribers on each party line, making it possible to pick up the phone and covertly listen to the conversation of others. Only one of the eight parties could use the phone at a time, and sometimes the wait to use the phone was unbearably long. There were times when the wait was so long that individuals could get into cars, drive to the home or the business of the person to whom they wished to speak, take care of their business face-to-face, and return home before their long-winded party line member was done talking!

I am not certain when the experimental system was recognized as a less than successful idea and stopped. What I do know is that my mother lived with, and paid for, a telephone that was considered to be less than satisfactory for a number of years. During one of our visits home, I learned that Mother was concerned (maybe even a little fearful) because she had been receiving telephone calls from someone who refused to speak or give their identity. She did not know if the caller was some perverted, evil person calling to frighten her, or if they had some other mischief in mind. I do not know where the idea came from, but I suggested that she place a Bible near the phone, and when the person called again, that she read a passage from the Scripture. Mother decided to do that. That plan must have provided at least some sense of peace, because the problem was not mentioned as often as before.

Some time later, we were in the country store at Emelle, where people met on sultry summer afternoons to enjoy a cold Coca-Cola. Several people were there, one of whom was Miss Mattie Stegall. At some point in the conversation, Miss Mattie laughed and said, "If you don't want to get the Bible read to you, you better not call Bessie's house. She just reads and reads and reads." It was then time for Mother to tell her story. She was so relieved that some "sick" individual had not targeted her, and Miss Mattie was happy to learn that my mother did not feel that she was in a dire state of sin and needed to be consciously brought face to face with the teachings of God.

The community honored Mother in 1993 for her seventy-five years of faithfulness as the church pianist. Not only did she play each week for Sunday school, church, evening worship, and revivals, but she also played for weddings, funerals, homecomings, and any other event to which she was invited, and sometimes she didn't wait for an invitation; she volunteered. Gerald Munday, her son-in-law, preached a wonderful sermon on "Remembering" for her special day. Miss Frances Mellen, my beloved piano teacher, accompanied us four siblings as we sang in four-part harmony:

> "Precious memories, how they linger;
> How they ever flood my soul.
> In the stillness of the midnight
> Precious, sacred scenes unfold."

Various community people spoke with loving appreciation of all that Mother had meant to the church and the community, as well as to adjoining communities. It was her day! She was truly honored! When the last person had spoken, it became Mother's time to respond. That small, demure, white-haired lady got to her feet and said:

> "If you think some praise is due me,
> Now's the time to shove it to me.
> I can't read my tombstone
> When I'm dead."

The capacity crowd in that little church broke into uproarious laughter. When some semblance of order was restored, Mother graciously thanked the congregation for their love and support through the years.

I was intrigued that day by a story told by Mr. Fred Stegall. He recalled days that he and Mother shared as children. He expressed his personal gratitude, as well as that of his family, for my grandfather, John Wesley Burton. He told how his father, James Solomon Stegall, had moved his very young family from Pontotoc, Mississippi, to Emelle in the early 1900s. My grandfather employed him as a clerk, and later set him up in his own store with a stock of goods. Mr. Fred reported that the Stegall family was truly grateful for that start in life.

(I interrupt the story here in order to express my own gratitude to Mr. Stegall's daughter, Miss Louise Lang, for hiring me to work as a clerk in that same store two generations later. Her daughter, Aileen, has remained one of my dearest friends through the years.)

Mr. Fred continued to extol the good qualities of my grandfather, finally telling a story that I had never heard even from my own family. According to Mr. Fred's story and information gathered from various other sources, my grandfather's first wife died in 1904. In 1906, he married Sallie Lillian Roberts from Kemper County, Mississippi, though he was twenty-five years her senior. Grannie was thirty-one years old when they married and had never been away from home. After the wedding she became very homesick. My grandfather was considered to be a wealthy man in his day, so in his concern for the happiness of his new bride, he set out to see that her homesickness would be cured as quickly as possible. He secured and put up poles upon which he later strung telephone wire all the way from their home in Alabama to the Roberts home in Mississippi, which was about twenty-five miles away. It was then possible for Grannie to talk with members of her family every day.

Building a phone line of such length was a monumental task. It followed the dirt road that crossed the prairie land west of Emelle and went through what we knew as the "Flatwoods," but that road could be used only in dry weather. The soil throughout that area was known as post-oak clay, and it became very sticky and heavy when it was wet. It was common knowledge that if a car became mired in it, it took a team of mules or horses to pull it from the mud-hole. In some of the worst places along the road, someone had cut saplings (small trees) and laid them side-by-side from one side of the road to the other. That was a method used to keep the roadbed from cutting down into deep ruts. Those strips of road were known as corduroy roads; and though wet places were made much better, the road was extremely rough when it became dry, and it felt as though your teeth were being jarred right out of your head as the car bounced along over it. This was the route we traveled as small children when we went to visit Grannie's brothers and sisters, who still lived in and around the old home place. We never went along that road if there was even a possibility of rain or if there had been rain in the past several days. A trip through the Flatwoods was long and challenging—almost unfriendly. Since the road was not heavily trafficked, many wild animals, birds, and snakes inhabited the woods and fields. Wildflowers bloomed profusely, especially wild phlox, which were known to us as "sweet Williams." Building a telephone line through those woods and along that route must certainly have been a daunting and rigorous task!

During our childhood, we played with those wonderful old telephones that had hung on the walls of our house and the store so many years before. The crank on the side was turned to ring up the person to whom you wished to speak, and the mouthpiece into which the caller spoke was located on the front of the wooden box. It was the best of that day! I suspect there were times when static caused considerable interference, making communications near impossible. Maybe the carefully strung lines were even blown down by strong winds. And there was absolutely no doubt that it was a good practice to stay off the phone during a thunderstorm. Yet even with all the negatives, the family could in no way diminish the great wonder of being able to ring up a party at another location to share news or simply to talk, even though it probably was necessary to frequently ask, "Can you hear me now?"

Margaret Elizabeth Burton Fuller, my mother

My Mother, "Miss" Bessie

Margaret Elizabeth Burton, my mother, was born on July 20, 1907 in Emelle, Alabama, to Rev. John Wesley Burton and Sallie Lillian Roberts Burton. She was born at home, as were most babies during that time. Her mother had complications during and following the birth, which later required surgery. Years later, when Sallie, my grandmother, told of those painful events, it was my suspicion that following her recovery, she decided then and there that there would be no more babies if she had to be a part of it.

The child, who quickly became known as Bessie, grew up in a home where she had everything that she needed and more. It is my opinion that my grandfather did not want his daughter to grow up as an only child. He was a deeply Christian man who took the Scriptures as literally as was humanly possible. For example, he believed in "caring for the widows and the orphans." So when he heard through the Methodist Children's home about a family in East Alabama whose children were being placed for adoption, he was impressed that he must look into the matter. I believe that when he learned of the breakup of that family unit, he received the news as God's call upon his life, and this became an occasion to care for "one of the least of these." Granddaddy went by train to Tuskegee, Alabama, to "adopt" one of the children. I do not know if the adoption process was legal by today's standards, but I do know that this girl, who was about nine years old, the same age as Bessie, came into the Burton home as Eleanor *Burton*, the name by which she became known.

The two girls played together as sisters, went to school together, took music lessons together, went to college together, wore each other's clothes, and went to parties together. They really became sisters, and biology had nothing to do with it. Bessie and Eleanor were treated equally in every way. Upon finishing the two years of college at State Normal School in Livingston, Alabama, Aunt Eleanor found employment in Atlanta. Mother went to Huntingdon College in

Montgomery.

Soon after Mother went away to school, her father became ill and died. Mother dropped out of college and moved back home because Grannie refused to live alone. This was the first of a number of important decisions in her life about which I cannot keep from thinking, If only... Mother was a bright young woman, and I grieve that she felt constrained to sacrifice her opportunity to complete her education to become a teacher or a nurse or...or...or...instead of allowing her life to become secondary to the requirements placed on her by another: her mother.

Mother met and married my father, Ed Fuller, two years after Granddaddy's death. The couple moved into the large farmhouse with Grannie because the same pressure of Grannie's living alone again became the focal point. The newlyweds built an additional room, porch, and small bathroom (with no bathroom fixtures) onto the already large house. It was not a house of their own, but in a real sense, it was their space. I suppose in a perfect world this would have been the solution to everybody's problems, but again I cannot help but think, If only...

As the years slipped by, the fact that Daddy was an alcoholic became apparent. Mother spent many nights alone, not knowing where Daddy was or when he was coming home. There were other nights when he did come home in a drunken state, when he cursed as he threatened to kill Mother, us four children, and himself. It goes without saying that Mother must surely have been disappointed in their relationship in addition to being fearful for herself and her children. She took all of the guns from our house to a neighbor's for safekeeping. And even with all these things, she still weakly attempted to be defensive of Daddy when Grannie firmly asserted her position as the owner of "this house," or when she loudly declared, "I do not have to put up with Ed Fuller's foolishness!" Mother was literally caught in the jaws of a vise! On the one hand, she was disappointed in her relationship with the man she loved, while on the other hand, she was obligated to her mother not only for providing a home for her husband, herself, and her children, but for providing the financial support required by her and the children. Pressure from these two people who should have been the closest to her destroyed any possibility of Mother's ever becoming a decisive person. She was blown about by whatever the two strong forces in her life dictated. My heart bleeds for her as again I think, If only…

Daddy spent more and more time away from home. When he did come home, he and Grannie were at each other's throats. Mother retreated more and more within herself. She did not do much cooking; Grannie or one of several black women did that. She did not clean house; on occasions Sally came to do that. Cleaning became Wrenn's and my job as we grew older. But Mother was not lazy. She took on huge projects, and I wonder now if those projects were a means of escape from existing problems that were much bigger than she. For example, she painted the interior of our house. That may not sound like such a big undertaking, but the rooms in Grannie's house were twenty by twenty feet with twelve-foot ceilings. Mother covered walls that had been dark gray for many years with a nice off-white color. Since Grannie paid her to do the work, this gave mother an opportunity to earn money, which she gladly used to provide for us children. I could not help but think that the real bonus, though, was the difference that the lighter paint made in those huge rooms.

The old house was filled with antique furniture that had been there from the mid-1800s. At first Mother decided to refinish a piece or two, but when she realized the beauty hidden beneath the several coats of different-colored enamel, she became captive to the prospect of refinishing it all! Her hard work and a number of gallons of paint remover worked miracles on some beautiful old pieces, some of which are in my home today. While refinishing one of the dressers from an upstairs bedroom, it was necessary for her to go through and empty the contents of drawers that had not been disturbed for years. They contained old letters from years before, sermon notes made by her father, old account books used to record debts made and repaid by tenants, and small scraps crumbled from the worn edges of very old paper, plus years of dust and a small amount of some kind of black powder.

Although it was summer, and very hot, Mother had a small fire in her fireplace to burn most of what she was finding. Upon reaching the bottom of one drawer, she lifted it, holding one end of it near her chest, while her other hand held it from the side. She dumped the small collection of dust and paper onto the flames in the fireplace. The explosion charred the inside of the dresser drawer and blew

Mother backward onto the floor. She had not realized that the black dust was gunpowder. Both hands were burned, as was her face and the lower parts of her legs that were not covered by the drawer. Her hair and eyebrows were singed. I was the one who drove her the seventeen miles to the doctor. I tried not to look at her blackened face. She instructed me to be very careful, but to go as fast as I could. She was in pain, which the hot day and sunshine only worsened.

Of course, she was out of the refinishing business for months; however, her hands were not idle. I was entering Asbury College that fall. Many on-campus jobs were performed by students who needed to earn money to apply to their expenses. We already knew that I would be working in the dining hall to defray the cost of my dormitory room. Both of Mother's hands were bandaged from the burns, but she somehow managed to sew a number of beautifully ruffled aprons from fabric left from clothes she had earlier sewn for our family. I felt very special as I went to work each day in the college dining room because I was the only working student with lovely aprons sewn with loving, bandaged hands.

Refinishing furniture, painting, and sewing were not the only skills my mother had. She crocheted, knitted, embroidered, quilted, and played the piano beautifully, for Sunday school and church each Sunday, and for weddings and funerals. And many times (when, I thought, she felt lonely), she went into the living room, opened the piano, and played. She played hymns, songs that were popular in her day, and popular songs of our day. She even composed a number of songs that told of her loneliness and heartache. She could play practically any song that she heard, and even though she read music, she usually exercised her special gift rather than go to the trouble of looking for certain hymns or sheet music. We children gathered round the piano and sang. We knew the words to songs from Mother's day as well as our own. She was also a lover of poetry, and she often quoted lines from many poets that she deemed appropriate for everyday occurrences and events. She loved teaching us poetry to recite each Friday at school. And though Mother did so many things with us, I cannot recall that she ever pulled us up onto her lap, or that she gave us a great big hug just because she loved us. Here again, I find myself thinking, If only...

Throughout the years, she did whatever she could to get us

through school and to adulthood. She drove the school bus, operated the school lunchroom, and later, when she worked a part-time job downtown, she also made pie crusts for the school lunchroom for five cents each. Those jobs worked well for her because she could accomplish them and still keep her job of driving the school bus. She finally got a job in the Probate Office, where she sold license plates and did most of the recording in the large record books for Sumter County, Alabama.

After the four of us were grown, Grannie became an invalid. For five years, Mother cared for her while continuing to work at the Probate Office. In watching Mother provide such loving care to Grannie, I could not help but see skills and traits that would have made her a wonderful nurse. The relentless pressure of those days was emotionally draining for her, and we knew it. There just never seemed to be any time for Mother until several years later, when on March 21, 1976, she married her childhood sweetheart, John Elliott. He adored Mother. He had never had children of his own, but when he married Mother, he cheerfully took us all. He was a giant of a man, and each year the gardens he planted became larger and larger. He was often heard to say that he had to "grow enough food for the children." Those years with John Pa were good years, years when Mother was loved for the person she was—years when Mother did not have to worry about every single penny and how it was spent, even though she always did anyway.

In looking back at Mother's life, it occurs to me that there are people who appear to ride the crest of the wave all the way through life, never wanting or needing anything; they already have it! Then there are those who bring so much potential to life, and somehow it all gets used up by the folks nearest to them; still they live and give with such grace! The latter was my mother. She never asked anything; she made do with leftovers. In looking at the beloved Scripture known as the Beatitudes (the poor in spirit, those who mourn, the meek, those who hunger and thirst after righteousness, the merciful, the peacemakers), I see Mother in many of those roles. The wonderful conclusion for those who paid the price of faithfulness was that every single person received a reward. Therefore, I shall endeavor to remember that my Mother may have done without some things, she may have been "all used up," but in the grand scheme of things, I am convinced that she had a delayed windfall, "for great is your reward in Heaven." And furthermore, I shall diligently work at erasing those wistful words "If only" from my mind!

If These Walls...

I find myself studying four snapshots taken several years ago by Jim Fuller, Uncle Albert's youngest child. Jim chanced to be at the site of the old Fuller homestead in Choctaw County, Alabama, as it was being taken down. It is interesting that I just wrote the words "taken down" instead of "torn down." The house could easily have been bulldozed or burned; rather, it was being taken apart piece by piece because somebody wanted to salvage the wood used in the old house's construction. As I continue to focus upon the remains of the house caught in the pictures, I realize that I am taking my memories of this spot apart, piece by piece, because I long to salvage the emotional ties binding me to this place. The oft-quoted phrase heard first in my childhood suddenly becomes my own personal query—"If these walls could talk..."—and so begins my journey.

Suns from many summers had bleached the sides of that old house. For nearly a century those walls kept the winds, frosts, and snows at bay for those they protected. The roof provided shelter from the scorching sun and countless rains. The front porch reached from one side of the house to the other. In the summer, it was a favorite resting place for both parents and children after long hours of backbreaking labor in the fields, or from the heat of the kitchen, where cooking, canning, and preserving were done on a wood-burning stove. The front porch was the place where Grandma and Grandpa Fuller sat and visited after Sunday dinner with their adult children and their families when they came home for a visit.

Throughout the years, countless breezes blew through the open hallway that divided one side of the house from the other. On scorching hot days in the summer, the family or visitors who often dropped by sought its cool refuge. Winter was a vastly different story, however. Family members avoided the open hallway because it became a broad avenue for the fierce winter winds that raced through from the north and east. As a result, when anyone went from one room to

31

The Fuller Homestead in Choctaw County, Alabama

another, it was done quickly, and the door hastily closed against the frigid blast.

James Benjamin Fuller (born February 6, 1876) and Tempie Annie Tew (born June 19, 1881) purchased the house from Mr. Cliff Tims before or around the time of their marriage on January 10, 1900. I do not know whether the house had been lived in previously, but the inside was not ceiled. I am told that Grandma and Grandpa Fuller traveled several miles in their mule-drawn wagon to a saw mill located on Scott Mountain, just south of their house. They pulled the best pieces of bead board from the scrap pile, loaded it onto their wagon, hauled it back over those few miles, and ceiled each room. Those walls were never painted. Colored walls were not a necessity, neither were they affordable, but snugly ceiled interior walls provided additional protection from the harsh winter winds and brought added comfort for the family. Grandma and Grandpa lived within those walls until they died—she in 1954 and he in October 1960. The house those two had shared for fifty-plus years stood at the top of a hill overlooking a small cemetery beside a rural Methodist Church. Grandma and Grandpa are buried there beside each other, within clear view of the place they knew as their home.

Jim and Annie Fuller were parents to eight children, who came along every two to three years from the birth of the first on June 23, 1901 until March 2, 1919, the birth of the last child. My father, Howard Edward Fuller, born June 21, 1903, was the second child in the line of eight. The Fullers were poor. They worked hard to scratch out a living for their large family. They were not able to hire out their farm work to tenant farmers or wage hands. They did it themselves. They grew or raised most of their food: vegetables, fruits, milk, butter, eggs, chickens, and pork. For many years, Grandma sold butter and eggs to the commissary on Scott Mountain. The small income from those sales was important to the family economy. In the summer and fall, the family gathered berries, plums, and grapes from nearby fields; in the winter, the men hunted birds, squirrels, rabbits, and deer.

Grandpa was a quiet man clad in overalls, a blue chambray work shirt, and high-topped, well-worn work shoes. Somehow he always

James Benjamin and Annie Tew Fuller, my paternal grandparents

seemed tired—maybe because his soft, slow speech gave the impression that he did not have enough energy to speak with any more enthusiasm or authority. Grandma, on the other hand, seemed to possess unlimited energy. She wore printed cotton dresses that she had likely made herself. If either of them was a leader and a motivator for the family, Grandma was it!

As children, my siblings and I knew a multitude of people much better than we knew the Fullers. There were a number of factors and circumstances that contributed to this sad fact. First, it was a long way to Grandma Fuller's house—approximately forty miles of dirt roads made difficult or sometimes impossible to traverse by rains—and we did not get to visit them very often. Although our cars were adequate and "road-worthy," the trip to Grandma's house always seemed to take a lot of effort. When five or six people were passengers in the same car, summer trips were *hot*. Winter trips were also *hot* because the heater seemed to operate at only hot or cold levels and there was no in-between! Rays from the winter sun spilling relentlessly through the car windows only added to our misery.

The second fact that contributed to this alienation from the Fullers was my maternal grandmother. While she was a jealous and possessive person, she was also a generous, caring, loving person. She brought stability into our lives. She provided a home for us and most of our clothes. Her contribution to us was not limited to finances, even though she gave what she had for as long as she could. She gave us more emotionally, ethically, and morally than I could ever repay in a thousand years. She loved us devotedly. I cannot reach any rational conclusion from my above contradictory statements. I continue to struggle with them as I attempt to reconcile all that I recall. Whatever her reasons and motivation, it was with great difficulty that Grannie shared us for even *one single day* to visit with Daddy's family, though she had us every day. It was she who tucked us into bed at night and prepared our breakfast every morning.

Grannie viewed Daddy and his family as being "beneath us" socially, educationally, and financially, as well as in any other actual or contrived sense. She conveyed her prejudice to me, Wrenn, Burton, and Howard, and when Daddy mentioned going to see his family, all of us knew that there would be the devil to pay. Grannie's disposition changed immediately. She became the injured, lonely old lady who was going to be left at home all day *by herself!* She never went with us. When she was out of earshot of Daddy, she muttered things in our presence about our going down there to see "Old Sunk Rump!"

Grandma Fuller was a hard worker. That was a necessity for a mother of eight children. Even though she was five years younger than Grandpa, she looked older. Her hair was completely white and was kept curled with Toni home permanents. When she was caught in an unexpected summer shower, or if her head became wet with sweat, her hair frizzed, but that didn't bother her. Her daily schedule did not include much time spent on personal grooming. There were always more pressing matters, such as two gardens to plant, fertilize, weed, and harvest, followed by the hard work of canning and preserving the surplus in preparation for the cold days ahead when the gardens lay dormant. Fruit trees and strawberries produced crops from which Grandma made jams, jellies, and preserves. Clothes were washed with water drawn from the well or caught in rain barrels. They were hung in the sun to dry, then brought inside and laid on the bed in the extra bedroom to be ironed later. After preparing a large breakfast, Grandma cooked an even larger dinner (the noon meal) with the express purpose of having enough left over for supper. Working people needed to eat regularly and drink plenty of water.

The water table was not far below the surface of the ground in Choctaw County's sandy land, so water for the family's use came from a shallow well. A wooden casing surrounded the small opening in the well through which a metal bucket, three to four feet tall with a diameter of approximately six inches, was lowered into the water. When the bucket reached the water, a valve in the bottom of it opened to allow the water to enter the bucket from the bottom. It was then lifted from the well by a windlass or hoist that consisted of a large wooden roller through which a metal hand crank ran. As the crank was turned, the rope lifting the bucket wound around the wooden roller; the bucket was drawn to the top of the well casing and emptied into other buckets that were placed into convenient locations for use.

Grandma Fuller was always happy to see us. It never mattered what she was doing when we came—that could wait. Soon after our arrival, she began preparation of a noon meal fit for royalty. In the meantime, there were usually teacakes in the pantry to tide us children over until dinner, just in case we were hungry from our long trip.

Dinner was always bountiful and delicious beyond description. Grandma was a wonderful cook. Summer meals usually consisted of fried chickens that had been fed in Grandma's yard that morning, accompanied by fresh vegetables, cornbread, biscuits, homemade pickles or relish, and iced tea or fresh milk, and there was never a time when we could not count on Grandma's wonderful homemade cakes and pies for dessert.

After dinner, the men retired to the front porch to talk. The women cleared the table, washed dishes, and put the food away. Sometimes after they finished in the kitchen, Grandma would take them into a back bedroom to show them a quilt or a bedspread that she had completed. When she opened the trunks where her treasures were kept, the aroma of mothballs filled the room. It remains a mystery to this day where Grandma found time or energy to sew, crochet, quilt, and embroider after completing her daily routine demands.

We children often wound up under the huge umbrella chinaberry tree in the front yard. The swing that hung from its branches was a perfect place to sit and visit with cousins. On rare occasions, the adult women went with us to a swimming hole in the beautiful creek that meandered through Grandpa's farm. Actually, none of us knew how to swim, but splashing in shady, cool water was all that it took to make a hot day perfect. The crystal-clear water flowed down the wide creek bed over a clean, sandy bottom. Branches from large trees growing along both banks met and formed a canopy over the hole which had been hollowed out by the currents in the bend of the creek. Large grapevines hung from branches and made wonderful swings. We loved that place because there was nothing like it at our home.

However, there was one negative to the swimming hole: sometimes the hogs wallowed in an area near where we played. That was obviously *off limits* for us. The polio epidemic of the late 1930s and early 1940s was at its worst during that time. Parents were urged on every hand to keep their children at home and away from crowds. Movies and public swimming pools were places to be avoided. One day at Grandma's when we went swimming, our cousin Jimmy climbed into the area where the pigs had been. Even though Aunt Mary (his mother) and Grandma quickly got him out of the muck, the adults always believed that he got the polio germ from that exposure. Jimmy never walked again after he became ill. He spent the early days of his tragic illness in an iron lung as he fought for his life. He had a bright mind, and though his educational progress was slowed, he continued to push forward. He was a student at Livingston State Teachers College when he died. What a sad time for our family!

Grandma loved taking the visiting womenfolk for a stroll in her yard or vegetable garden to see what was growing there. Her yard and potted plants were her pride and joy. Considering both of my grandmothers' interest in and love of flowers, it is easy to explain my own affinity for plants. The front walk at Grandma's, leading from the front gate to the steps, was a clean, sandy path bordered on both sides by flowerbeds carefully outlined with brick. The yard itself had no grass in it—not one blade! Rather, it was sandy soil swept clean by brush brooms made from a brushy shrub (often wild plum bushes) found nearby.

As the day grew late, the time came to begin our homeward trek. Grandma brought out things that she wanted us to take home with us. She was one of the most generous people I have ever known. Throughout the day, she placed things to be given to us in one spot so she would not forget anything. Our bounty consisted of strawberry preserves, canned soup mix, and pickles or relish. Sometimes there were fresh vegetables that we might not have in our garden at home or a quilt or bedspread or a small piece of embroidery. There were occasions when Grandma generously sent Grannie cuttings from her beautiful flowers. I wonder now if she ever suspected that Grannie found it so difficult to share us with her.

That was a long time ago. As I continue gazing at the pictures of the old Fuller house in its process of being demolished, my heart is deeply pained, for I am finally accepting the fact that it is all gone! All of those people are gone: Grandma, Grandpa, and their eight children. There remains no physical evidence that any of this history ever occurred. As I look again at the list of children, I realize that so much more than my few happy times took place within that Choctaw County, Alabama, house. That old house and each of those within knew deep and tragic sorrow. Two little boys at about the age of eighteen months died inside those walls. They were both buried at the foot of the hill in the Old Cyril Cemetery, just down a long drive from the house. Maybe there was some sad comfort in knowing that the babies rested nearby. The oldest child and the youngest child were "afflicted" and severely challenged. Louise, who was the youngest, died at the age of nineteen. Three sons (one was my father) were alcoholics and died in their fifties and early sixties.

My sister, brothers, and I experienced genuine unhappiness related to Daddy's alcoholism. Now I know that Grandma Fuller also knew about and understood alcohol-related horrors. Her own father fell victim to the alcohol demon. There were countless nights when her mother quickly gathered her large family of children and fled to escape her husband's mean tantrums and fits of rage. She went to the woods, where she would build a fire to keep the children safe and warm for the night with the hope that her husband would have slept off the effects of the liquor by daylight. Grandma Fuller's father was later murdered because of his involvement with a married woman.

Today I am taking a long, introspective look backward. I am making a genuine effort to put everything that I know together, but all of the pieces do not seem to fit. As I continue to dig into memories long buried, I cannot help asking, "What or who could have made a difference? Was there anyone or anything?" I am delving into areas filled with many empty holes. I am struggling with questions that seem to have no answers. In looking at those walls I am again asking, "If these walls could talk, what would they say?"

I have drawn one profound conclusion: Grandma Fuller was a dear, hardworking, generous person who did over and above all that was required or expected of her. I now understand that the real tragedy—the one that I am feeling so keenly—is that I never got to really know her! I never had the chance! During my childhood, she was put down and underrated! Any deep and lasting relationship with her was short-circuited by Grannie's attitude, my father's irresponsible alcoholism, and lastly, my own youthful inability to create opportunities to spend time with her. I can only hope that somewhere in God's boundless sea of grace, there will be a time and place for me to meet Grandma again, and that this time I will get to know her for the person she was! Today I feel empty and miserably cheated!

Dearest Daddy

Dearest Daddy,

So much time has passed since September 21, 1964, the day you died. So many thoughts have come and gone, while still others have lingered to haunt me. Today is the day when I shall finally attempt to bring my thoughts and feelings (as much as I know of them) into focus, and I want to share them with you.

How can it be that you were actually such an infinitesimal part of my life and my growing up, and yet you were and continue to be so huge? In my memory, you were not home for so much of my childhood. Your jobs took you away from us for two-week time periods, and when you came home, it was for short weekends. You worked for the ABC (Alcoholic Beverage Control) Board and lived in Montgomery until you were fired. You were an agent whose duty it was to locate stills, put them out of business, and arrest their operators. We always suspected that you were let go because of your drinking. You then worked in the shipyards in Mobile during World War II. Please understand that I was young, and I don't really know how much you contributed to the financial stability of our family, but I could not help overhearing Mother and Grannie talk, and there never seemed to be enough money to make life easy. Our family lived with Grannie Burton in her house, so we never feared that we would be homeless. Grannie assured us that we would never be without anything as long as she was able to provide.

Do you remember that you were always moody? You sat a lot of times with your head in your hands and said nothing. I always felt that you were unhappy. You were not easy to talk to—you seemed surrounded on all sides by tall walls—and there were no visible doors to get inside. One day I went with you to cut wood in the hog pasture. I was thrilled beyond measure to be spending time alone with you. I loved you, and longed for your attention. I had come to believe that perhaps I could earn your love and attention if I could help you com-

Howard Edward Fuller Sr., my father

plete whatever task you were doing. I was a good worker, and I worked as hard as I could that day. My childish heart yearned for you to be proud of me, and to notice that I had done a good job. I loaded the wood that you cut into the wagon. I was dead tired as we rode home, and I could barely drag my weary body into the house when we arrived. You went silently about your work all day. You whistled softly to yourself, but you never seemed to notice that I was there. You never said that we had a good day, never said "Thanks," never told Mother or the others in the family that I had been a lot of help. I was crushed. As the years have slipped past and I have recalled "our" day, I wonder if you simply did not know how to say "thank you" or how to give praise—or further still, did not know how to say "I love you." Could it be, Daddy, that for a long time nobody had noticed you? The passage of years has helped me understand that it is sometimes difficult, maybe even impossible, to share secrets and dreams known only to our heart. Is it because we are afraid that the listening heart might not understand and reciprocate? I know now how frightening it can be to risk deep personal emotions.

It must have been difficult beyond measure for you to come to live in your mother-in-law's house when you and Mother married. The two of you graciously moved in so Grannie would not be left to live alone in her large country home. Even though you built your own bedroom as an extension to the original house, I understand now that you were never the "man of the house." You were caught between Mother and Grannie, and Mother was caught between you and Grannie. You must have loved Mother to stay as long as you did, even though you made those years almost unbearable for us because of your alcoholism. You had two other brothers (Uncle Leon and Uncle Albert) who were also victims of the same dreadful addiction.

No point in telling you how much you embarrassed us! I was certain that my friends and classmates felt that they were "better than me" because I was the child of a drunk. You stayed away from home a lot, sometimes several days at a time. We didn't know where you were, or when you would come home, and often when you came home, you were drunk and threatening to kill us all. We took your guns to Travis Wooldridge's house so at least you would not have a weapon available. When it was dark and you came home after everybody was in bed, I used to lie in my bed and listen to you curse and verbally abuse Mother. We were all so afraid! We were embarrassed! We did without things many times because you were too irresponsible to earn money—or at least to bring any home.

Even though you had bottles of liquor hidden in the corncrib, under the seat of your truck, and probably other places that we did not know, none of us ever saw you take a single drink. Why? Was that because you were not allowed to drink in Grannie's house? Did you feel guilty? Would things have been different if you had not been forced to drink away from home? Who knows? I remember that Grannie despised liquor or anything related to it, but I also remember that when she became bedfast, you used to bring her wine, and she asked for it throughout the day when she had a "sinking spell." You two became friends in your last days. That was good! How different our lives could have been if that had happened earlier!

I must have been a real irritant to you when I became a Christian because you thought that all religion was hypocritical and you never refrained from clearly stating your opinion. You refused to go to church because of all of the hypocrites there. When I committed my life to Christ and answered a call into some form of Christian service, we began making plans for me to go to Asbury College for my education. One night, you came home after the rest of us had eaten our evening meal—drunk again. Even when you were some distance from the house, we could always tell when you were drinking because your "pinkie" fingers curled and stood apart from the rest of your fingers. You never had to speak a word. Mother asked me to go to the kitchen and get you supper that night. We had been told that tomatoes or tomato juice helped to sober a person who was drinking, so I made sure that you had a bowl of canned tomatoes.

You always had big plans, and that night was no exception. You were going to open a barbershop in Livingston, and there would be enough room in the back of the shop for a bedroom and kitchen. You asked if I wanted to go to live there, along with the rest of our family. It was obvious that there would not be enough room in one bedroom and kitchen for you, Mother, and us children. I knew that if we all went with you, Grannie would be left alone. She had taken care of us as long as I could remember, and as sad as it was, you were not dependable in any area of your life. I had to say, "No." Your response killed me! You said, "Then do not consider yourself to be my daughter any longer!" As a young and zealous Christian, I felt that I was being "persecuted for Christ's sake." I determined then and there to stand firm in what I believed. As it turned out, none of your plans came to fruition except the barbershop, the bedroom, and the kitchen in which you lived and worked. Mother and Howard occasionally went and spent the night with you. Mother really wanted you to come back home, you know.

I shall never forget the day when you left home for good. I was a senior in high school, and by that time I was very protective of both Mother and Grannie. Please believe me, Daddy, when I tell you that I had no concept of the loneliness and pain you must have felt. You had literally been closed out of the family circle. As you walked unsteadily across the front yard, you said in your slurred, drunken voice, "You think I'm coming back, but I'm not!" Mother was crying. I mustered all my courage as I answered you. I said, "Nobody cares!" You didn't hear what I said, and even though you asked what had been said, Mother asked me not to repeat it. I didn't.

You did not attend my graduation from high school. I was hurt again. All the other fathers were there. On the other hand, I was thankful that you did not come in a drunken state and humiliate us. I graduated from Asbury College, and you were not present for that milestone either. During my college years, I always came to see you when I was home for holidays. Usually I swept up hair that had fallen to the floor from the haircuts done that day—I was still begging for your attention. When I finished, I just sat and watched you work. You were good at what you did! You built the finest brooder house any-where around, where we raised our baby chicks. People in and around the community used to hire you to put up wire fences because they knew you would make them strong and straight.

While I was away at college, I became engaged to a wonderful young man who was preparing for the Methodist ministry. I brought him to meet you and you later referred to him as "a damn preacher" whenever you made reference to him. Nevertheless, I brought Gerald to your shop the day before our wedding to get a haircut from you, the best barber in town. You did a perfect job! Thank you! Nothing had changed between us, though, and I still considered myself *not* to be your daughter. I did not ask you to give me away at our wedding because I felt that you had already done that. You did come to our wedding, however, and you sat behind Mother. I'm glad you came.

In 1957 or '58, Mother called to tell me that you were in the hospital in Mobile following a critical heart attack. You had divorced Mother by that time, had married a woman named Agnes, and were living in Mobile. Gerald was a seminary student at Emory. We did not have an extra penny for anything, but I knew in my heart that I must go to Mobile to see you. Gerald came home from school to keep Lynn (three years old) and Mark (less than a year), and we somehow managed to come up with enough money for a bus ticket to Mobile and cab fare to the hospital. It was in the wee hours of the morning that I boarded the bus in Opelika, Alabama, bound for Mobile.

You recognized me immediately as I entered your room. I don't think that I had ever seen you smile as broadly as you did that day. You turned to the nurse and said proudly, "This is my oldest daughter, Sara Ann!" I don't remember what we talked about during the brief visit that we shared, but as I left your room, I recall feeling much more accepted by you than I had earlier on my bus ride toward Mobile. You had actually introduced me as your daughter. I heard those words with my own ears!

There were not a lot of visits or letters after that, but you did come to visit once when we lived in Phenix City. The children loved you, and you commented on how well behaved they were. We went to the farmers' market while you were there, and you bought some black-eyed peas, which you shelled in the car on the way home, and you threw the hulls out the window. The children loved that because they were not allowed to throw anything from the car windows. They loved the time you were there, and they wished for you to come more often.

Years passed, and the family was at Grannie's house. You also came that day. You were divorced again and living alone in a little storefront building nearby. We were busily greeting each other as we gathered, and when you came into the house you gave me a small brown paper bag with the instructions, "Don't let anybody see this. It's just something I wanted you to have." I could hardly wait to open it. When I was finally able to peek inside, I found six beautiful dessert dishes with a single paper napkin separating each from the other. You had packed them with such special care. The dishes had belonged to your mother—my grandmother—and you brought them to me! What a treasure!

As I write today, I know without a doubt that you reinstated me as your daughter in that hospital room in the Mobile Infirmary, and you acknowledged me as the firstborn in my generation of Fullers when you gave me Grandma Fuller's dishes. Thank you! Please know how much I love you. I'm sorry you were so lonely, and I'm sorry I was so deprived! My prayer is that somewhere in God's great beyond, I'll be able to give you a hug that is long overdue, you will smile that great big smile again, and you'll hug me back!

Your Oldest Child,

Sara Ann

Days of Grace

We lived at the end of the dirt road, and it was an exciting event when we heard a car motor down by the woods or when we could see billows of dust that clearly indicated a car was coming in our direction. My sister Wrenn, my brother Burton, and I were always eager for someone—anyone, any age—to come and visit. We were allowed to sit quietly and listen to adult conversation when visitors came, and we never tired of that.

Perhaps the person we most wanted to see coming was Sally McDaniel, wife of a tenant farmer on our place. She never came in a car; she always walked. She lived on the next hill from us—close enough that we could call her if we "hollered loud."

When we saw Sally coming, we always called loudly to Mother or Grannie, "Can we go meet Sally?" There was never a time when we were not allowed to go, and we ran as fast as our legs would go to meet her. When Sally came from her house, she always carried a bucket because the purpose of her trip was usually to get water. There was no water well or cistern at her house, so the source of their drinking water was our well. She caught rainwater in barrels for other purposes such as bathing or washing clothes, and if it did not rain for a long time, her husband Ed hauled water from the small pool that was nearby.

There were always countless fun things to do when Sally came. Probably the thing we liked best was going to look for eggs. Our chickens were not in pens, so they laid their eggs wherever they found a nest to their liking. One even made her nest in a large patch of garlic at the back of the orchard.

The best place to look for eggs, though, was in the barn, up in the hayloft. To get up into the hayloft, we stuck our toes between the boards that formed the walls of the stables, almost like climbing a ladder, and there it was: the musty, dusty, wonderful smell from all those bales of hay, and sunlight streaming through nail holes in the tin roof. We loved putting our hands under the small beams of light, and as we took the radiance from the floor, we held it for a while in our hands.

Sally always seemed to know exactly where the hens would make their nests, and though we never knew it, she skillfully guided us to their hidden treasure. She let us believe that we had found the eggs "all by ourselves" as we eagerly pulled them from the nest. It was like having an Easter egg hunt without color on the eggs. Sometimes we found an egg that was still warm, and that meant that it had not been very long since the hen laid it. Some of the places where the hens laid were dark, and all three of us children were scared to death that there might be a big snake curled up in the nest, so we always held back and waited for Sally to go ahead of us. If there were any eggs there, Sally's long, graceful black hands slipped carefully into the shadowy places and came back with the treasure which we sought—sometimes three or four. We were constantly aware of Sally's protective presence, her smile, and her sparkling eyes.

We never wanted Sally to go home. Her departure always came much too soon. But when she had to leave, and the water was drawn from the well and in the bucket, all three of us children walked as far as we could with her, fussing over who would hold Sally's free hand. She knew that each of our childish hearts did not want her to go, so she would stop in the middle of the road and set her bucket of water down. We would talk for a while, then she would say, "Now y'all go on home 'fo it gits dark. I'll be back tomorrow."

The dust on the road was like warm, dry powder beneath our bare feet as we turned toward home. All the way we called over our shoulders, "Bye, Sally! We love you!" until we reached our front steps and home. We would make plans a little later about seeing Sally the next day, but it was just getting dark enough for the fireflies to light the evening as they silently flew from one dark spot to another. They captured and held our attention. They never seemed to grow weary of doing what they were created to do, and they did not stop because the entire world did not glow with brilliant light from their individual effort. Long after we were in bed and sound asleep, millions of little lights continued to blink on and off. Those were days filled with grace and nights wrapped in promise.

I'm Jus' Waitin'

"Advice is something that everybody wants to give and nobody wants to take," declared a girl with whom I went to college. It seems to me that persons who give advice need a sound undergirding of facts, knowledge, and experience. I question whether many of us are qualified to dispense advice as seriously and as frequently as we do, particularly on so wide an assortment of subjects and circumstances.

I cannot possibly count the times that I have needed and sought advice—times when I tearfully poured out my heart and soul while hoping against hope that my confidant would clearly and concisely outline exactly what I should do. During those times, I listened and heard wonderful directives; some worked while others did not. It is highly possible that the sage and wise counsel so graciously and generously administered was not the vehicle needed to move me toward an acceptable conclusion; rather, it was the simple act of talking through the problem that made the difference.

This is in no way to be considered a blanket declaration that advice is not helpful, nor is it intended to say that lots and lots of advice never found its way into my life, whether I sought it or not. I was literally brainwashed from an early age with all kinds of advice and platitudes. My grandmother admonished me daily to "hitch your wagon to a star." Mother, on the other hand, taught me that attitude plays a huge role in moving toward success. She often sang a little ditty that she learned in her early years:

> "When you are down in luck,
> Just buck right up
> And sing away your blues!"

Mother loved saying, "Give to the world the best that you have and the best will come back to you!" I heard that so many times I thought it was in the Bible.

I adored Aunt Sarah, an elderly black woman who lived across the orchard from our kitchen. Wherever she went, I followed on her heels as closely as I could. She used to sing under her breath as she went about her chores, and even though her song was barely a whisper, I heard every word. It went like this:

"I been strivin' tryin' to make a hundred—
Ninety-nine and a half won't do!"

Even as a child, I understood the admonition contained in that plaintive little song. It was saying that even though we are good people and on our way to perfection, as long as there is any small imperfection, there is still reason to strive to reach the 100 percent mark. I felt that because Aunt Sarah was so old, she was preparing her soul and spirit to present them blameless before God on "that great gittin' up morning."

Others people, not just family, also gave good advice. For example, my English teacher wrote on the inside cover of my senior playbook, "Perseverance wins out!" I interpreted that to mean: "Consistent, energetic pursuit of a goal always produces winners." As a high school senior, those words gave me unlimited assurance. I decided then and there that I would be an achiever—a conqueror! Still others along the way assured me that "good things come to those who wait!" Of course the basis for that encouragement was unquestionably sound since it came from the pages of Holy Writ. Actually, there was never a time in my life when I was not inundated with good advice and encouraged to be the best of whatever or whoever I was.

Seeking advice and good counsel, though difficult for me, is usually done after I have exhausted every option that seemed attractive to me. I hope against hope that my wise confidant will validate what I have already been doing, and that I will be assured I have been on the right path all along. However, a real tug-of-war occurs when the one solution I have tried to ignore surfaces time and again. I recognize that course of action as difficult, possibly even painful or distasteful; yet I also recognize it as inevitable. During sleepless nights I often pray for more pleasant and less demanding options, but the solution remains constant; and even after having gone through the long and tedious process of determining the road I must take, I still resist. Why is it so difficult to just get on with it? There must be something in my humanity that does not lend itself well to direction and advice—especially when it is not what I already had in mind. However, all advice is not hard to accept.

Possibly the wisest advice that has ever come to me was neither given nor recognized as advice. It became a part of me even though I did not know it had come. I actually was not aware of its presence through the years, but it has been a kind of underpinning in my life that I have simply taken for granted. I was so young when this event took place that I am not certain whether I actually can recall what happened or whether I heard the story so often that I consider myself to have been a witness to it. Whatever the facts, the wisdom of the experience is mine, and I cherish it as good and sound advice.

The words that were spoken were not considered to be "wise" words then. They came from a man who was considered to be nearly an idiot by those who knew him. He was a poor man with limited skills and abilities; a man whose limitations reduced him to a simple, basic honesty—the kind of honesty to which we are seldom exposed, and tragically, an honesty that may be a vanishing commodity. Let me share what I recall.

Some of the big trees along the creeks were selected, felled, trimmed, cut to the proper length, and hauled to our house by mules and wagon to be used as our supply of firewood during the cold winter months. One final step remained before the wood was ready: the large pieces must be split into small pieces that could be easily lifted and placed into the fireplace.

An elderly black man named Muff did chores and odd jobs for white families in the community. Either my father or my grandmother had contacted him, and it was agreed that he would come to our house and split the wood. I don't know where Muff lived; I don't even know if he had a family or a last name. I do have a few faded memories of how he looked. He usually wore a happy smile that revealed empty spaces where teeth had once been. His pleasant, round face conjured up images of a sprightly leprechaun as he went about accomplishing the chores that were assigned him. His head was covered with an ample supply of curly white hair that looked almost like cotton. His clothes were old and well worn. They most likely had been previously worn by someone who gave them to Muff as payment for work he had done. His shoes may or may not have fit him at one time. They had been worn so long that they had come apart and were in several pieces. Muff had carefully tied the pieces back together with twine. He wore no socks.

The day arrived for "Old Muff" to come and split the wood. One by one, the hours slipped past until it was the late afternoon. Still, Muff had made no appearance. As I recall, nobody was particularly upset by his absence; quite the contrary! It was casually dismissed because "what more could you expect from somebody who just wasn't right? Besides, when he gets hungry, he'll show up!"

I don't know who discovered Muff sitting calmly on the woodpile. It was near sundown, and it made no sense at all that he had come to split wood at that late hour. As Grannie approached him, she said, "Muff, it's getting mighty late. What are you doing sitting here on the woodpile?" Muff turned his happy face in her direction, and a wide, toothless grin made his face almost shine. He replied haltingly, but convincingly, "I'm jus' sittin' here—waitin' fo' de Lawd to send me some light." And so he sat, as though he had been assigned a task, and he had arrived to do his job. His answer was not altogether clear to Grannie, but then Muff was not always a clear and logical person.

We ate our supper. As was her custom, Grannie prepared Old Muff a plate piled high with some of the food that we were eating. Never was there anyone at our house at mealtime who was not fed or at least invited to eat. Muff sat on the kitchen steps while he ate, and then returned to the pile of wood that needed splitting. He sat down on the wood and waited patiently. The lengthening shadows of the evening began to gently wrap the earth in soft shades of twilight; but that was soon to change. Out of the east, the harvest moon began to rise—at first just an orange glow followed by a huge orange ball as it peeked over the horizon. Slowly, deliberately, it made its way further from the dark edge of the earth as it began to climb into the night sky. What a dramatic appearance! The majesty and brilliance of its entry into the evening left no question as to who ruled the night—and there on the woodpile, silhouetted against the moon, was the figure of Muff as he faced the source of the light that the Lord had sent him.

The fall night was cool as we slept; that is, all of us except Muff. He split wood all night while it was cool, and the moon provided the illumination for his task. I have faint memories of waking in the night and hearing Muff through the open windows as he hummed or talked to himself, accompanied by the thud of the ax as it hit and split the wood for our winter use. Sometimes when Muff needed to rest, he did. As he sat there on the wood, he appeared to have a simple reverence and appreciation for the cool night, the glorious moon, and work to do.

How often we have heard that "Fools rush in where angels fear to tread!" Perhaps that night we were in the presence of an angel—the divine. There was no rushing in, no hustle and bustle, no mad dashing about to complete a big job, no anxiety about food or pay. Instead, there was a simple man who had every appearance of being familiar with God and His creation; a man who, in his simplicity, had learned to use the best of what was available to him. Often my own life is filled with confusion, turmoil, and doubts, and sometimes I feel completely empty, maybe even hopeless, and it is then that my own soul cries for the faith and serenity to sit with Muff—to understand that I also have work to do—and as I recognize my own finiteness, may I answer with Muff, "I'm jus' waitin' on de Lawd!"

"But they that wait upon the Lord shall renew their strength;
they shall mount up with wings as eagles;
they shall run, and not be weary;
they shall walk, and not faint." (Isa. 40:31)

My First Job

It was not much as jobs go. But it was my first job, and it had many of the elements found in today's good, sophisticated jobs. Circumstances and conditions qualified my job as a genuine service provided for a particular and specific small group, and I was paid for my efforts. There was an agreement between the employer and the employee as to the wage to be paid, as well as to what would be expected in the work to be accomplished. My first job was not even close to that time when the workplace would be made as comfortable as possible and working conditions would be scrutinized to make them safe and more humane; however, all of these things were taken into consideration for me.

My job was one to which I was not required to report every day; I did the work on an "as needed" basis. And what was this job? It was churning, as in churning milk to make butter. Certain things had to take place before churning became necessary.

When I grew up, we did not feed our cows year-round in order that we could have milk. That was far too expensive for most farmers. It was not nearly as costly for us to do without; and sometimes that was exactly what we did. During the summer months, cows grazed happily on the lush green grass in the pastures. That worked well until extended periods of drought came and grass for grazing became sparse. During those times, water levels in the ponds dropped, and sometimes water was hauled or drawn from the well at the barn to water the animals. There was little wonder then that at times, the cows went "dry," which meant that they were not producing milk. When baby calves were born, it was always a good time to start milking, since the calf usually did not need all the milk that the mother produced, especially if she were considered to be a good milk cow.

After considering all of the above mentioned conditions, it is understandable that there were days when it was not necessary to churn because there was no milk to churn. Besides the lack of milk, there was a process that must be completed before milk was ready to churn. First, the family used the milk they needed for drinking and cooking. Any and all remaining milk was set aside to sour and turn to clabber. For anyone who does not understand the term "clabber," Webster defines it as "thickly curdled sour milk."[1] The soured cream was then carefully scooped from the top of the clabber with a large spoon or scoop and put into the churn.

Webster says that a "churn is a container or contrivance in which milk or cream is beaten, stirred or shaken to form butter."[2] Our churns varied in size, but the one that we used most often was probably eighteen to twenty inches tall with a diameter of eight to ten inches. Churns were made of some form of crockery and were covered with a top of the same material that fitted into a lip around the top of the churn. There was a round hole in the center of the top through which the handle of the churn dasher fitted.

The dasher was made from two wooden pieces chiseled and fitted together in the shape of a plus sign (+) and fastened onto an upright wooden handle about the size of a broomstick. The dasher was placed into the churn, the top of the churn was slipped over the handle to cover the milk, and the process of beating the milk or cream into butter began.

By no means could this be considered easy work! It was not at all easy for my grandmother to stand or sit beside that churn and raise and lower the dasher into the cream enough times to beat the butter out of it. It was hard work for arms and backs that were already tired from all the years, and it was not much easier for young arms that were not quite yet formed and strong. But this was my first job, and I did it well. I did it as regularly as it was required. And I was paid five cents for every churn.

My work was made easier when Grannie placed a small wooden box beside the churn. Upon stepping onto that box, the extra three or four inches gave just enough lift to my young torso to make me feel in charge. Up and down! Up and down! Up and down! It seemed to take a very long time to make the butter "come," but during those

---

[1] *Webster's New World Dictonary*, 2nd college ed., s.v. "clabber."
[2] Ibid., s.v. "churn."

times, I was free to let my imagination escape the restraints of daily routine and visit places that existed only in my thoughts. And yes, there were opportunities to dream of how I would spend all that money I was earning!

When the butter finally was "made" and gathered on top of the milk that had become buttermilk, it was scooped from the churn and placed into a cool bowl. With a wooden paddle, the milk was quickly worked out of the butter, which was then salted and placed into a wooden mold to cool and harden.

My job was completed for the day, and I had earned another nickel. There were real fringe benefits to this job. There probably was nothing better in the whole wide world than Grannie's hot biscuits, yellow with all the melted butter that had taken such intense labor to bring into being.

A Cup of Cold Water

There were always chores for a farm girl to do if she was willing and available. Much of the work was routine, as was much of our daily living, and much of our work was hard. Bed making was done every day before we left for school. In the summer, beds were made as soon as breakfast was over. Clothes were hung in the closet or placed into dresser drawers, and dirty items were placed into the clothesbasket to be laundered on the next washday. The long front porch was the summer dwelling place of countless pots of flowers that continually dropped their spent blossoms, so that meant the porch needed to be swept. In addition to sweeping their blossoms, they needed regular watering. That was a real chore because the water we used was not available through a hose. On washdays, we brought water that had been used to rinse the clothes, a bucketful at a time from the large zinc tubs, to the front porch, where it was dipped from the bucket and poured carefully on every single plant. All of our water was drawn from the large cistern at the end of the kitchen porch.

Cleaning out the chicken house and carrying chicken manure to the garden was a chore that none of us ever volunteered to do. Extra care was always taken to ensure that the young plants did not receive too much "fertilizer" because there was danger of burning them since chicken manure is very strong chemically. Gardens always seemed to have weeds that needed pulling, and that was really hard work. We usually worked early and late in the day because it was not as hot then as when the noonday sun burned relentlessly and without mercy upon our backs and heads. When the vegetables were mature, they had to be gathered, either for a meal or for canning and preserving. Cleaning and preparing the vegetables came next, and that took lots of water. The cistern was on the kitchen porch, so that task was usually done on that porch, which was cooler than the kitchen.

One of the worst chores in the entire world, however, was emptying the slop-jars or "thunder jugs," as they were called by some, and that job had to be done every morning. Chamber pots were essential. They were washed each day and left on a shelf to dry. At the close of the day, they were brought back into the house and placed in their conveniently assigned spots where they were available for the relief of those resting within the house for the night. Though we did not like that chore, it was much better than a long, dark trek to the outside toilet in all kinds of wind and weather. And besides, the tenant farmers on our place believed and convinced us that our house was haunted, so we guarded against getting very far away from the protection of the adult members of our household—especially after dark.

On bright, sunny summer days, we periodically took all the quilts and blankets from the quilt closet, all the feather pillows, the feather beds, and all of the mattresses outside to spend the day in the purifying, deodorizing rays of the sun. Every piece was turned over at midday. Late in the afternoon, the bedclothes were brought back inside, folded, and put away. All the beds were made for the night, and no bed ever smelled as fresh as one that has spent the day outside in the sunshine.

Our food was cooked on a wood stove, so stove wood also had to be brought in almost every day. In the winter, fireplaces heated the house, which necessitated that wood also be brought inside for fireplaces. Before any of that could take place, trees were felled, sawed, and cut into proper sizes for stove and fireplace. The woodpile was on one end of the house, and the kitchen on the other, so bringing in stove wood required a lot of effort, especially in cold or wet weather.

Kitchen scraps and dishwater were saved in a large five-gallon bucket that was carried each evening to the hog pen to "slop" the hogs. Cows had to be milked, milk had to be churned, hay had to be thrown down from the loft to feed the cows and mules, corn had to be shucked to feed the horses and cows, corn had to be shelled for chicken feed, and eggs had to be gathered. Chores and work never seemed to end on the farm.

However, the chore that I liked most of all was really not a chore. It always happened when company came, most especially in the summer. We did not have Cokes or Oreo cookies to offer our guests, but it can never be said that we were not hospitable. I can almost hear my grandmother call to me as she did so often, "Sara Ann, go get a bucket of fresh water!" We didn't have ice, but the water was cool as it was

SARA F. MUNDAY

pulled from the deep, dark cistern. I loved being asked to bring fresh water. Going to the well alone to draw fresh water gave me a sense of being trusted, and then to offer its cooling comfort to those who had come to visit on a hot day gave me a sense of responsible maturity. It was a huge bonus when I spilled some of those cooling waters onto my bare feet, but the real joy was in knowing that I had been privileged to give "a cup of cold water" to our friends.

Starting to School

The county did not own and operate school buses when I started to school. They were owned by individuals who either drove the buses themselves or hired drivers. My father owned two buses, and as a result, one of the routes began and ended at our house. Scheduling the route was a part of the owner's responsibility, and they, of course, made every effort to get the children to and from school in a safe and timely manner.

Our bus route covered many miles. Since it took a long time to get to school, it was necessary to start early to be at school when the eight o'clock bell signaled the beginning of the school day. Several communities through which we passed had their own school, though they were considerably smaller than the school in Livingston. Some families kept their children in local community schools, while others chose to have their children transported to the larger, better-equipped school where there was a teacher for every grade. Those who opted not to stay in the public schools in their local community were charged a monthly fare to ride the bus to Livingston. Although I am not certain, I assume that the county contracted with school bus owners to provide transportation for children who lived in the country and had no neighborhood school available to them.

Our bus driver was a college student who lived upstairs at our house. He was paid a small monthly salary plus being provided a room and meals. Thomas Earl Roberts, my mother's first cousin, was the driver when I first started to school. He had already completed two years of college at Scooba, Mississippi. Since the family had no means of transportation, he rode back and forth daily from his home to school on the Doodle Bug, a small commuter train. Upon completion of his work at the Junior College in Scooba, he registered at Livingston State Teachers College to complete his degree in education. There was a strong sense of family in the mid-1930s, and that probably figured heavily into Thomas Earl's being hired as the bus driver. Besides, having a respected family member living in the home was far better than bringing in a student who was a stranger and virtually unknown to any of us. Thomas Earl's sense of responsibility and maturity were strong qualities that he brought to this job. He was a good student, and he took his education quite seriously.

My sheltered childhood made going to school as a first-grader quite intimidating. Thomas Earl and I were the first people on and the last off the bus every day, so our days began very early and ended very late. I sat in the first seat directly behind him, and I knew with great assurance that he would take care of me in any and all circumstances. I know now that sitting near him helped to ease some of my first grade apprehension. He was my security blanket.

Grannie was the first person up every morning. Since those early winter mornings were always cold, the first thing she did was to get the fire blazing in the fireplace to provide warmth for me to get dressed. Mother saw to it that I had my bath the night before, and that I was in bed as early as six thirty or seven P.M. Mornings seemed to come so early, and in the winter, it was always dark. Before going to bed each night, all of my clothes for the next day were laid out on a chair, along with anything else that I was going to take to school. Mother made certain that I was always dressed warmly, and that meant putting on several layers, so having everything ready made the dressing process move along a bit more expeditiously. Having my clothes laid out also meant that I could move quickly from my flannel pajamas into my school clothes, and I would not be cold quite so long with my change of clothing at my fingertips.

When Grannie had the fire going in the bedroom, she went to the kitchen to start the fire in the wood stove and get breakfast ready. We could always count on hot biscuits, grits, and fig preserves or plum jelly. The "hot tea" that Grannie made for me from hot milk, water, and lots and lots of sugar made me feel warmer with each swallow, all the way to my "tummy."

The bus route was not only long, but the roads were quite treacherous in wet weather. It was not at all unusual for the bus to get stuck in deep ruts or to slide off the road into a ditch. When this happened and it was obvious by our tardiness that something was wrong with the bus, another bus came to pick us up. The driver always stayed with the bus until it was pulled back onto the road by another vehicle, a tractor, or mules, at which time he would drive the bus on to school to be ready for the afternoon return trip. There were times in the winter that the last mile before reaching our house was so bad that it was impossible to negotiate in the bus. The winter rains caused the roads to wear down into deep ruts and mud holes, and the mud was deep and sticky—but we were always able to go home, even though the bus could not.

Sam and Lindy Bradley, an elderly black couple, lived at the last turn off the main road. They had known and worked for my grandfather for many years, and even though he had been dead several years, Sam and Lindy still spoke of him with deep respect. Sam was a master at odd jobs, and he told the best ghost stories of anyone we knew. The Bradleys had enough space in their yard for us to back the school bus in each afternoon, and leave it overnight.

After making sure that all of our belongings were off the bus, we disembarked and prepared for the next stretch of the journey toward home. Our transportation from that point was a farm wagon pulled by mules and driven by Norah Orman, a black tenant farmer who lived on our place. Due to an accident of some sort, one of Norah's arms was off at the shoulder. I recall watching him as he clutched the mules' reins in his one hand while at the same time carefully putting his foot on the ends of them as they fell to the floor of the wagon. I always felt perfectly safe in his care, though I wondered how he was able to manage without one entire arm and hand.

Thomas Earl stood with Norah at the front of the wagon while I sat behind them in a straight (ladder back with a cane bottom) chair. Dear, sweet, black Lindy took one of her handmade quilts and wrapped it around the chair with me sitting in it, carefully tucking it into all of the spaces that might let in cold air. Only my eyes were left uncovered so I could see the treacherous, muddy road over which we must travel to reach home. I never felt fear or concern, but I can still remember how loved and warm I felt, even though it was freezing cold and almost dark, and for the moment it did not matter that it was not possible to travel the last mile home on the school bus; Lindy, Norah, and Thomas Earl had taken care of everything that I needed.

School Days

Today's schools are far and away more advanced and sophisticated than the schools when I grew up. However, in my considered opinion, I personally benefited by the very factors that gave the educational process such a simple appearance. I entered first grade and graduated from high school with most of the same students. Our families had lived in and around Livingston for generations. Nobody thought much about "going home again" because they were already there. There was little faculty turnover, and it was not unusual for all of the children in a family to be taught by the same teacher.

I can still remember the names of all my teachers, although it was many years ago (in 1937) when I began the first grade at Livingston Elementary School. Miss Tilford was my first grade teacher, followed by Miss Everett in the second grade. Miss Lois Bowden, who was very strict, taught us in the third and fourth grades. There was no third grade teacher when I was in the fourth grade, and as a result, Miss Bowden taught half of the third-graders in our fourth grade classroom. I still have trouble understanding how one teacher could teach two classes, let alone how one person could ever be responsible for all age levels in a one-room school. It was in Miss Bowden's room that we learned poetry to be recited every Friday. We stood before the class, announced the title and author of the poem that had been chosen, and in order to receive any credit at all, it was necessary to recite four lines with every "a," "and," and "the" in the correct place. After the first four lines, we received credit for all additional lines quoted in a "letter perfect" manner. The first incorrect word was the signal to discontinue credit, even though the pupil might complete the poem without another error. Special recognition was given in chapel at the close of each year to those students who earned credit for the most lines of poetry correctly recited, and the names of all students who had correctly recited three hundred lines or more were read. It was also in Miss Bowden's room that we constructed a cutaway model of a coalmine.

Miss Carrie Lee Smith, severely crippled by arthritis, taught us in the fifth grade. She ruled with an iron hand and always maintained strict order. I think that most of us were afraid of her—at least I was! Most of us had waited for five years to reach the sixth grade, because everybody knew that Miss Mignon Pitts was a wonderful teacher! She laughed a lot, and we loved being in her room. We raised a garden that year and prepared a meal for our class from the fruits of our labor. In preparation for the meal, we went on a field trip to a small creek behind the school in search of watercress. Our search was rewarded, for we found plenty of it in the fresh water that trickled between the moss-covered banks. We had watercress leaves in our salad. That was a brand-new experience for me. I was convinced that Miss Pitts was very knowledgeable when it came to social graces and the "finer" ways of the city—certainly, nobody I knew in Sumter County knew anything about watercress salad! In retrospect, I think Miss Pitts was likely considered rather liberal for those times: she smoked, and maybe even drank wine! However, this made little difference in how her pupils felt about her. Those of us who were fortunate enough to sit in her classroom for a year thought that Eufaula, Alabama, must be a wonderful place because that was the place of her origin.

All of my elementary teachers had several things in common: each of them was single ("unclaimed blessings); each of them lived in the girls' dormitory at the College; each walked the short distance to school every day; and none of them were local.

Those same observations were also true of our principal, Miss Lucille Foust. She was a small, thin person and extremely stooped. Her white hair was cut short in what was then called a "mannish bob." She always dressed in what we thought were very nice clothes. When she visited in different classes, the pupils were always happy to see her. Besides briefly taking us away from our lesson, it was fun just to listen to her because she knew so many interesting facts and stories. She was the only person who could get away with taking "precious" class time to talk to us. We children liked Miss Foust well enough, but we also had a healthy respect for her; after all, she was the principal. The words "Old Lady Foust chased a mouse all around the schoolhouse" were known and oft-quoted by us—particularly when we thought we were getting even with her in some childish way.

The elementary school was known then as the training school, and in later years as the lab school. It was related to Livingston State Teachers College, and it was very convenient for many of the students majoring in education to do their practice teaching, later called internship.

After the first big milestone that came on the first day of the first grade, Graduation Day from the sixth grade was our next. Completion of the elementary grades was an exciting time for us. No more chapel once a week in the college auditorium, and no more weekly reciting of poems for credit. Even so, I felt remorseful about leaving such wonderfully qualified and dedicated teachers who faced the daily task of molding us into good and productive citizens. But we were off to bigger and better things!

Livingston High School (grades 7–12) was not a large school— fewer than two hundred students. However, the size of the student body in no way diminished the quality of the faculty, which consisted of teachers who were highly skilled and educated, most of them with master's degrees. An example of the quality of the faculty was Miss Eltie Haynie, my seventh grade homeroom teacher. She taught me English in grades 7–9, and Latin for two years. Upon graduating from high school and going to Asbury College, I was placed in the most advanced class of freshman English after taking the placement tests. Our teachers were qualified as critic teachers, which meant that they were capable of supervising college students who were assigned to do their practice teaching at the high school as well as the elementary school. Both schools were coveted assignments. The young prospective teachers had only to cross the football field to the high school or walk a brief distance across campus to the elementary school instead of going to a school located out of town, in which case it would be necessary to make arrangements for housing and other needs.

I don't know just how old Mrs. Susie Moon was, but she seemed ancient to me as a teenager. She taught tenth-, eleventh-, and twelfth-grade math. I was good in math, and I took all of the math classes she taught. Mrs. Moon also appreciated and enjoyed potted plants, and as a result her classroom (along with the auditorium) was filled with beautiful plants. She quickly discovered my love of plants and recruited me to help care for the many, many pots needing to be watered or to have dead leaves removed.

As the senior class of 1949, we chose pink and white gladioli as our class flowers. I conceived the idea of growing the flowers to be used for our graduation, and Mrs. Moon agreed. We found a space for a flowerbed just outside our homeroom window, and we decided that the glads would be grown there. After the bulbs were purchased with class funds, Mrs. Moon commissioned me to direct some of the senior boys in the digging and planting process. What an enviable spot that placed me in! The plants grew well, but we soon discovered that we had a problem. They didn't bloom at the same time, and some of them bloomed far too soon to last until graduation. Fortunately, the local florist had a solution to our dilemma. She suggested that each stem be cut as it was ready, and she would keep them in her cooler. We followed her instructions to the letter, and when the time came, she arranged them into a lovely bouquet. A large basket of beautiful pink and white glads, the labors of our own hands, graced the stage for our commencement.

I was in the seventh grade the year that Mother started driving the school bus, and although I knew Mrs. Moon, she was not my teacher until I was a ninth-grader. Mrs. Moon and her husband, whom she called "Father," lived about a mile from the school. They had no car; therefore, getting to school was difficult for her. It occurred to me that we could pick Mrs. Moon up at her home each morning and return her each afternoon. After all, we drove directly in front of her house. Mother thought it was a great idea, and agreed to the plan. Delighted, Mrs. Moon graciously accepted the invitation. From that time on, as long as I was in school, it was my responsibility to go quickly into her house each morning, help her gather her books and her purse, and get her safely aboard the bus and into the front seat reserved for her. She left her front door unlocked for me because her deafness made it difficult for her to hear a knock. The same responsibility was reversed in the afternoon when I went to her classroom, walked her to the bus, and carried her things into the house and placed them on the dining room table. It was never any trouble, and I loved every minute that I spent with her.

The Moons lived in an antebellum house. The upstairs rooms were used for tourists. A sign in the front yard identified the beautiful old residence as a "Tourist Home." Numerous travelers came through Livingston in those days since Federal Highway 80 (east/west artery) and Federal Highway 11 (north/south artery) intersected there. In addition to Mrs. Moon's income from teaching, there was income from the tourist home. There was yet a third income: Father Moon had a dairy. He was a short man with a pleasant countenance and a soft voice with just a touch of humor in it. He wore blue chambray work shirts that made his eyes even more blue, and khaki trousers kept comfortably around his waist by means of wide suspenders. He was most generally shod with black rubber boots. All of these enterprises kept Mr. and Mrs. Moon busy much of the day, and must have been very demanding, especially since they were elderly.

Mrs. Moon's deafness was a daily challenge, especially in the classroom. A wire ran from the earpiece of her hearing aid to a battery-powered case carried in her bosom. There were sometimes noises and static, probably caused by her clothes rubbing against the case, but she usually attributed those disturbances to some of the "bad" boys in the classroom. In addition to her deafness, she also suffered vertigo attacks. On those days, I was especially careful to help her safely down the steps and onto the bus.

Mrs. Moon was a staunch Baptist. She knew a lot about the Bible, and each of our school days began with a Scripture reading and prayer. Sometimes she did the devotional; on other days, pupils volunteered. Mrs. Moon and I frequently talked about the Scriptures as we walked to and from the bus—usually because I asked her questions. There were so many things to discuss with her about what God expected of me; about my going away to Asbury College in Kentucky; about hard work and good grades; about social and moral issues.

Our high school did not have an alma mater, and young visionary that I was, I wanted our graduating class of 1949 to leave an alma mater as a part of our legacy. I shared my concern and my dream with Mrs. Moon. I can almost hear her soft voice as she said, "Now, Sara Ann, you are the class poet. You write the words, and I know Frances Mellen will help with the music." If Mrs. Moon thought I could do something, then I could! And that was that!

Miss Frances Mellen, whom I adored, was my piano teacher. She had played the organ for silent movies when she was a teenager, and she often told her piano students with a smile, "I have perfect pitch, you know." I believed that she could do anything. She knew every song that we knew—and many more—and could play them all in a manner that would "steal your heart away." It was as though she poured her soul through her fingertips onto the keys of the piano, and she deliberately shared that inner part of herself with us as we listened with our hearts. She was a giving person, and she agreed to set my words to music. Our class of 1949 graduated from a school with no alma mater, but a year later, I heard the alma mater left by my class as a gift as it was played and sung by the student body at the graduation exercises for my sister's class of 1950. What a thrill!

Late afternoon and night activities at the school were limited since many students lived a good distance out in the country; consequently, each activity was special. Mrs. Moon was aware that it was impossible for me to participate in any activity scheduled outside the regular school day. I was one of those who lived a long way out of town, and Mother simply could not bring me back. I loved it when Mrs. Moon would say, "Sara Ann, why don't you just spend the night with Father and me?" Mother and Grannie were never anxious about me when I was with Mrs. Moon. In the senior play, I was cast in the role of the black cook, Demopolis Demijohn, and I spent all of the rehearsal nights with Mrs. Moon and Father. I shall always be grateful for the countless opportunities that were mine, made possible because of the generous hearts of two wonderful people!

Today the Moon House has been beautifully restored, and the LHS Class of 1949 celebrated our fiftieth class reunion there. The house is presently available for special occasions and celebrations. Mrs. Moon and Father died many years ago, but our fiftieth reunion was a wonderful trip down memory lane for me. I climbed the stairs (though not as easily as I used to); I walked from room to room; I recalled the mornings when we shared breakfast together—Mrs. Moon, Father, and me—and after we gathered Mrs. Moon's books and her purse, we waited for the school bus, and Mother.

Summer Fun

Our home in rural Alabama was a large two-story white house built in the early 1800s. It was surrounded by a thousand acres divided into pastures, wooded areas, and fields cultivated by black farmers. In the Old South, there were written and unwritten rules regarding the "shoulds" and "should nots" for people who were not white. Though I understand now that black people were sorely oppressed, I am still amazed and extremely grateful for the wisdom, insights, and inspiration with which they blessed my life at a very early age.

Days in the country in Alabama did not arrive with a multiple choice of fun things to do, and unless one was ingenious and creative, life could sometimes get boring. There were no TVs, the movie theater was eighteen miles away, and our only radio was operated by a large battery. This meant that we listened only to those radio programs that the entire family enjoyed.

One summer, the three of us—sister Wrenn, brother Burton, and I—decided to create a new and wonderful activity that would keep us entertained for the entire summer. Since Wrenn was seventeen months younger than I and Burton was four years younger, the two of them decided that it would be fair if they competed against me. We agreed that we would have a cotton-picking contest, and that at the end of the summer, whoever had the most pounds of cotton would be declared the winner. Unlike many white Southern young people, we had never been required to work in the fields, but that in no way says that we were

The Fuller children
Wrenn, Sara Ann and Burton

never in the fields. We had been there many times while the black people worked. We loved the wonderful stories they told and the rich, plaintive harmonies in the songs they sang.

So it was officially decided! The contest was on! "Let the games begin!"

Mother and Grannie made cotton sacks for the three of us. Each sack was made with a strap that was worn over the shoulder and went diagonally across the chest. The sack was long enough that it fell to the ground and dragged between the cotton rows behind the person picking the cotton, therefore taking much of the weight off the person as the bag filled. So we had our own bags, and it was then that the real work began.

We learned several things that summer. It quickly became painfully apparent that *picking cotton is really hard work*. In addition to that, we learned: the sun gets very hot when a person is surrounded by plants that are head high and so dense that not one breath of air can penetrate; cotton bolls are very sharp and can cause injury to young, tender hands that have not been exposed to hard labor; it takes a long time to fill a bag with cotton, especially if the picker works only brief periods; a full bag of cotton never weighs as much as the person picking thinks.

I worked hard that summer—at least, harder than my competition. I wanted to win this contest. The fact that I was competing against two people (even though they were younger) would be a real "feather in my cap" if I should win. Aunt Sarah Shaver, an elderly black woman, watched with interest as the three of us competed. She had been like a member of our family for years. She was our cook. She stayed with us when Mother and Daddy were away, and I always slept with her. I was her favorite of all of Miss Bessie's children and she referred to me as Miss Bessie's "first born." In no way could she have ever been considered a disinterested bystander; so in her own way, she decided to level the playing field.

Early one morning, in the quiet gray hours just before dawn, I became aware that the sheet under which I was sleeping was slowly moving toward my feet. Half asleep, I pulled it back beneath my chin. The same thing happened a second and a third time. As I finally managed to open my sleepy eyes, I focused on the stooped form of Aunt Sarah standing at the foot of my bed. In her gentle voice, she softly whispered, "Git up, baby. Go pick yo' cotton while de dew is on it. It weighs mo' when it's wet."

From Aunt Sarah's early morning word of advice until the end of the cotton-picking season, I picked very early in the mornings, when it was cooler and when the cotton was damp with dew. But there was nothing (not even dew) that could dampen the joy of my undisputed victory!

I Love a Rainy Day

A premier group of musicians known as the Ink Spots recorded at least two (maybe more) songs that talked about rain. Their tunes were always high on the hit list. One of those songs, loaded with appropriate melancholy and sung with great feeling, tunefully declared:

> "I get the blues when it rains...
> The blues I can't lose when it rains."

During some of my growing-up years, those words were my theme song: "the blues I can't lose when it rains." My days, my nights, my heart were all filled with yearning...and longing...and hope! Besides that, my heart broke with regularity—and usually for no reason. Now in the words of Forrest Gump, "That's all I want to say about that!"

The question that I want to ask is whatever happened to those wonderful rains that used to come and stay awhile? Sometimes it rained all day—even overnight. They were quiet rains—no thunder and lightning; it just rained! And since there were no TVs then, there were no watches or warnings to alert us that terrible weather was approaching. I suppose those long, quiet rains were winter rains. Even as a child, I looked forward to those days. They felt cozy.

It was not hard for my sister Wrenn and me to clean our room till it fairly glistened on a rainy day. We dumped contents from dresser drawers in order to carefully fold and straighten every single piece. Colored pictures of movie stars cut from movie magazines covered our bedroom walls, and we arranged, rearranged, and added to our collection on a rainy day. A rainy day was a wonderful day to read a library book for the book report that was required each month at school. If we could find something interesting to do upstairs, the sound of rain on the tin roof made the day even cozier. There were old trunks up there filled with all kind of things from old letters to beautifully crocheted pieces. They were always good for an afternoon

71

of exploration. Rainy days were—and still are—wonderful.

The storms that came in the summer, however, were significantly different. They were accompanied by thunder, lightning, and sometimes hail, and although we had no televised watches and warnings, Grannie never failed to deliver fearful warnings while she paced from room to room announcing that "there is a bad cloud making up in the west!" Those storms were frightening to us children because Grannie was so terrified of "bad weather," and she taught us by example to be fearful when clouds approached. We were quiet and respectful of "Ole Massa's work" until the storm passed. What a relief when the lightning flashes were less sharp and the thunder grew less boisterous as it moved further and further away. As soon as "the worst" was over, we children ventured out to the front porch, where we climbed into the swing and swung as high as the swing would swing. That was our happy expression that the storm was over.

I felt a little cheated as a child because there was no lovely creek on our farm in which we could wade. So before the raindrops actually stopped falling, all three of us knew exactly what we wanted to do. Uncle Johnnie's pasture lay just across the road in front of our house. It was fenced with barbed wire to keep the cows inside; however, a gap allowed entry into the pasture. A narrow road meandered through the field to where some tenant farmers lived. A short distance down that road, on the right side, there were two or three small sinkholes that could be easily seen by anyone sitting on our front porch. Those holes caught and held water when it rained, and were to us the perfect place to wade. Sticky post oak clay surrounded and lined the bottom of those small earthen cups, and that clay was very slick when it was wet.

As soon as the storm was over, we asked permission to go wade in those holes of water. Mother usually said yes with one restriction: "Don't get muddy!" So off we went, all three of us, down the drive, across the road, through the gap, and to our favorite wading place. The sides of the largest hole were sloped just enough that if we wet and smoothed them, they became slick enough for us to slide down them into the water—which, by the way, quickly became muddy from the activity. The longer we slid, the slicker our slides became. Before long, one of us would slip and fall into the water—mud and all. After the initial fall, it was only a matter of time until all of us were very wet and very muddy; sometimes we just sat down in "our mud hole."

Not only was it possible for Mother and Grannie to see us from the front porch, but the two of them were equally visible to us from where we were having the time of our lives. Sitting there in the mud and mire, we remembered Mother's admonition "not to get muddy." However, we reasoned that since we were already wet, we might just as well go ahead and enjoy the time we had left—no matter that the water was getting thicker and thicker with mud. So there we were, looking at Mother and Grannie while they were looking at us getting filthy—and loving every moment of it!

Mother called us when it was time to come home. We were as dirty as pigs. As we walked the short distance back to the house, we knew instinctively what was coming. We knew that we needed to go by the rain barrel on the east end of the house and attempt to wash off some of the mud. If we were lucky, the worst that was coming to us was a huge tongue lashing, at which both Mother and Grannie were very accomplished. There were days, however, that verbal chastisement simply did not seem adequate; so we were instructed to go bring a switch. It was difficult to be sent on that errand, but the trip back from the "switch tree" was even worse. Our punishment was never unexpected, but we were always hopeful for the lesser consequence for our disobedience.

Just thinking about our mud hole still brings smiles. It is still crystal clear that we understood that we were not to get muddy (though I have not the vaguest idea how we could have accomplished that in a mud hole), yet we were not content to get just a little muddy—we wallowed in it like pigs, all the while knowing there would be consequences! Does that same child still live within me? I shamefully confess that I have since eaten like a pig, and then greedily topped it off with a huge, rich dessert. My reasoning was exactly the same as when I was a child: I had already broken the law, so I might just as well go ahead and really blow it—just wallow in it! I could mention other times and places when the same thought process possessed me, but there is no need. "And that's all I want to say about that!"

So much for mud holes, muddy children, chocolate cake, and overweight adults, for switches and bathroom scales—I still love a rainy day!

Vacations

I can count on one hand the number of vacations that we took as a family. Maybe it was because we were poor and could not afford to travel to new and distant places, or maybe it was because our family was dysfunctional.

We did, however, go on a family vacation to Pensacola, Florida, when I was about six or seven years old. Mother, Daddy, Grannie, Grandma Fuller, three of us children, and Sally (our wonderful black nanny) piled into our car along with our luggage. Sally was going to do all of the cooking and attend to us children while we were away. We loved being with Sally anywhere and under any set of circumstances. It sounded as if this would be a wonderful time because she was going to be with us all day and all night until we returned home.

Vacation in Pensacola, Florida
Adults standing: Mrs. Kerr, Grannie, Daddy, Grandma Fuller, Sally
Children: Wrenn, Sara Ann and Burton

Maybe it was because I did not have much fun that I have so few memories about a vacation that should have been remembered and relished. Without question, the best thing about those days was Sally! Other than that, I remember that we stayed in a concrete block cottage that was very hot, and it became even hotter when Sally cooked our meals.

I have another memory from that same excursion that does not evoke any joy. Daddy wanted to go deep-sea fishing, so we did—all of us. Mother, Grannie, Grandma Fuller, and Sally all wore dresses, and my father wore a sport shirt and long trousers. We children were more appropriately dressed in shorts that Mother had made especially for vacation. I am certain that everyone who saw us knew at a glance that we were not accustomed to taking vacations, and that we were most assuredly from someplace where fishing in the Gulf of Mexico was not a daily happening.

We all got aboard the charter boat and found places to sit. The air was heavy with diesel fumes and when the smell of bait fish was added, it became almost unbearable. I began to feel queasy, and the motion of the boat added significantly to my discomfort and upset. There was a tense air of uneasiness surrounding Grannie, and she had the uncanny ability to convince us children, without saying a single word, that her anxieties were authentic and that we should be as frightened as she was. She was afraid of water; she could not swim and had no intention of learning at her age. To make a bad situation worse, a storm blew up and began to toss the boat about. Sometimes the waves even washed over the deck. I looked to Sally for some assurance from my fear, but there was none. Her face was ashen and her eyes wide with terror. She fearfully moved closer to Grannie and sat down on the deck at Grannie's feet. In a voice choked with fear, Grannie said, "Don't come over here by me, Sally! I'm scared to death!" Mercifully, my memory does not pick up again until we were back at the dock, and even though the earth continued moving beneath my feet much as the motion of the boat earlier in the storm, there has never been a time in my life when I was happier to be on solid ground. The remaining days of the vacation remain a blank; maybe because I had no fun at all.

There were, however, some times, places, and experiences that I enjoyed and considered to be delightful vacations. Those experiences came when school was over for the year, and three months stretched before us until we were again accountable to the school bell. Wrenn and I had two cousins who were our age, so we eagerly planned times when we could visit together in each other's homes. We lived about forty-five miles apart, so when we got together in the summer, it was for two weeks in each home. I am still puzzled as to how our mothers lasted through four weeks of Monopoly games that were finished not because somebody won, but because we always got into a fight; or the times we played bridge and smoked rabbit tobacco like the ladies smoked while they played bridge; or the midnight raids on our kerosene-operated icebox; or all those moonlit nights when we thought everyone was asleep and we sneaked out the upstairs bedroom windows onto the roof and wrote letters to our boyfriends; or the ghost stories we told until we had ourselves so scared that we ended up waking Grannie and going downstairs to sleep; or us getting Mother to let us have the car to go to Emelle because I had my license, and often ending up going further. One summer, after we had been drilled and schooled in the graces of table etiquette, Grannie took Mother, the four of us girls, and my two younger brothers to dinner (the noon meal) at Rosenbush's Café in Livingston. For days before we went, we critiqued each other's etiquette often, chiding the offender by saying, "You can't do that at Bush's!"

In looking back at so many happy memories while at the same time being completely objective, I have come to several conclusions:

One does not need to be any special place to be on vacation ("A bird with feathers of blue is waiting for you, right in your own back yard").

Fun vacations do not have to cost a lot of money.

There is a strong possibility that vacations can and do happen within us.

Those summer days of long ago shared by us four cousins were some of the best vacations I could ever imagine!

All Day with Took

His name was Josh Mitchell, but everyone knew him as "Took." He was a black tenant farmer who lived just across the bottom and on top of the hill behind our house. His wife's name was Julia Mae. She had a lovely soprano voice and could often be heard singing spirituals and old hymns. They had no children, and they were getting to be up in years—"ageable" as Took described it. They had lived on our place and raised their crops there since before my grandfather died. Took had been reliable from the time that Grannie first knew him, and she depended on him for advice in making decisions as to which tenant families she should rent to, or for a report on the wellbeing of the live stock, or when the pools on the place needed to be cleaned out. He

Josh (Took) Mitchell

77

was deliberate and objective in forming his opinions, and Grannie never once considered him anything other than trustworthy.

There were times when Took felt that he needed to come to talk with Grannie about things that were happening on the farm. He always came to the back door, knocked on the doorstep, and called in a loud voice, "Mrs. Burton! Mrs. Burton!" When she admitted him to the house, he removed his hat and rolled it in his hands, thus revealing his white hair, which had been cut very close to his scalp. He always stood just inside the door, and sometimes he rested one of his rough hands on the corner of the mantle. One of Took's eyes turned toward the outside, giving the appearance that he was looking up at the ceiling as he talked. He had a large, booming voice and he stuttered, but his manners were always courtly. He would rather have died than say anything that would in any way seem vulgar or "off-color." He came one day to talk to Grannie about the bull that had been purchased for breeding purposes. It was Took's recommendation that a new bull was needed. He tried to say in every way that he knew that the bull was no longer capable of breeding. Grannie insisted on knowing the exact reason for the bull's inability to procreate. Finally a most embarrassed Took blurted out, "Ahhhh, Mrs. Burton, he done broke dat thang!" Grannie pushed the matter no further. She trusted his judgment, followed his recommendation, and a new bull was purchased without further discussion.

The day dawned clear, not a cloud to be seen anywhere in the sky. It was not difficult to tell that it was going to be blisteringly hot. We were delighted with this new day because we had a plan that had been completed the day before. The plan was that Took could take us to Emelle in his mule-drawn wagon if it did not look like rain, and there was no sign of rain anywhere. We were up early in order to get our beds made, pick up any clothes that had not been hung, eat a good breakfast, and get dressed and ready to go.

Vivian and Elizabeth, our cousins from Meridian, Mississippi, were spending two weeks with us. We looked forward to their visits because Mother and Grannie allowed us to do "special" things when they came—and going to Emelle in Took's wagon was a very special thing. Sister Wrenn, brother Burton, Vivian, Elizabeth, and I made up the passenger list. I cannot imagine what could have possibly persuaded Took to agree to spend a day entertaining us. Surely there must have been some way he could have wiggled out of it, but he did not.

When Took drove his wagon up to our house that morning, we were ready, even to having enough nickels for everybody to have a "Co-cola." We were quickly seated on the floor of the wagon. We were off on our day's journey amid peals of laughter and continuous giggles. Since Burton was the only male, he rode beside Took on the spring seat. Nothing could have convinced us that there were any girls anywhere in the world who were happier or more excited than we.

Took clucked to the mules, slapped them with the reins, and we were finally on our way. Down the drive, onto the farm road that wound its way through our plantation, across the bridge that spanned the ditch behind the house, up the hill, and we were at the first of many gates that had to be opened. I was the official gate opener because I was the oldest child in our family, and our visitors were city girls. It just seemed right that I should jump out of the wagon and open the gates. It was very important to keep the gates closed; otherwise the cows might get out of the pasture and into the crops, or worse yet, they might even wander away, get into the road, and be hit by a car. We made it safely through the first gate and left it securely closed.

By that time, the sun was already hot, and the wagon was moving at a snail's pace. Took had pulled his well-worn felt hat down over his eyes and face, and had begun to doze. The mules most likely had been in the barn overnight without water, so when they became aware of the pool of water ahead of us, they picked up their gait and did not stop until they were at least knee-deep in the water, where they drank deeply. In the process, Took jerked to attention, appearing to be completely surprised, and after the animals had drunk their thirsty fill, he cracked the whip and skillfully got the team back onto the road. We were again on our way. Took spent most of the trip asleep—or so we thought. He showed no signs that he was paying any attention to his passengers or to their ceaseless chatter.

My memories of our time in Emelle are not as clear as that of our mode of transportation or of our wonderful driver. We all had a nickel, so we happily enjoyed our "Co-colas" fished from the icy cold water in the drink box. Emelle was a small rural town with few accommodations. There were no public bathrooms (or toilets as they were called then). Finally, as the day wore on, Took told us it was time to start home, and we did not argue nor beg to stay any longer. We did not have anything else that we needed to do since we had spent our money and enjoyed a cold drink.

The trip back home was much the same, only in reverse; however, it had gotten much hotter. We were completely wet with sweat. Even our hair dripped. The mules were hot. They switched their tails to keep the flies off their backs while they slowly pulled the wagon, whose passengers were not having nearly as much fun as they had earlier. Besides the heat and the flies, we really needed to go to the bathroom, but under no circumstances would it have been considered "proper" for us girls to tell Took that we had to stop to go to the bathroom. Besides, there was no place for us to go unless we went into the woods where we could not be observed. No! No! No! That could never be considered an answer.

Vivian, the oldest of us all, decided that we could probably work the problem out to some degree of satisfaction, and Took would never need to know. After all, he was asleep and the mules were faithfully plodding toward home. Vivian carefully pulled up her dress, pulled down her pants, and perched herself on the tailgate of the wagon. For a moment, this seemed like the answer, and the process was in motion, when alas and alack!—the road went through a sand bed, the wagon lurched, and with one swift motion Vivian flipped off the wagon onto the ground. As surprised as she was to find herself there with her pants down around her knees and her dress up, she quickly made every possible effort to get her clothes adjusted, while at the same time making a mad dash for the back of the wagon, which continued to move at a snail's pace. The challenge of getting her back on board was accomplished by the three of us girls left in the wagon extending our hands and dragging her back on.

And Took! What did Took do? He never indicated that he was aware of any problem. His hat was still pulled down over his eyes, and he appeared to be dozing there on the spring seat as the sun relentlessly beat down upon us. The team of mules plodded on toward home. There was another gate or two to open and we were home. What a day it had been! The shade of the front porch offered such comfort, but not nearly as much as our outhouse.

I miss those days when there was never a thought given about children's safety when they left home for the day in the company of a black tenant farmer. When we finally had the courage to share our experiences of that trip with Mother and Aunt Nina, it became a page in their memory book also. They never once expressed any regret that we had gone on that memorable excursion, nor did Mother feel that she had made a wrong decision in allowing us to go. Days were simpler then. Trust was a part of our culture. We knew and partially understood even then that "it takes a village to raise a child." What good fortune that Took was one who lived in our village!

Depending on the Weather

Weather is an element whose importance is held in common by all mankind of present and past generations. It is ours, yet we do not control it. It is and has been the topic of countless conversations since time began. Difficult and awkward moments sometimes occur when two or more people struggle feverishly in an attempt to make conversation, and when all else fails, the weather is always a viable topic for good conversation. The old standby! Weather is a subject that never fails to introduce diversity: some think it is too hot, while others complain about how cold it's been, or the sunny days have been perfect, but the farmer complains that his crops are in dire need of rain. And so goes the conversation that is limited neither by age, sex, race, social status, financial security, nor personal ignorance. All people, great and small, are able to comfortably participate in a conversation centered around the weather, because all mankind experiences it.

Some of my earliest recollections are of severe thunderstorms that occurred during hot, sultry nights in the summer. I am not certain what awakened me—whether it was the sharp claps of thunder or the low, rhythmic moans coming from my grandmother as she sat on the side of her bed, fully awake and frightened to death. My sister and I slept in Grannie's large twenty by twenty–foot bedroom, which accommodated two full-sized beds quite adequately. Grannie was paralyzed with fear even as clouds began to gather, and most assuredly when a storm appeared to be imminent. We children grew up watching her suffer through any weather that was not sunny or moonlit. As the lightening flashed and the thunder rolled, her silhouetted figure, clad in her long white cotton nightgown, rocked slowly back and forth as she cried in a pleading, almost pitiful voice, "Ooooooh, Lord! Have mercy, Lord! Ooooooh, Lord!" We were taught from an early age to have a genuine respect for "old Massa's workings."

I remember one particularly violent Alabama storm that was in process one afternoon just as we were getting out of school. On really bad weather days, we did not walk from the school building to the buses; rather, each bus was identified as it came to the front door of the school, where we waited until our bus was called to load. Everybody was finally on our bus that day and we had begun the trip toward home when the earth and sky were suddenly illuminated by a brilliant flash of lightening, accompanied by a fireball that danced along the power lines. The sky was black, and night appeared to be rapidly approaching long before the clock indicated that it was time. Rain came down in torrents. The ride home was treacherous. At long last, we were on the final mile of our trip. The dirt roads were very muddy and slick from all of the rain that had fallen, and driving was difficult at best. However, Mother was an experienced and careful driver, and we reached home safely even though we arrived in a downpour.

The storm continued to be extremely violent, and I felt a real sense of uneasiness in the pit of my stomach all the way home. I was acutely aware of how terrified Grannie was during such a storm, especially if she were alone. As it turned out, she was not exactly alone because my little brother Howard had not yet started to school, and he was there with her. Howard told me recently that he and Grannie had gotten on the bed when things became really bad. According to Grannie, the bed was always the safest place during a thunderstorm, because lightening was not supposed to strike the feathers used in pillows and feather mattresses. So when storms came, Grannie usually summoned us to her bed, where we remained until the storm subsided.

We children felt very protective of Grannie, and it seemed to me that some of her anxiety would be relieved if one of us were inside the house with her. It was a given that anyone would be drenched to the skin before reaching the shelter of the front porch; nevertheless, I told Mother I was going to make a dash for it. Upon getting inside, I found Grannie a nervous wreck! She was blurting out something about there having been a terrible noise somewhere near the kitchen end of the house. It did not take long to discover what the noise had been. Only a pile of splintered wood remained where the smokehouse had once stood. Located very near the house was a large building that had been built many years earlier by my grandfather. It was used as a smokehouse where fresh pork was smoked, cured, packed into large wooden boxes, and covered with salt to preserve it. It had been the storage place for our year's meat supply—and in seconds it had become a pile of rubble.

Mother, Wrenn, and Burton came inside a few minutes later, when there was slight letup in the rain. Though the storm had not fully abated, Grannie was noticeably better than when I had first entered the house. We were all safe! As we viewed the wreckage of the smokehouse, we were in total agreement that it must have been some bad storm to cause such total destruction to a building that had survived so many other storms through the years. And we were amazed that though it had sat so close to the house, there appeared to be no damage at all to the house.

Our attention was quickly diverted by a highly excited voice that we immediately recognized as Sally's. She was calling to us as she ran up the front walk, up the steps, and onto the front porch. Between gasps, for she had run all the way, Sally told us that their house had been blown down, and that her husband Ed and Aunt Sarah were trapped inside.

There was no time to waste! Sally and I ran back along the muddy road. Upon reaching their yard, our hearts filled with thanksgiving as we saw Ed and Aunt Sarah standing safely in the yard, outside and away from the demolished house. They had crawled through an opening made by the chimney as it fell away from the house. Ed, who had recently had an appendectomy, was still recovering, and was extremely weak. Aunt Sarah was a very old woman, and my love. It was she who taught me how to make a toothbrush out of a twig from the plum bush, and she who made me "play-like snuff" from cocoa and sugar and put it into one of her snuff boxes that she had washed ever so clean. I carried it in my pocket just like Aunt Sarah. When Aunt Sarah dipped snuff, so did I.

By that time, the rain was falling much more softly. Mother and Burton joined us. We were soaked to the skin, but rejoiced that we were safe. Surely it was a small tornado that touched down on the west side of our house, destroying the smokehouse, then somehow lifting over our house only to strike Sally and Ed's house. Though there was a sense of relief that we had been spared, there was a pressing need that had to be immediately addressed: Where were Sally, Ed, and Aunt Sarah going to spend the night, for it would not be long until dark? Having grown up in the Old South, I understood that there was a line drawn between the black and white races across which we did not go. We did not live together nor did we visit socially. Yet it was quite acceptable for Aunt Sarah or Sally to come and spend the night with Grannie and us children if Mother and Daddy were away. All the pieces did not seem to fit. It did not make sense to me.

I am not sure who issued the invitation—I don't even know the words that were said—but what I do know is that three wonderful black people spent the night in our house that night—in the house that all of the black tenants vowed was haunted by Miss Lou Amerson. They were there every night after that until they were able to make whatever living arrangements they needed to make until their house was rebuilt. They stayed upstairs while they were with us, and Sally took at least part of their food upstairs in order that Aunt Sarah and Ed did not have to walk downstairs. And each morning before anyone was awake, Sally was up, dressed, and at the old house site clearing away the rubble, cleaning brick, and helping in the rebuilding process. I loved having them with us, but they were so happy when they were finally able to get back into their own place.

Don't ask me how it happened; I don't know. Those events were highly unusual for that time and place. Perhaps it was simply the perfect time to experience the fact that it was a loving God who made us all, regardless of the color of our skin. If anyone is interested in what I really think, I think it was a miracle. It was a miracle that we were all safe! It was a miracle that we shared bed and board with people whose skin was a different color from our own. There is an interesting saying that goes like this: "It is an ill wind that blows no good," and though the splintered buildings were a reality, it was also a reality that Sally, Ed, and Aunt Sarah were welcomed guests in our home. These events would be far from noteworthy in today's world, but those kinds of things simply did not happen in that time and in that place.

There has been lots of weather since that storm, and I am still learning new and interesting facts about this phenomenon. I have been exposed to terms like "dew point" and "wind chill"—terms that are much more sophisticated and concepts that are much more accurate than what our science teacher told us in seventh- or eighth-grade science. He explained that God created the world and that everything was perfectly balanced. Maybe because he was a Baptist preacher, he felt as though he would betray his faith if he did not mention God in relation to creation. But, he explained, there were times when the earth became unbalanced. This occurred when one side of the earth suffered a drought, thus causing the soil to become dry and lighter in weight on that side. The solution always came in the form of rain that soaked the parched earth and made the dry side of the earth heavy enough to bring things back into balance once more. I suppose it all made sense to me when I was in the seventh grade!

As television was coming upon the scene, and more and more people were experiencing the joys of owning their own sets, two people in the little town of Emelle were heard discussing the daily weather forecasts. They agreed that forecasting was in no way a perfect science. The conclusion to the conversation came when one of them said, "You know, we used to have pretty good weather till Mr. Bob Holland [a local meteorologist] started messin' with it!"

And now a word of advice: If and when the party grows dull and the conversation lags as it sometimes does, introduce a topic about which everybody is informed and can speak, and they will surely let you know what they think—depending on the weather!

One Cherished Bike

It was Christmas morning, probably 1942 or 1943. It was cold, but Mother had made a fire in the living room fireplace, and the room was filled with flickering light from the flames, even though there was not much heat yet. A kerosene lamp had been lighted and placed on the upright piano near the Christmas tree. The tree was a large cedar that had been cut and brought in from our pasture. It was mounted on a wooden foot made from two pieces of two-by-four notched and fitted into each other to form a cross. A huge nail through the center of the foot was driven into the tree trunk to hold the tree upright.

All of our decorations were old—used year after year—but we loved them. We made snow from Ivory Soap Flakes by adding a small amount of water and beating them with a handheld eggbeater until the mixture formed stiff peaks. This process produced a concoction similar to stiff egg whites, and we tipped all the branches of the tree with it so that the tree had the appearance of being frosted with freshly fallen snow. Our tree was beautiful beyond description, and the aroma of fresh cedar filled the room. The glow of the kerosene lamp, the flickering light from the fireplace, and the wonderful odor of fresh evergreens transformed our living room into a place where we went only in our dreams—or maybe on occasions like that day.

It was, however, the item in front of the tree that captured and held our undivided attention. Our eyes were fixed in disbelief upon it. There, with kickstand down, stood a blue-and-white America's Best girl's bicycle! The tubular metal frame mounted on two wheels with wire spokes assumed a proud posture that immediately convinced us that this was a bike second to none, and the best thing about it was that it was ours! It wasn't that this was the first bicycle in the community, for practically everybody except us had one. Each of us—Wrenn, Burton, and I—had wished for and wanted one so badly, but we knew that bicycles were expensive. We also knew that our family did not have a lot of money to spend on nonessentials. Though we did not discuss it, we were all aware of the great sacrifice on Mother's part that such a gift required. We were filled with an overwhelming sense of love and gratitude for her that day, and even though we knew better, we could almost envision Santa as he happily placed that blue-and-white beauty beside the tree for us—all of us—on Christmas Eve as we slept.

It occurs to me now that there was only *one* bike, yet there were *three* children! We never had a thought of to which of us this gift belonged. *It was ours!* All that day we took turns riding up to Uncle Johnnie's house and back. Two of us sat on the front steps until the rider returned for the next one in line to have a turn. The road was dirt and was muddy in spots, so when dark came, we cleaned the tires and carefully saw that our new possession was as shiny as it had been that morning. Since it was a full-sized bike and our front steps were steep, it required two of us to get it up the steps, onto the front porch, and into the front hall. Even though we were exhausted from riding all day, we checked on our new bike several times before we went to sleep that night, and it was the first thing we saw the next morning.

I cannot say how long this shared means of transportation lasted. We never rode it to any particular destination unless it was up to Uncle Johnnie's house on one side of us or to Sally McDaniel's house on the other. Each of us hoped that one of our neighbors would be in the yard or on their front porch so we could visit for a while. I think that sometimes we rode just to get away; to be free; to find a new and interesting spot in the road or to discover a plant that we had not seen before. Though it did not happen often, we were aware of the possibility of meeting a car, so we rode with great care.

We took good care of our bike, but finally the aging process began to take its toll. Even though it had spent every night inside, rust began to develop and some rattles and squeaks became evident. Finally we took both the front and back fenders off. We decided that their removal did not deal much of a blow to its overall appearance; in fact, it gave the bike a "faster," sleeker look. The seat and handle-bars seemed to need adjusting far too often. Flat tires or a broken chain were common occurrences. Thank goodness there were no gears to complicate matters. Large parts of my summer days were spent repairing our bicycle, but that was not a bad thing.

Uncle Johnnie was my mother's half-brother. He was twenty-six years older than she and was much like a grandfather to me. He had a work shop and lots of wonderful tools—at least my childhood mind understood that his shop was well equipped with tools. We had a special relationship, Uncle Johnnie and I; we called each other "Partner." He suffered from a disease known as myasthenia gravis, and sometimes he wore a neck brace. When he did not have the brace on, he held his chin up manually. He was tall but slight, and he walked with a rolling kind of motion. He had patience beyond measure. So Partner and I spent lots of hot summer afternoons (after his nap) at the workbench outside his shop under the hackberry tree. Sometimes we could make the bike go again, and other times we failed. We did not have money to buy new parts that would have made repairs a snap, but the upside of it all was that I learned a lot from Uncle Johnnie about tools and improvising. I also came to realize just how wonderful it was to have someone take the time to help in solving my problems. My "Partner" died when I was thirteen, and I experienced grief like I had not known before. Many repairs went undone and long hours spent under the hackberry tree with him were over. There were times later when I tried to accomplish tasks on my own, only to realize that it was not working, and I remembered how Uncle Johnnie would quietly say to himself, "Hot brown you!" I said it, too; maybe because I missed him so, and just remembering him for a moment brought comfort.

The bicycle outlived Uncle Johnnie, and we continued to ride it a long time after he was gone, going no place in particular; just riding. I have no memory of what happened to the "final remains" of that wonderful means of mobility. There should have been at least a slight pause to recognize and appreciate the hours of joy it brought to three children, and though Mother never hinted that it had been a sacrifice for her, I am convinced that she struggled to make that bike a reality for us.

Life would have been different without that blue-and-white America's Best bicycle. How could we ever have managed without it? In recalling the joys and challenges shared by the three of us, I am aware that today's children have their own individual bikes—or two or three. I do not feel one bit deprived that the three of us shared one bike. I am grateful that I learned to share and to take care of my possessions, and I value the lessons learned from "Partner" as we so often attempted "the impossible" at his workbench in the shade of the hackberry tree.

...And Lilac in the Spring

"Be careful, now, or you'll hurt yourself running around that flower pit." This parental warning was undoubtedly justified, for we often played rag-tag baseball or football in our front yard, and on occasion, we experienced some painful scrapes and cuts. Whatever the game, we always ran and played with complete abandon, and exercising good judgment never occurred to us until it was too late. The flower pit was right in the middle of our field of play, and we knew to play carefully around it—but we always had to be reminded.

My Grannie was the original "Mrs. Green Thumb." Everything that she placed into a new pot grew as though being moved had in no way interrupted its life cycle. It was as if the small plant taken from its parent plant had been delivered at birth and the growth process was at that point set in motion. From the moment she got the baby settled into its new environment, it busied itself to outperform all of the neighboring plants. It never seemed to matter to her plants that other plants grew larger, or were prettier, or smelled sweeter: "they just bloomed where they were planted."

The big open front porch that stretched across the front of the house was the perfect place for Grannie's countless potted plants, clothed in their spectacular summer dress. Several benches rested just inside the banister; each bench was covered with flowerpots. Being so near the edge of the porch allowed the plants to catch some of the sun's rays as well as the balmy breezes that occasionally stirred their leaves and branches. A magnificent bench, made from a single piece of wood that measured eighteen inches wide and sixteen feet long, stretched from the front door toward the west end of the porch. It was probably constructed when the house was built in 1840. Even though that special bench was built for heavy duty, it sagged a little when Grannie got all of her flowers arranged and settled on it.

The long porch served as home for Grannie's "children" from early spring through the summer until fall began to arrive and the nights turned cooler. Actually, the flowers appeared to like the cooler nights, which came as a welcome relief from the sultry nights of summer, which cooled only slightly and brought only slight relief from the languid, hot days. The cooler nights were also a warning to Grannie that cold days and nights were soon to come, and her beautiful plants that had brought such joy all summer would need a warmer place in order to survive until the next spring.

We children looked forward to the moving day when all of the flowers were taken one at a time to the side of the flower pit and set carefully on the ground. My grandfather had built the pit for Grannie many years earlier. It was nothing elaborate, just a square hole in the ground that Granddaddy had the black tenant farmers dig. It was located in a place in the yard that sloped slightly, which meant that one end of the pit was deeper than the other. The large begonias were placed at the deeper end of the pit because they were tall and required the extra depth. Smaller plants were nestled in wherever there was room. Two wooden benches were in the bottom of the pit to keep as many plants as possible off the ground. A small pipe placed in the lower part of the pit ran underground to drain any water that might collect and stand on the floor of the pit. One of the black men who lived on the place always came to help with the move. He stood in the bottom of the flower pit while Grannie stood at the side of the pit and directed the entire process. We children knew our assigned tasks. We were charged with bringing the plants from the front porch to Took or Ed, who would in turn carefully place them into the pit. When they were all tucked in and safe for the winter, we could no longer see any of the dirt floor; it had all been covered with flowers— a wonderful bouquet!

A piece of wood was placed from side to side across the opening of the pit to support pieces of tin roofing that covered the entire opening. The pieces of roofing overlapped each other, thus assuring that there were no leaks. Pieces of wood were laid along the outside edges of the tin to keep it from blowing off the pit when the wind blew. But flowers need sunshine. Grannie knew that, so on warm, sunny days, she directed us to "uncover the flower pit" and let the sun shine in on her plants. Opening the flower pit always brought a longing for spring as we gazed upon the green leaves and a few remaining blossoms nestled away in their safe, sheltered place where they were protected from the cold blast of winter. But about mid-afternoon, as the day begin to cool, we were trotted out again, this time to "cover up the flowers."

Our winter landscapes were bleak and bare. Sometimes if the day was warmer, and if the sunshine tugged at us until we were no longer able to remain indoors, we took to the fields and pastures for a walk. Whether conscious or unconscious, we were actually in search of some sign of spring. As we walked, our hearts kept asking with the poet, "If winter come, can spring be far behind?"[3] We walked along the banks of Big Creek where we knew the shy little violets grew and became even more aware of our yearning for some clue that might indicate that the new life of spring was only days away. Our hearts sang with joy at the first sight of violets and their little purple faces that pushed their way up through the brown blanket of leaves that had covered and warmed them through the winter. About the same time each spring, the wild plums and haws began to show their lacy white blossoms as well.

Flowering quince was among the first of the shrubs to bloom in our yard. Signs began to quietly announce that winter was loosening her icy grip, and we knew warmer days would come very soon. The sun did not run away in the evening as early as it had been doing, robins appeared in numbers and diligently scratched for worms, and bluebirds gathered material for their nests in preparation for the arrival of babies. The real proof of spring, for me, was going into the yard and discovering that the lilacs were celebrating this long-awaited season as they flaunted their showy lilac blossoms, so filled with their lovely delicate perfume that all who passed were compelled to breathe a little deeper than normal in order to capture its fragrance.

Then Grannie began to be restless, for it was getting to be time. The days were finally warm enough. The cover was removed from the pit, and the flowers lifted gently from their winter bed. The porch had been bare all winter, but no longer. The underground benches in the pit were uncovered, and the benches on the front porch were covered with flowers. Dead and tired leaves and blossoms were removed, and Grannie again had her babies where she could water, feed, repot, and take proper care of them. It was not unusual to hear her speak to

---

[3] Percy Bysshe Shelley, "Ode to the West Wind."

them and assure them of just how beautiful they were.

After the flower pit was emptied and every flower was assigned its special place on the porch, the pit was carefully covered for the summer. The inside of it was dark and cool, and we children feared that it then became the summer home for snakes, since several had been killed near its outside edges.

Grannie's love of plants moved next to my mother, then to me and my sister. My own house is heavily populated with plants—some very old, but they seem to know that they are safe, and that they will not be discarded because of their age, just as the babies that come on parent plants know that they will be birthed, potted, and tended with care. My love for flowers is the same: the anticipation of wishing winter goodbye has not changed; my hopeful anticipation of spring days is still vibrant; and I still look for lilac in the spring!

What If and Play Like

What if the moon really were made of green cheese? And what if the man in the moon has always lived there? What if a watermelon really did grow out of your mouth every time you swallowed a watermelon seed? What if drinking coffee really would turn you black? What if you really did have seven years of bad luck when you broke a mirror? None of these "what ifs" allow much wiggle room. They state a circumstance and give the results of it. The "what ifs" that I am thinking about allow a person to declare his or her own circumstance as well as envision the ultimate outcome. My idea of "what ifs" would place the world and its riches at my disposal. If I had wings, I could mount to the sky like an eagle! What if I had a million dollars—or two?

The philosophy of "what if" is not far removed from the idea that "wishing will make it so." My high school English teacher used to frequently quote a four-line ditty that should have reminded us that wishes and reality are not now and never have been one and the same. The rhyme went like this:

> If wishes were horses
> Beggars could ride.
> If wishes were fishes
> We'd have them all fried.

I cannot help thinking that perhaps life would be a lot more fun and living would be so much easier if everything just happened the way that we played like it would. I never plan or dream things that are difficult, discouraging, or depressing, yet I know full well that life sometimes goes in those directions. When I pamper myself and do some authentic daydreaming, the outcome is nothing but pleasant, beautiful, and perfect, because I chose it to be so.

I am convinced that planning and dreaming are vital parts of any healthy child's growing up process. In glancing back to the years of my childhood, I still remember some dreams that I sincerely hoped would become a part of my real life when I grew up. Much of our childhood play was built on what we believed or hoped our adult life might be. It was an escape from where we were, I suppose. We didn't play like we were children, because that is what we were; we played like we were somebody else, or like we were all grown up, and life was not just good, it was perfect.

I was not overly unhappy as a child. There were many occasions when I was perfectly happy just being a child. I loved playing hide-and-seek or hopscotch, or sitting on Grannie's lap while she read to me, or riding our bike up and down our country road. But there were other times when I wanted to break those chains of childhood. So I mentally ran away into the land of "play like," and as if by magic, I could become whomever I chose!

Since I was a tomboy, there were many times when I played soldier with my younger brother. There were other days when I really thought that I wanted to be a cowboy (or cowgirl) because I loved riding Old Gray. I enjoyed the solitude of riding through the pasture in the evenings, during that time after the sun had set but before darkness wrapped the earth in soft shades of night. Other times my brother and I would go hunting. We never killed anything, but we wandered about the fields armed with air rifles and slingshots. We felt very grown up because we were away from the ever-present watchful eyes of the adults in our family. We had been allowed to carry "firearms" into the fields unsupervised!

As time slipped past, my tomboyish-ness took a different turn. I began to dream of the time when my handsome prince charming would come for me, and I would go away with him to some place where we would live happily ever after. I spent a lot of hours and lived a lot of "play like" dreams as I looked toward my future of becoming a wife and mother with a family of my own. But before I ever thought about my true love, I played countless games about lots of other things.

Children, I think, are naturally creative, and with a little effort, we children were always able to find a suitable spot to play house. There were several choice places at our house. Just outside Mother's bedroom window was a huge mulberry tree whose large branches provided cool shade most of the day: a perfect place for a house. When it rained, our playhouse was moved under the back of our real house, which was about three feet off the ground. It didn't matter that the taller we grew, the more we had to stoop to get inside our imaginary house. On winter days when it was too cold to play outside, we moved our "play like" house to the toy closet, the space underneath the stairs. We played house when there was no one around but us, and we played house when friends came to visit.

We played house most of all when our cousins, Vivian and Elizabeth, came to visit us each summer. Not only did we have a "play like" house at our house, but we also had one in Meridian at their house. None of our playhouses had walls except in our minds. The outside walls of our houses were carefully outlined with bricks. Broken spaces in the line of brick indicated doors. Sometimes we divided our houses into rooms. This allowed us to play like we were sitting on the front porch or eating breakfast or whatever the day's activities might dictate. Of course, cleaning and cooking were important parts of keeping house and demanded attention every single day.

The Meridian playhouse was not inside our cousins' back yard like the one at our house. A drain ditch bordered one side of their property, and a railroad crosstie had been carefully placed across the ditch as a means of crossing. A very large oak tree stood across the ditch from their house, and anybody could tell that it was the perfect place for a playhouse. Wrenn and Elizabeth were the chief builders of that very special place, and they were the ones who spent most of their days within its "play like" walls.

One day those little girls spent most of the morning in their house. They were very busy. They were canning! Adult women always canned and preserved as much of the summer crops as possible to provide for their households during winter's cold days when the gardens and fields lay dormant as they rested in preparation for spring planting. Aunt Nina allowed the girls to take some canning jars, some of which they filled with green leaves (their "play like" turnip greens) and others with green chinaberries (their "play like" peas). Their hard work was interrupted only long enough to go to the bathroom or to come inside for the noon meal.

About mid-afternoon, Vivian and I decided to visit those two busy "p'like" (Southern pronunciation of "play like") ladies. When we reached the footbridge across the drain ditch, we found Wrenn and Elizabeth sitting about halfway across it. Their legs dangled from the bridge and swung back and forth from time to time. They were no longer canning "play like greens" and "play like peas"—they were cleaning chitterlings! They knew exactly how to clean chitterlings because we watched every step of that process every time hogs were butchered for our family's supply of pork.

For anyone who does not know, chitterlings are the small intestine of the hog, and are used for food. The first step of the cleaning process was to empty the contents of the intestine by "slinging" it. One end of the intestine was then closed off with one hand while the other end was filled with clean water that was washed back and forth from one end to the other until it was clean. We children loved to watch Sally perform that rather unpleasant task when we had a hog killing. She did it with such grace and efficiency that we children thought of the entire process as a really fun experience. The old folks used to say, "We eat all of the pig but his squeal," and so far as I am concerned, I would have much preferred the squeal to the chitterlings.

But back to Wrenn and Elizabeth—what were they using as their "p'like" chitterlings? Aunt Nina raised chickens that ran free in the back yard. They were fed and watered daily, so the one taking care of those birds got to know them on a rather up-close and personal basis. Thoughts of killing and eating them could sometimes be troubling— maybe even problematic! Catching and killing them, plucking their feathers, removing the parts that were not edible, cutting the whole chickens into pieces, and finally frying them was quite a process, and we children had no idea how much work was involved. We were only aware of how delicious it was when Aunt Nina called us to eat. She was a wonderful cook, and that day at noon, we were delighted to see a large dish of crispy brown fried chicken on the table. We devoured it in short order, then licked our fingers and wished that we were able to eat just one more piece.

Some time later, Vivian and I decided to visit Elizabeth and Wrenn in their playhouse, only to learn that our intended hostesses were busily cleaning chitterlings. We also made other discoveries. They had quietly sought and retrieved the discarded, inedible innards of the chickens earlier that day as Aunt Nina prepared for our noon meal. And there they sat, those "play like" Southern ladies who had been so innocently playing house a few hours earlier—cleaning chicken guts for their "p'like" chitterlings.

I do not remember exactly who blew the whistle on the girls' new endeavor, but I do know that Aunt Nina was a mighty unhappy lady, and that was not a good thing! Wrenn and Elizabeth were not allowed to play in their grand house for the remainder of the day—maybe longer. Possibly the best thing that came from that experience was the joy that we four girls still share as we tell and retell every sordid detail over and again.

We grew up when there was no money for expensive store-bought toys and there were no TVs or video games. The absence of manufactured playthings was our motivation to look for new and different kinds of entertainment. We learned to be creative with what we had. Hours of "what if" and "play like" provided opportunities to resist boredom while embracing a time and place where we could be anybody we chose; we could do whatever we wanted to do; we could go wherever we decided to go—but "p'like" chitterlings? You must be kidding!

Gray, the Color of Mud

Not everybody who lived in the country had a horse. We didn't. Grannie had a team of mules named Rhodie and Dolly. They were fine animals used for pulling a wagon or a plow, but they were not for riding. The black tenant farmers used to sit sideways on their mules' backs sometimes when they came from the field, but we were never allowed to ride the mules. They were for work.

When I was a really little girl, Daddy brought home a Shetland pony named Ted. Until that time, whenever there was an opportunity to ride a regular-sized horse, I had to be lifted by strong adult arms from the ground to the horse's back, and suddenly, there I sat atop that magnificent animal whose riding place had been far above my head just a moment earlier. My legs were too short to reach the stirrups from the ground; neither could I touch the stirrups from my perch in the saddle. As I sat there on top of the world, my hands clutched the horn of the saddle with a death grip.

I had always, always wanted a horse, and the Shetland pony that Daddy brought home was surely the realization of all my dreams. Shetland ponies are a small breed of horse only about forty inches high at the shoulder, so I assumed immediately that I would be able to mount him without difficulty, and my feet would reach the stirrups in the small saddle that came with him. Finally, at long last, I would be able to ride *my* horse *anytime* I wanted to ride and for *as long* as I wanted. Perfect.

It did not take long, however, to realize that Ted was not going to be the perfect pony for the three of us children. Every time we approached him from the left side (the side from which one mounts a horse), Ted quickly turned his head and bit us. Mother and Daddy finally agreed that this beautiful gray Shetland pony was much too mean for us to be around. I don't remember what happened to Ted, but somehow, at some point, he just wasn't there anymore.

I loved visiting with Jane Ramsey because her family had two or three horses we were allowed to ride. Some of their names elude me now, but the horse I rode was called Whistle-breeches. He was a bit more spirited than the other horses, and at times he was quite "skittish." I felt completely in charge and as free as a bird when I climbed upon the back of that beautiful roan horse. There was only one downside to those weekends: they ended, and we went home to no horse.

Then came the day when we were no longer deprived! We saw a huge white horse eating grass in our pasture. He then came to our barn to be fed. I cannot tell when or whence he came. My best remembrance is that Daddy got him as a work horse. He was probably part Percheron: massive and strong. He certainly had every appearance of being capable of doing heavy work. This acquisition of a work horse somehow makes no sense now because my father was a barber and never did any work with a horse; however, it was not unusual for Daddy to bring things home that might or might not be useful.

The three of us children quickly became acquainted with this fine new animal. Even though he was completely white, his name was Gray. He soon came to be known to us as Old Gray. Though he was large, he was very gentle. Permission was asked and granted by our parents for us to ride him. At first, he allowed us to walk up to him in the pasture and slip the bit into his mouth; however, he was neither worked nor ridden regularly, and he became more and more difficult to catch. Approaching him was not the difficult part, for he allowed us to get close enough to extend the bridle toward his head, but just as we were about to slip the bit into his mouth, he would turn, gallop a short distance away, and stand looking at us. It was almost as though he were laughing at us because he had fooled us again! After several failed attempts, I decided to ride our bike and chase him into a fence corner. It worked, but only after I had ridden as fast as I could over terraces and through thick grass, and was completely exhausted.

Our cousin Elizabeth from Mississippi was visiting us one summer. We had grown sick and tired of playing Monopoly and Chinese checkers, and our best option for something else to do was to go riding on Old Gray. We finally ran our playful friend down and got the bridle on him. We led him back to the barn since none of us could mount him bareback because of his large stature. We usually threw a saddle blanket or a quilt across his back in humid weather to protect us from his hot, sweaty back and hair. We could have used a saddle, but since there would be three of us riding, an old quilt was just fine.

While we were at the barn, Grannie called to us, "Don't forget to water that horse, and don't ride him into the pool! He might bog up!" We clearly understood what that meant. In the summertime, the water level in the small pools on the place would lower because of the water consumption by livestock, horses, mules, cows, etc., as well as from the evaporation caused by the sun's hot rays. As the water level receded, the clay soil surrounding the water was wet (or at least damp) and became very slick and boggy. Sometimes in really hot weather, cows waded out until the water covered their backs to keep cool and to get away from the swarms of torturous flies. On occasion, the cows bogged up in the mud and could not get out. It then became necessary for the men on the farm to pull them out, and if they could not, then it took mules and horses to get the job done.

That day, after the quilt was smoothly on Gray's back, we led him into the loading chute normally used for loading cattle into a truck. Once we had Gray in the chute, we climbed up the outside walls and slid easily onto his broad back. I was in front, Elizabeth was next, and Wrenn was on the back, with each one holding on to the one in front. Finally, the three of us were in place.

After some discussion, we decided to get the watering detail over with at the beginning of our ride, so we headed slowly toward the small pool that was near the barn. The pool was surrounded by willow trees, which gave the appearance of coolness; however, it was not cool anywhere that day. Water had covered the dried soil around the edge of the pool only a few days before—and it would again as soon as the fall and winter rains came. In our considered judgment there was no danger in letting Gray wade into the edge of the water to drink. We had done it many times before—and besides, if we dismounted, we would never get back up onto Gray's back—so very slowly and carefully, we rode into the water. However, before we knew it, Gray's front legs were mired up to his stomach, and he was struggling to free himself. In a split second Wrenn slid off Gray's tail, with Elizabeth not far behind. Somehow the quilt fell into the water's edge as the two girls slipped to the ground. I vaguely remember Wrenn and Elizabeth as they ran toward the barn, around the curve, and past the mock orange trees that formed a thick hedge. Gray was still struggling and I was still on his back when suddenly he pulled himself free and fell onto the solid ground surrounding the pool. I shudder now when I think that I could easily have been beneath that massive horse when he fell.

Gray quickly got to his feet. He was not hurt. I do not know what brought Wrenn and Elizabeth back to the pool, but they returned. We stood for a bit just to catch our breath, and there before us was the muddiest horse we had ever seen—and it wasn't just muddy water. It was thick, sticky mud! We earnestly set about assessing our situation. It would have been such an easy solution if only we had had running water and a hose. We could have simply given Gray a bath. We decided that the water in the pool was one option; but alas, it was as muddy as Gray since so much mud had been stirred up in his attempt to pull himself free. This obviously was not the answer. Maybe the leafy branches of the willow trees would do it. We quickly broke a number of them. Holding one end of the branch tightly in each hand, we pulled the branches along Gray's muddy legs toward the ground, but that did not work. We were dealing with really sticky mud. We made no progress at all in removing that thick goop from Gray's beautiful white coat that was now the color of mud. We were in deep trouble, and we all three knew it.

After much wasted effort and a lot of careful deliberations, we gave up! Just simply gave up! Poor muddy Gray still stood patiently, almost as if he were waiting for us to finish cleaning him up. But that was not to be. Instead, we led him back toward the barn, stopping at the gate to the pasture where he was kept. We hastily opened the gate, gave him a sharp slap on his muddy hindquarter and called out, "Giddy-up!" He turned quickly and galloped away beneath the trees and across the open field.

We carefully hung the quilt in the barn to dry. After a reasonable time, we went back to the house. I don't think there was a lot of conversation about our horseback ride that day. I clearly recall the anxious uneasiness that shrouded each of us. We were acutely aware of the real possibility that Gray would come to the barn, muddy as he was! Or what if Grannie should see Gray as he grazed in the pasture? He was no longer a white horse; he was the color of mud!

I think there must have been countless bargaining moments with

God as we subconsciously prayed that it would rain—rain hard, maybe even for a day and a night, long enough to wash the mud and stain from Gray's coat, long enough to restore his pure white color, and most of all, long enough to wash away any and all evidence that might incriminate us.

Pass It On

The days of the Great Depression of the '30s finally ended, and people everywhere began looking for a better day. Countless individuals and businesses had gone bankrupt. Bread lines were the rule instead of the exception in many places. I am told that when I was lying in my cradle as an infant, my adopted aunt came home after having been to Livingston. Upon entering the house, she walked to my cradle, bent over and whispered in my ear, "Honey, the Bank of Sumter just went busted!" Actually, I never became much more aware of the severity of those difficult days than I was when Aunt Eleanor whispered that tragic news when I was only a few weeks old.

Recovery from the financial devastation was long and arduous. As a result, money was never spent frivolously. Bare necessities were often difficult to obtain. But this was the world into which I had been born. I had never known any other way of life, and so I accepted that way of life as being "normal." Besides, everybody else was poor, so at that young age, we didn't know that times were tough. One might suppose that as I grew, I would have become more aware of how extremely frugal Grannie and Mother were, but those were the times when adults took care of business matters and children spent their days running carefree and loving being children.

Recreation was not considered a necessity; consequently, little to none of our hard-earned money was ever spent for such things. Going to a picture show (now called movies) was a treat, but tickets cost a dime. My grandmother had come from a very strict, conservative, religious background, and she never liked for us to go to movies. To her, it was not a wholesome activity. On those rare occasions when we did see a movie, she always recalled that she had been to a movie once. Then after a pause, she would continue that as she entered the darkened theater and walked down the aisle to her seat, she felt strongly impressed that she was on the downward road to perdition. Under no circumstances would we ever get permission to attend a

Sunday movie! In Grannie's mind, movies and sin were synonymous.

There was no money to pay admission into any of the other recreational activities of the day; besides, we lived a long distance from town, and even though gasoline cost only seventeen or eighteen cents a gallon, it was never wasted! Even with all of these factors coming into play, it must never be construed that we had nothing entertaining to do—quite the contrary! We learned at an early age to be both resourceful and creative when it came to entertainment. We played Chinese checkers, Monopoly, Parcheesi, and Rook. We even learned how to play bridge a little. We also entertained ourselves for hours at a time when Grannie pulled out the bag filled with leftover scraps of fabric used to patch torn items or to make quilt tops. If time allowed, under Grannie's tutelage, we sometimes pieced squares of fabric together to make a quilt—even though we never finished one.

Of all the things from which we could choose, probably the thing we liked to do most was to spend weekends with friends, and there was a proper protocol for those special weekends:

We asked permission from our parents to invite a friend or several friends to our house for the weekend.

Only after permission was given was the invitation issued to the prospective guest or guests.

Our friends then asked permission from their parents to come.

The parents of the visiting child wrote a note to the principal requesting permission for their child to ride the bus to the friend's house if it was different from her regular bus.

Usually the parents participating in this process of a child's visiting in another's home either knew or knew something about the other family involved. We understood that we were accountable to the parents where we were visiting, whether at our house or in the home of a friend. We were usually allowed to stay up a little later than normal, but even after the lights were extinguished and we were tucked in bed, there was always lots of giggling.

The Ramseys lived about three miles from our house. We were good friends from early childhood. Our parents liked for us to visit in each other's home because our families had been neighbors and friends for three generations. The proximity of our houses plus our longtime friendships brought an added dimension of comfort as we visited back and forth. So it was not surprising that when my sister Wrenn and I were invited to spend the weekend with Jane, our mother agreed. The day finally arrived. It seemed that school would never end that Friday, but at long last we climbed aboard the bus and were on our way home. We had planned a thousand things to do that weekend.

A beautiful little stream ran through the pasture in front of the Ramseys' antebellum home. We decided that we would spend Saturday morning damming up the creek that meandered through its damp, lush bed nestled between deep banks. As in many of the pastures, the creek was lined with trees and bushes that created a shady, cool, private play area. This was the perfect place for our "hideout." Since we knew that we would be hungry before we returned home, we took a jar of peanut butter, some crackers, and a knife from the dining room with us. There was only one thing wrong with this picture: Aunt Lally, Jane's mother, had warned us about going into that particular pasture because that was where the bull was. We had always been taught to have a healthy respect for the male gender of that species, which meant: "Avoid getting inside the same fence with a bull!" But somehow that day seemed different, and we felt that we would be just fine. So we proceeded with haste to the pasture where the bull was!

We worked hard on the dam, and it grew quickly. Water began to back up and get deeper between the rows of fern that covered both banks of the creek. Searching for rocks, bringing them to the construction site, and laying them in place was hard work, so we took time out to sit along the shady bank and have a snack. All the while the water backed up behind our dam, and it was a perfect place to wade.

Suddenly from above the dam there came the sound of small bushes breaking as though being trampled and crushed beneath the feet of a huge monster. The threat came closer and closer—right down the creek bed. As it came nearer, we clearly heard a low, guttural sound accompanied by heavy breathing. It was the bull! In instantaneous concert, three little girls, scared out of their minds, scampered to their feet and ran as fast as legs weak from fear were able to move them. We stopped to catch our breath only after we were safely on the opposite side of the barbed-wire fence from our previously unseen assailant. The Scripture we heard Mother quote so often as she related it to guilty consciences seems appropriate now as I recall the events of that day: "The wicked flee when no man pursueth; but the righteous are bold as a lion" (Prov. 28:1).

We looked at each other with great relief when we realized we were safe. Actually, we felt rather proud of ourselves when we considered how brave we had been. We were on the verge of celebration when, like a bolt out of the blue, we came face to face with the reality that we had left the jar of peanut butter behind on the creek bank in our shady picnic area. I suppose that would not have been of such great concern for us under today's circumstances; however, what we knew was that every evening for supper at the Ramseys' house, we always had a bowl of clabber, along with peanut butter and crackers. Clabber is thickly curdled sour milk, and can be eaten with either salt or sugar, and we knew without a doubt that the clabber would be there. But what if there was not another jar of peanut butter? There was no money to be spent on spare jars of peanut butter or other food items to be placed in reserve on a pantry shelf; consequently, items were purchased only as they were needed. What were we going to do?

After considerable deep thought, we knew that we had only one choice: we had to get that jar of peanut butter, and I was the one to retrieve this lost treasure. That seemed to be the best plan. After all, I was the oldest, I could run the fastest, and I would most assuredly be on the lookout for that raging bull. My heart was beating like a tom-tom. We knew that if Aunt Lally found out where we had been, we would be in some kind of big trouble. As bravely as I could, I made my way to the spot along the creek bank from which we had fled only a short time earlier. The jar was right where we left it. We had left the lid off as we ate, and luckily it was lying nearby. I quickly grabbed up both pieces, along with the knife and the box of crackers. I somehow managed to close the jar while running like the wind, for I was now headed in the direction of safety.

Safely through the fence for a second time, we quickly discovered that there was something different about the peanut butter jar. There was a thick, slimy coating on the outside of it. Upon opening it to take a peek, we saw that the peanut butter had been pressed down into the jar and was very smooth. We slowly began to understand what had happened. We knew that cows ate peanuts and peanut products. It seemed reasonable to us that our bull friend had smelled the peanut butter and tried to get it out of the jar with his tongue, thus smoothing and packing it inside the jar. It was only natural that his big tongue reaching toward the peanut butter inside the jar caused saliva to drip off his tongue and run down the outside of the jar.

We didn't make a lot of noise as we went back into the house that day. Two of us kept watch while the other one washed the outside of the jar. Then, removing the lid, we carefully stirred the smooth peanut butter so that it had the appearance of having been dipped into by many knives.

We held our breath that night as we sat at supper and bowed our heads for the blessing. We were so tired we could hardly move. We gladly and thankfully accepted our bowl of clabber. However, as the peanut butter was passed, we stifled our giggles. When it came to us, each in turn quietly and politely said, "No, thank you!" and we quickly passed it on.

The Ghost Became Flesh and Blood

Everybody knew that our house was haunted. At least, it was a fact known to all the black tenant farmers who lived on our plantation. My sister, brothers, and I loved the times when one of the tenants came to discuss business with Grannie. There was always the chance that we might get to talk with them before they left, and sometimes the conversation would drift to discussions of spirits, ghosts, or "haints" which could be either good or bad.

When Sam Bradley talked about "Mr. Burton's spir't," everyone who heard his stories instinctively knew that he was speaking of a *good* spirit. Mr. Burton was my grandfather and the owner of the land that Sam farmed. The loving expression in Sam's eyes and the gentleness in his voice were indications that Sam knew Mr. Burton to be a *good* spirit. Sam remembered him as a good man who was fair in his dealings both with the tenant farmers and in his business practices in the community. My grandfather preached somewhere every Sunday, many times in a black church. It was a given that such a good man's spirit would never return to harm or get even with anyone. Sam told us that there were many times when he had spoken with Mr. Burton after he "passed," and he was not frightened at all; rather, he was glad for any opportunity to talk with him.

On the other hand, he told of experiences with spirits that were not so good. For example, one night while Sam was hunting, his hound dog treed a big possum. Delighted that he would not return home empty-handed, he clamored up the tree to retrieve his catch. After climbing some distance up into the branches of the tree, there was unexpected trouble, and a fight broke out—a terrible fight. After a hectic scuffle, Sam was thrown from the tree by an unexplained presence that he described as a "one-legged baby." It was a bruised, battered, and badly shaken Sam who went home that night—empty-handed.

When these stories and other conversations took place in our presence near sunset or just before dark, our childish imaginations began working overtime. And if we thought long enough, we remembered that there was a cemetery just behind our barn. My grandfather had given space years earlier as a burying place for local black folk. Their funerals were long and deliberate and usually required most of the day. Riders on horseback and those in mule-drawn wagons entered the pasture by a gap located at the top of the next hill where Ed and Sally lived. It was a long, slow, solemn procession that wound its way along the narrow pasture road as they approached the grave that had been opened earlier. As I became more and more uneasy about our close proximity to the cemetery, I remembered that some of the graves were sunken, and I wondered if that might be a passageway from within that grave to the outside world where we lived that would allow the spirit of the deceased to move in and out. Spirits were different, you know, and were not limited by flesh and blood.

Eli and Lou Amerson (my grandfather's sister) lived in our large two-story farmhouse before it belonged to my grandparents. Mr. Eli was a "ne'er do well" kind of fellow, and as a result, much unhappiness, bitterness, and just plain hard times were housed within those walls. Because of Mr. Eli's irresponsibility, Aunt Lou became the strong, dominant person of the pair. There was another dimension to this woman that set her further apart from "normal" folk: She possessed the gift of divination. Aunt Alice Thomas, an elderly black woman who lived on our place, told the story of losing her hen and chickens. She visited Aunt Lou and inquired as to where her chickens were. Aunt Lou told her that the chickens were under a cotton basket in the chimney corner of a neighbor's house. Aunt Lou was right. Aunt Alice Thomas went to the neighboring house, found her chickens, and took them home with her. Countless other such accounts served as testimony to Aunt Lou's "powers."

Word was that late one night Aunt Lou thought she heard someone breaking into the living room window, which was across a wide hall from her bedroom. Arming herself with a hatchet, she crossed the hall. Opening the door to the empty room made a vacuum-like sound, and if there was actually an intruder, he fled! That was a wise move on his part, else he might well have had a hatchet buried in his skull had he proceeded to enter. The community knew about all of these stories, and after both Eli and Lou were dead and gone, it was firmly believed and discussed in the black community that "Miss Lou" still walked about her house at night.

While none of us children ever actually saw a ghost, stories surrounding our house were rich with events that were not always easily explained or forgotten—by us anyway. But late at night when the house creaked and moaned and groaned, our hearts raced and our mouths became dry as cotton, and we wondered if it might be Miss Lou just walking about. It was during those times that all of us children would have felt much safer if we had been in bed with Grannie.

My sister and I planned during the winter months for the two weeks during the summer when our two cousins from Mississippi came to our house on their annual visit. Playing Monopoly was one of our favorite things to do. As I recall those animated games, I am compelled to add that next to playing Monopoly, we must have enjoyed fighting, for seldom did we ever finish a game without first having a vocal confrontation followed by someone kicking the board, and then the fight was on.

During those visits, we four girls slept upstairs in the east bedroom, just above Grannie's bedroom. My sister Wrenn and I grew up sleeping in Grannie's large bedroom, which resulted in our feeling much more secure and protected while in the presence of an adult, particularly when it was dark. Sleeping upstairs all night with no adult present was a bold venture that required all the courage we were able to muster. Telling and retelling ghost stories only reinforced our ever-present feelings of uneasiness.

When Vivian and Elizabeth came, we were allowed to stay up later than usual. One night after going upstairs, we decided to play Monopoly till we went to bed. Almost immediately there were some disagreements related to the game. As the discussion progressed, our conversation became more and more boisterous, then became physical, and then a chase began. First we ran in wide circles around the room, then one of us jumped onto the bed and crossed it with a big step or two before jumping off on the other side, only to run a few steps and cross the second bed in the same manner, followed by the other three girls. Our voices were at high pitch by that time. Running the circles continued until the one being chased stopped dead in her tracks, and the other three piled in behind her. As we faced the open door, it was impossible to miss the figure clad in white from head to toe—just standing there as big as life. It had appeared suddenly and without a sound. Since we were so thoroughly brainwashed and acquainted with the world of the supernatural—and since we were already scared because we were out of the company of an adult—we were not at all certain just what we were seeing. Without a word, two of us walked reverently to the side of our bed and quietly sat side by side, never taking our eyes off the presence in the door. The other two girls followed suit on their bed.

A profound silence filled the room, but did not last long. The stillness was suddenly replaced by the pounding sounds of two bare feet on the wooden floors as the white-clad presence stomped her way into the room, round and round, running in circles, interrupted only by larger thuds made by occasional jumps. A casual observer would surely have thought a member of some ancient tribe had returned and was doing a rain dance or some other ceremonial ritual. As the dance continued, a single long braid of white hair rose and fell upon her back with each stomp.

Finally, in a breathless yet explosive voice, Grannie said, "Now do you understand what this sounds like downstairs? [gasp] Who could sleep with all of this going on up here? [gasp] Get your pajamas on right this minute, and that light had better be out before I get to the bottom of the steps!" We followed every direction just as Grannie had ordered. There was no further discussion that night—not even any girlish giggles beneath the covers. It was not long until four little girls were sound asleep.

I don't know if there is a moral to be drawn from this story. I do know that many years have come and gone since that night. I know further that the four of us girls still recall the events of that evening with lots of laughter, and more fond memories than we can count of a much-loved woman who for a moment convinced us that at least one of our ghosts had become flesh and blood.

Tardy Treasures

Our families had been friends for three generations. When my grandmother moved to the area as a new bride in the early 1900s, Mrs. Fulton was already there. Their homes were about three miles from each other, but they were not more than acquaintances until their daughters came along. They quickly became better acquainted when my mother and Aunt Lally went to school together. Those two girls grew up together, went to college together, married about the same time, and, as fate would have it, their children were born close enough together that they became the best of friends, just as the generation before them had done.

Jane and I were the oldest. We entered the first grade together in the fall of 1937. Wrenn began school the next fall. Drew and Burton started first grade in 1940. Then came Lawrence, and nobody was his age! My brother Howard (eleven years younger than I) and Margaret Annie Ramsey were exactly one year apart in age, and they often came and went places together. The Fuller children and the Ramsey children were predestined to become the best of friends, and our friendships were blessed and encouraged by our parents' stamp of approval.

Though our families had ever so much in common, there was one significant difference: Without fail, the Ramseys were late for everything. Their tardiness was one of those things that everybody knew about and made allowances for. I think this flaw came into the family when Aunt Lally married Mr. Andrew, whom she affectionately called Hobo. He called her Gal. My grandmother used to say that she believed the Ramseys were the slowest folks she had ever known. She continued by adding that Mr. Andrew just didn't know how to leave when it was time to go home. He would rise from his chair and start toward the door; however, before reaching the door, he managed to find a convenient chair upon which to lean, all the while turning his hat round and round in his hands, and there he stood…and stood…and stood! He was ever so pleasant, as was evidenced by the slight smile that played comfortably about his lips. He spoke slowly, even for a Southerner, and sometimes it was mighty tempting to urge him to just "get on with it."

Once, Mr. Andrew and Aunt Lally were invited to a community barbeque. The hour grew late—and later—and Mr. Andrew still had not gotten home. Aunt Lally bathed and dressed, all the while becoming more and more agitated. She sat quietly stewing in the swing on the front porch as evening shadows began to lengthen and night slowly wrapped the earth in darkness. And finally, there he was! At long last! The Ramseys' white Ford car sped up the drive with a huge cloud of dust rising behind and around it. There was another well-known fact about the Ramseys: Their cars never had any brakes. After his rapid approach, Mr. Andrew skillfully geared the car down to slow its speed, and it ultimately came to rest at the log placed across the drive for that exact purpose. He jumped from the car, slammed the door, and made a mad dash for the house. He rushed up the steps, across the porch, and through the screen doors. In his haste, he failed to notice Aunt Lally sitting silently in the swing.

She arose from the swing and quietly but firmly gave the directions, "Hobo, go get in the car!" Without a word, he turned toward the front door and started for the car. Aunt Lally followed with a basin of water, a bar of soap, a towel, a washcloth, and clean clothes. She nodded for Mr. Andrew to get into the back seat. "I'll drive," she said. And drive she did. She was well aware that they were already late, so she did not waste any more time. She fairly flew along those dark country roads, up and down hills, around curves, and when she hit a bump in the road, the water sloshed and splashed over the sides of the basin while Mr. Andrew reached and struggled to keep everything in place. When they arrived, Mr. Andrew was bathed (sort of) and dressed. They enjoyed the perfectly delicious food, loved every minute of visiting with good friends, and at the close of the evening, returned home. They adored each other until they were parted by death many years later.

Mother drove our school bus, and the Ramsey children were the first to be picked up—in good weather, that is. We drove the short distance from our house to theirs, turned the bus around at the end of their drive, then backtracked that distance before going on to pick up the Little children. I cannot recall a single time that all of the

Ramseys were waiting at the road when the bus arrived. Either Drew or Lawrence was first out of the house, but never together. Whoever was first would be near or on the bus when the other one jumped down the steps and started down the drive. And lastly, Jane appeared. She was rushing and in such a hurry, sometime even hitting a slight trot before reaching the bus. Out of breath, she pulled herself aboard and collapsed in a seat with one of us. But that was the good weather route.

When it rained, or if rain appeared to be imminent, the Ramseys met the bus at Sumterville. The road between our house and theirs was treacherous and could not be traveled when it was wet; however, there was a road that ran in the opposite direction from their house to Sumterville that could be traveled in bad weather. Of course, there were days when we got our signals crossed, when the Ramseys thought that we were coming to their house to pick them up and Mother thought the roads were too bad to travel. We did not have a telephone then. That would have made things too easy. As they waited for the bus that was not coming, the Ramseys became even later than they would normally have been. Mother always waited at the bus stop in Sumterville as long as she could for Jane, Drew, and Lawrence without causing the rest of us to be late for school. Sometimes they made it before we pulled away, and sometimes they didn't. Whether they were late or *very* late, their white Ford car always appeared to be traveling very fast (Grannie described it as "breakneck speed"). Perhaps their reason for going so fast was that they were always late and forever trying to catch up.

As they drove into Sumterville from the north, they came up a small hill and just sort of bounced into view. I loved the times when it was dry enough for us to tell that they were coming by the huge billows of dust rising behind their car. It was one thing if they arrived to catch the bus in Sumterville. But if we had to leave them, we knew exactly what would happen next. The children sitting in the back seats always turned to face the back of the bus. From that position, they could keep a sharp lookout for the Ramseys' car as they attempted to overtake the bus. As soon as the car was sighted, whoever saw it first yelled in glee that the Ramseys were in hot pursuit. Mother slowed the bus, pulled to the side of the road, and allowed their car to pass. She followed behind until their brakeless car could be brought to a stop.

Jane, Drew, and Lawrence, along with books and lunches, quickly climbed aboard the bus. We relaxed during the rest of the ride to school. Everybody who was supposed to be there was finally there.

My grandmother often declared in a voice so solemn that it could well have been recognized as the voice of a prophet, "Time and tide wait for no man!" Those words brought a deep sense of dread and gloom to me, because I felt Grannie was weighing the remaining days of her life with great seriousness—maybe even reluctance. On a lighter note, however, maybe our family arrived on or ahead of time because of Mother's attitude of anticipation expressed in the old adage "The early bird gets the worm." (Incidentally, my response to that would be "But who wants a worm?") I am convinced, however, that the most appropriate and accurate phrase for the Ramseys was "Better late than never!" If they were not present when things began, we firmly believed that they were somewhere on their way. We learned not to be angry when they were late; we were just delighted when they arrived. They were such good friends. There was never a question as to our deep love and appreciation for them. In traveling back to those wonderful days beyond recall, I know beyond a shadow of a doubt that the Ramseys were and continue to be our timeless (though tardy) treasures.

"Sumterville Siftings"

The Sumterville that I remember was a quaint little village nestled near the state line of western Alabama, about midway north and south in the state. It was a small, sleepy, peaceful Southern town that appeared to have been gently set in place many years earlier. To get there from our house, we traveled narrow dirt roads toward the east. It was about five miles through farm and pasture land with a scattering of tenant houses along the way.

Mr. Charlie and Miss Hannah Little were the only white family living between us and Sumterville. They were a wonderful family with three children: Eddie, Nell, and Roma Jean. Alice came along much later. They were very poor and did not own a car, so they often went places with Mr. Charlie's brother, Martin. Eddie was the proud owner of a handsome black horse named Pharaoh, and most of his travel in the community was done on horseback. Eddie and I were teenage sweethearts. We both worked on Saturdays at Miss Louise Lang's country store. Eddie rode Pharaoh to our house each week and left him in our barn. Mother or Daddy took us from home to work in our car. Eddie came home with us after work, and then rode his horse the remainder of the way to his house. One Saturday night after work as we arrived at home, we saw that our barn was ablaze, and tragically, Pharaoh burned in it. There was no one there to lead him out of the flames. The entire community grieved, both for the loss of our barn and for Eddie's handsome horse.

Another two miles or so past the Littles' house, a large, square, one-room building appeared on the right. It rested upon a small hill just as the road made a slight turn to the left. That was the Baptist church. It was surrounded by dark green cedar trees and had large windows covered with shutters. The slats in the shutters were always closed. There was no steeple and no church spire, and my childish mind wished for a cross or some symbol that identified it as a House of God.

Just a short distance from the Baptist church, across the road on the left, was the abandoned Methodist church, which had long ago fallen into disrepair. There had been no regular worship there for years. The property was surrounded by a rusty iron fence that appeared to set it apart as a special place. Behind the church was an overgrown cemetery. Many who had earlier worshipped within the walls of that church and had faithfully supported the work of the congregation now rested quietly in the hallowed grounds behind it. The road turned rather sharply to the right, went up a small hill, and we were there—in Sumterville. From that point, it was possible to observe the entire village.

Miss Willie Ramsey's house was up a small embankment on the right. Her small country store sat beside the road in front of her house. Miss Willie was postmistress and the post office was in one corner of her store. From the front porch of her store and off to the right, the Presbyterian church, nestled against a small hillside, was in full view. The dirt tennis court with its sagging net lay to the right of the small dirt road leading to the church. The court seldom had lines except those drawn in the dirt by those folks who played. Countless hours were spent in what might be considered a losing battle in an effort to keep the court free of grass.

On the left of the church and at the crest of the hill sat the old one-room schoolhouse that had long been abandoned. The community children were bused to Livingston to bigger and better school buildings. A teacher for every grade was even more progress! A long, steep set of concrete steps led from the schoolhouse down to the heart of Sumterville, the place where two dirt roads crossed each other: one running east and west, the other running north and south. Right there in the middle of town was a well-worn old windmill that turned and moved as the winds directed it. It had stood there for years as though it had been assigned the task of marking the heart of this special little place.

Both Miss Kate Bayless's store and house were across the road in front of the old school building. A giant hackberry tree stood in her front yard. It was stark and bare during the winter, but in the hot, humid summers, it covered the yard with dark, cool shade. To the east of Miss Kate's house and across the road running north and south was an abandoned store used by the Baker brothers, who raised bees.

They took orders for queen bees and shipped them as far away as Canada. Of course, they always had honey for sale.

The Ozments' house was in the corner across the eastbound road from the bee house and across the southbound road from the schoolhouse. Mr. Ozment and Miss Hassie had seventeen children, and all of them were loved by their peers. Possibly out of necessity, each had developed a sense of independence. They all had chores to do around the house and barn, and not a single one of them was spoiled. Annie Lou was our age and was the second youngest child in the family. Her brother Gump was just older than she and was the heartthrob of countless teenaged girls. He was captain of the football team and was the jitterbug champion. His sense of humor was unmatched by anyone that we knew. If the party was dull or even dead, Gump could change that simply by walking into the room. He was "the life of any party."

Wrenn and I often spent the weekend with Jane Ramsey, one of our closest friends. During one of those visits, Aunt Lally, Jane's mother, allowed us to go to Sumterville on Saturday afternoon. We were left in the care of Jane's grandmother, Miss Willie Ramsey. She was very busy on that day because local tenant farmers went to town on Saturday to do what shopping they could afford and maybe pick up their mail. We three girls played at her house until there was nothing else left to do; then, deciding to stroll up and down the dirt streets, we somehow wound up at the old one-room schoolhouse. Some of the community folk had been talking of possibly converting that building into a community house to be used for meetings and social occasions, but nothing had been done up to that point. The building was kept locked, but we discovered one window that was not. Up went the window, and in went the girls for a peek into this onetime school that now held great intrigue for us.

Though the building appeared to be a simple box from the outside, we were delighted to find that there was a stage on one end with small rooms on each side of the stage for costuming, entering, and exiting. There were lots of dirt daubers and wasps, but they held no fear for us. We even discovered a small pile of cotton in one of the rooms beside the stage. My guess is that it was left over from a government-sponsored program that provided materials for people who were needy and were willing to make mattresses. The room was dark since it had no windows, and we were curious as to what this pile of cotton might be hiding. I have no idea where the match came from, but we struck it to investigate. In so doing, the head of the match flew off and into the cotton. The entire pile of cotton ignited and flashed as if it had kerosene on it. At exactly the same time, three girls tumbled out the window that had earlier been their entry, running in all directions and screaming as loudly as we could, "Fire! Fire! Fire! Help! Please, help!"

Fortunately, Gump Ozment was in the basement of his house across the street cutting potatoes to be planted. Hearing our cries for help and yelling back and forth to discover what was happening, he came with a bucket of water. Word of fire spread rapidly throughout Sumterville. Soon Miss Kate Bayless and others brought buckets of water up the steep flight of concrete steps. The fire was soon out with no harm done. Throughout the entire ordeal, Gump's good sense of humor was evident, and we probably would have been laughing uproariously if we had not been scared to death. Miss Kate wore her stoic expression until the last flame was extinguished. I suspect that she was thankful for her status as an old maid, and she was doubly thankful that she had never had children who could quickly and without warning bring trials and tribulations capable of turning parents gray much before their time.

We girls feared for our lives, but for the life of me, I cannot recall that we were punished. Perhaps Aunt Lally thought that the embarrassment and humiliation were enough. Everybody in Sumterville knew about the fire, and they looked at us in that knowing way. And besides, Mother was going to find out. Our lives seemed to be much simpler then. Mischief was treated as just that, and accidents were overlooked and forgiven; in the spirit of the times, there was never a police report filed regarding that fire in Sumterville. Neither was there a news story listing the offenders and the heroes.

But as with most things, we survived and time has healed the wounds. While I don't really think that the Saturday afternoon fire hastened the conversion of that old schoolhouse into a much-needed community house, it was not long until exactly that happened. As part of the youth of the community, we enjoyed a place for ice cream socials, dances, moonlight picnics, and parties, and a stage for skits and plays was a bonus.

Sumterville still exists, but not exactly as I remember it. Miss Willie Ramsey and Miss Kate Bayless are both dead. The faithful old windmill in the heart of town has been gone for many years. But the one-room school turned community house still resides on the hilltop and continues to be the center of social activities. I shudder when I recall the events of that day so long ago. It is difficult not to dwell upon what might have happened, but I must not leave my thoughts there. I am ever so grateful for the bucket brigade that came to the rescue; for the community of Sumterville; for the wonderful people who lived there and loved us; for that wonderful old building where children learned and played long ago and where community folks still gather. Not only am I grateful, but I am also joyful as I realize again that even though the old landmark may have been a bit scorched, it was not burned to the ground. And that's a fact!

ADDENDUM: The title of this story is borrowed from the *Southern Home*, a county paper printed in Sumter County, Alabama, when I was a child. Communities and neighborhoods throughout the county submitted news for weekly printings. Those contributions were identified by titles that made them readily visible for the reader. Emelle's news was titled "Emelle Events," Gainsville's news was "Gainsville Gleanings," Geiger's news was "Geiger Glimpses," and Sumterville's news was "Sumterville Siftings." I am grateful to Mrs. Lawrence (now deceased), editor of the *Southern Home*, for the perfect title for these ramblings and siftings.

Twice My Childhood Friend

I was born, grew up, graduated from high school, went away to college, and married in the same small community of Emelle, Alabama. My mother had the same experience before me. For three generations my family had been a part of that community, and as a result, we knew everybody. This, however, did not mean that we knew thousands of people, because it was a rural area and the population was far from dense. We were born with generational ties, but we still had the option of choosing who would be our closest and dearest friend. Those choices were not always deliberate ones, but sometimes they came as a direct result of the circumstances of who and where we were.

Aileen Lang was a few months younger than I. We were in the same grade though not in the same school. She went to school for the first six grades in the one-room schoolhouse in Emelle, while I went to school in Livingston, where there was a teacher for each grade. I went to Livingston because my father owned the school bus, and the route began at our house. Aileen would have had to pay to ride the bus to school in Livingston because there was a public school in her community, and she was expected to attend there. Upon entering the seventh grade she came to Livingston, and I was thrilled at her coming. We competed for the best grades, participated in all of the school activities, and were a part of the tight-knit group of girls who called themselves "The Big Four."

Aileen's mother gave me a job in her general merchandise store, where I worked each Saturday from a little after noon until nine thirty or ten P.M. I earned a dollar per day when I started my job. Aileen also worked on Saturdays. Miss Louise was a wonderful employer. She increased my pay with time and experience. There were a few occasions during the summer when she needed to be away during the week, and I tended the store for her. She left the keys with me so that I could open up and lock up daily. She trusted me.

My job also had some real fringe benefits. During World War II, many items were rationed. Tires and gasoline were purchased according to the automobile owner's placement in the war effort. For instance, a farmer was allowed more gasoline and tires than a person who lived in town and whose work was not considered vital to the war effort. Sugar, meats, butter, and canned goods were also rationed, and stamps issued by the government according to the number of family members were required to purchase them. Items such as chewing gum, chocolate candy bars, and nylon stockings were not rationed, but they were very hard to come by. When Miss Louise was able to get shipments of those coveted items, she put them under the counter for special people. I was one of those.

Many of our "sloppy-joe" sweaters, penny loafers, and yards and yards of fabric came from her store. Mother made most of our clothes, and Miss Louise made most of Aileen's. In fact, Miss Louise's sewing machine was kept at the store, and when she was not busy with customers, she was frequently sewing.

Those Saturday afternoons were long and busy, unlike days during the week when Emelle's merchants were seldom busy. In the afternoons, some of the local white folk often came to the store for a cold Coca-Cola and pleasant conversation, but on Saturday, all of the black folks who were physically able got cleaned up, dressed up, and came to town. There were small groups of them standing and visiting under large oak trees, while others were gathered in the shade from buildings. In the winter, as many as possible huddled around the coal stoves inside the stores. They worked all week, and on Saturday, they walked, rode mules or horses, rode in wagons, or caught rides with friends as they made their way to Emelle in great numbers. Only a few black people owned cars then.

Taking care of so many customers was hard and tiring, and it was easy for us to work up quite an appetite. Of course, there were no restaurants in Emelle, so when suppertime came, we became creative. There were the ever-present items from the store such as sardines, onions, and crackers; bologna that we cut from a long stick packed and wrapped in cloth; crackers and cheese cut from a large round hoop; or perhaps a pickled pig's foot.

There was one other option in which we did not often indulge. Becky Eason was a middle-aged black woman who ordered fish out of Mobile each week. The fish arrived around noon each Saturday on the train that ran through the heart of Emelle. It did not take long for Becky to get her fire going behind the store, and soon the melted lard in a large black kettle was hot enough to fry fish. There was no need to advertise, for the wonderful aroma of cooking fish filled the entire town and people followed their noses to Becky's kettle. The fish was sold with a slice of light bread that probably had been purchased earlier from Miss Louise's store. Sliced white bread was usually referred to as light bread, maybe because it was made with yeast and was light in texture as compared to corn pone, which was made with cornmeal. An entire loaf of bread cost ten cents, and bottled soft drinks were sold for a nickel.

We did not have a phone at our house, but very early one Sunday morning my mother received a phone call at a neighbor's house that brought distressing news. My father had not come home the night before; however, when Mother returned from the neighbor's house, she had an explanation for his absence. Daddy had been in a drunken brawl the night before and was in the York Hospital, about twenty miles away. Mother took us to Sunday school, where she made arrangements with Miss Louise for Wrenn and me to go home with her after church. Mother promised to come for us after she had been to the hospital to check on Daddy.

After we had eaten dinner and were playing, Aileen looked at me and asked, "Aren't you afraid of what people will say about you?" I knew exactly what she was asking. She was referring to my father's drunken irresponsibility. I was crushed. Of course I was afraid of that. That thought plagued me daily! It hung over me like a storm cloud every waking moment. But what could I do about it? I was a child, and children did not tell their parents how to behave—no matter how much they may have wanted to. That question no longer haunts me as it did, but it does give me insight into children who have problem parents.

The miracle of the friendship shared by Aileen and me through the years is that she knew about the painful and embarrassing part of my life resulting from my father's alcoholism, made allowances for it, and loved and accepted me still. Even though our lives went in different directions after we graduated from high school, we continued to keep in touch with periodic visits and phone calls. Special occasions like homecomings at the church or community barbeques were each made even more special by Aileen's presence.

For almost twenty-five years, I nurtured the dream of being one in a group of community folk who would go to Bethel Church to celebrate Christmas. I envisioned taking gasoline lanterns for light and afghans or quilts to wrap around us for warmth. I imagined that I could hear a small group of worshippers as they sang carol after carol a capella. Bethel is a very small church that was built in 1908 as a memorial. It was never wired for electricity; consequently, there are no lights, heat, or cooling in the building. There have never been regularly scheduled times of worship there—only homecomings and funerals. Behind the building lies a very old cemetery where rest the bodies of our forebears who "have finished their course" and moved to a higher level of "things thought eternal."

At Christmas 2002, my dream of long ago came true. It happened when Bethel Church was filled with worshippers from the community. There was no minister. The Good News of Great Joy was proclaimed and sung by local common folk. Small clear Christmas lights shone overhead, powered by electricity from an extension chord that ran to a power pole outside the church.

Aileen was there with Bud, her husband. What a difference from our teenage years. While the years have been good to us, we both have white hair. We hugged like always, sat together, and chattered like girls in school. As we worshipped there, we may have heard the angels sing again—of peace and love and a Savior. As perfect as it all was, the time came for us to return to everyday things and home. As Aileen left, she said to me, "Now I've had my Christmas!" And so, dear Friend, had I!

It has been said, "Once a man and twice a child." If that statement is true, and since I have reached or am nearing my second childhood, does this mean that Aileen is becoming my "childhood" friend again? Or maybe "lifelong" (as in my "always friend") describes it more accurately.

The Mellen Mystique

I am not a psychologist; however, I have watched life and lived long enough to suggest with some certainty that childhood dreams and imaginations are essential to the development of every child growing toward maturity. Little girls who imagine being a princess or the little boy who sees himself as big enough and strong enough to conquer any foe are classic examples of such dreams.

It occurs to me that as time passes and lives change, these dreams and visions also change to span the breach between reality and the extravagant goal that children believed would make life perfect. So many years have intervened since my childhood and today's reality that I am not able to assign a time or an age to any of my specific dreams and wishes. I am coming to understand that personal dreams and wishful thinking are also a part of our mature as well as our maturing years.

I think often of Ann Mellen, one of the children who entered the first grade with me in September 1937. Ann was overwhelmed, as was I. Not one of us in the first grade had been to kindergarten, because there was no such class available to us then. Consequently, we entered elementary school with no prior experience of formal education, although I suppose that attendance at Sunday school was helpful to those who had some exposure to church and socialization. The entire process of education was daunting, for we knew that completion of high school would require at least twelve long years, and our entire life to that point was only half of that. We believed that real life did not actually begin until we finished high school.

Children began school the September after their sixth birthday. At that time, the new school year always began the Tuesday after Labor Day; the date changed, but the day never did. My summers were lonely because I lived in the country, and we did not go to town often, and I did not always get to see my friends when we did. As the years passed, however, I began to form deep and lasting friendships; among those friends was Ann Mellen. She was cute, smart, and among the first to be chosen for teams at recess.

Ann had lots of good friends who lived in "town"—Livingston, Alabama. Town held such intrigue for me. There were inside bathrooms, warm houses, and electric lights—all of which, I believed, would make life wonderful. Children walked or rode their bikes to and from school, and sometimes they walked home for lunch. I recall the days when the black lady who worked for the Mellens brought Ann's lunch to school, and knocked softly on the classroom door. The teacher would answer and bring Ann's lunch, packed in a new brown bag, back to her. The sandwiches were made of fresh bread and wrapped in waxed paper that had been purchased just for that purpose. My sandwich was wrapped in waxed paper from the bags in which our loaf of bread had been purchased. If I ever forgot my lunch, there was no way to have it brought to me. But in town, it was possible to walk back and forth to school or to have someone bring a lunch. What a grand convenience.

Moreover, each trip from the country to Livingston confirmed my notion that Livingston was the perfect Southern village, with its quiet, tree-lined streets that separated houses that had stood facing each other for generations—maybe even a century. Upon reaching town, we passed Miss Lucille Leonard's house, then the Markhams' home on the right and the Storys' house on the left, then came the Grubbs' house, the Scotts', the George Flukers', the Thomas Tartts', and Moons' Tourist Home. Just past there was the lovely old Jones house, set well away from the street, easily rivaling Tara of *Gone with the Wind* fame. Across the street from the Joneses' home was Livingston State Teachers College. Downtown was next.

The old brick court house in the center of town was bordered on all four sides by businesses including Scruggs for Drugs, Shorty Bryan's service station, the bus station (owned and operated by Robert Ennis), and Bullock's dry goods store, later owned by Mr. Tartt Mellen, Ann's father. The Ruby Pickens Tartt Library was located in the courthouse square along with the covered bored well. People believed there were curative and medicinal benefits from the bored well water, which was shipped in five-gallon jugs to many customers who firmly believed that those foul-tasting mineral waters were good for them. The D.U.D.'s (Damned Ugly Devils') Parade was centered each New Year around the bored well. I only heard that it was quite a celebration; I never got to go.

"Time, like an ever-rolling stream," moved silently and steadily, carrying us into junior high school, another intimidating milestone. The best thing that happened to me in the seventh grade was that I began taking piano lessons from Miss Frances Mellen, Ann's mother. My former teacher was an austere, impersonal lady who was highly impatient when a lesson was not all that she expected. What a marked difference in the two teachers! It was not long until Miss Frances became one of my favorite people in the whole wide world! I adored her. Not only did she play the most gorgeous piano music I had ever heard, but she taught me more about life, caring, and relating to others than she did about music.

I looked forward to my two half-hour lessons each week, for which Miss Frances was paid five dollars per month. I realize now just how underpaid she was. She was actually a therapist for me. Many times during my lesson, I sat on the piano bench with my back to Miss Frances, and she listened to the bottled-up pain pour from my heart. I was painfully sensitive about my father's alcoholism, and I always felt safe when Miss Frances listened with such deep and sympathetic understanding. I loved it when she stood behind me and reached around me to show me how to play those notes that I failed so miserably to play. Sometimes I was tempted to make another mistake so she would hug me again.

Lunch hour at Livingston High School was always fun. Upon finishing our lunches, we gathered as quickly as we could in the front part of the auditorium, where we were allowed to dance in the space between the stage and the first row of seats. Anyone who could play a boogie woogie, or any other dance tune, soon found themselves sitting on the piano bench, playing for the students gathered to dance. It was not unusual for two girls to dance together, because the boys did not always show up in sufficient numbers. Ann was a wonderful dancer, and she loved dancing with Gump Ozment. They were quite a presence on the dance floor as they laughed and moved in perfect rhythm, all the while making it appear so effortless! What a gift when Miss Frances came back from lunch early and sat at the piano, playing for the few remaining minutes until the bell rang! As she played, the number of students in the auditorium grew. She was like the Pied

Piper of our dance time! She graciously shared herself and her gift with each student as he or she listened. We remember her as a true artist. My heart longs to hear again those lovely melodies filled with rich harmonies and shared with such grace by Miss Frances.

When the student body assembled in the auditorium for chapel, it was Miss Frances who played "God Bless America" or "Peggy O'Neal" for us to sing. If Miss Frances was not available, Mrs. Mettie D. Seale, Ann's maternal grandmother, marched firmly to the piano, adjusted the bench, tucked her handkerchief inside the watchband on her left arm, and began to play "The Star-Spangled Banner" with great conviction—and the student body sang with inspired fervor. Mrs. Seale was a patriot, and at a moment's notice she could and did speak with stirring zeal about democracy and patriotism. She loved these United States of America, and she taught us to proudly do the same.

Little Frances, Ann's younger sister, was three or four years younger than Ann. Like Ann, she was smart, played the piano, had lots of friends, and wore nice clothes. The sweaters, plaid skirts, penny loafers, saddle oxfords, and socks worn by both girls likely came from their father's store. I recall going to Mr. Mellen's store on several occasions when I needed shoes or an item of clothing. I politely requested that they be charged to my grandmother's account. I had no charge card or a written statement from Grannie, but I was allowed to make the purchases. What a privilege to grow up in that small community and to be affirmed by the trust placed in me by the man who owned the store. If there was a downside to this arrangement, it was that everybody knew everybody else, and not only was I trusted, but I was also accountable. When a child or youth misbehaved, it was not unusual that a responsible adult felt obligated to speak to the offender or at least to make their parent aware of what had transpired.

Ann's father, Tartt, was a pleasant, soft-spoken man. I think he was a deacon in the Livingston Baptist Church. If he was not, he certainly should have been. It seemed to me that he was the kind of man who would have been a perfect church official. Miss Frances was the organist at that church for years, and was known and loved by folks from the entire area. I did not attend worship at that church, but I am certain that Ann and Little Frances were regular participants in all the appropriate congregational programs.

Each morning, Mr. Tartt walked the three blocks to his store, opened it, and went inside to begin the day's business. Miss Frances was off to teach piano lessons at the high school, and the two girls went to school. Thus their day began. The family members went home together for lunch. Following their afternoon activities, they came home again and ate supper together.

I recognize this now as my childhood fantasy: the Mellen Mystique. Mr. Tartt was a loving father who faithfully provided for his family and came home every night. Miss Frances was a mother who listened, demonstrated her love with grace, and was such fun to be around. Ann and Little Frances loved each other and their parents. Their physical and emotional needs were recognized and provided for daily. It seemed to me that each one of them respected every other member of their family. That was everything of which my childish heart dreamed.

One of the most wonderful weeks of my life was spent in the Mellen home. I had an appendectomy just before school began, and the consensus was that I would make better progress healing if I did not have to ride the school bus back and forth over those rough country roads. Miss Frances, whose compassion made it impossible to turn away children and strays, took me in! I now see myself as a dry sponge soaking up all the love, kindness, and acceptance that I could hold during those healing days.

Years later, I was moved when Little Frances asked me to sit with Miss Frances in the hospital just before her death. Frances needed to go to the airport to pick up Leon, who later became her husband. Left alone, Miss Frances and I talked about days that we had shared—she as a parent, and I as a child. We talked about Ann, Little Frances, and Mr. Tartt. We listened to a tape of music performed by the Central United Methodist Church choir, of which I was a member. The songs were music that was a part of my past, and I had heard Miss Frances play many of them. It was a wonderful evening of music and I loved sharing it with Miss Frances. I am not sure just why she told me that she was proud of me, but she did. Wow! My own mother had never done that. At that moment I felt loved and accepted by a lady I deeply admired. Miss Frances died on November 19, 1986—my birthday.

The Mellens were married for well over fifty years, and it was only natural that Mr. Tartt felt lost when Miss Frances died. After her death, he included me, with Ann, in an invitation once for lunch. We feasted on hamburgers made the old-fashioned way, and chocolate milkshakes. There was no mention of or concern for the caloric value of those delicious morsels. Our folly brought back countless fun-filled memories, and we were peacefully content to drift there for a while. I was privileged to be included in that family moment.

Little Frances (who has grown to be Frances #2) has called me her "angel of mercy" since the time I sat with Miss Frances. None of my siblings ever referred to me in such heavenly terms! Little Frances feels like my little sister, and that feels right.

And Ann! Who could have guessed that this cute, happy girl who was a wonderful student and could jitterbug like crazy would become a nurse after her children, Bill and Barbara, were born? And who could have guessed that the girl who sewed only "required" garments for home economics class would immerse herself and her resources in sewing countless dolls and caps for cancer patients? It comes as no surprise that she is a patriotic American because she is the grand-daughter of Mettie D. Seale. As Miss Frances's first-born, she was des-tined to play the piano, and to appreciate beautiful melodies filled with feelings too deep and too personal to be contaminated by words. Observing Ann's deep faith and hearing her talk personally and freely of Jesus reminds me of the practice and example set by Mr. Tartt. It is not at all surprising that Ann Davidson Mellen Dutton is a special lady, for she is the combination of priceless ingredients.

Generations have come and gone, and I am becoming more con-vinced of the old cliché: "Wishing will make it so!" The dreams of my childhood have come true—only better! I have learned through the years that people are born into families for better or worse. They can change some circumstances related to their position in the family, but they can never change the fact that they are a part of that family. Perhaps it is better that I was not born into the Mellen family, because I might never have known the Mellen Mystique. I am indebted to each member of that wonderful family, for each accepted me for the per-son I am. I was not forced upon them through an accident of birth; rather, I was chosen—accepted—and that, for me, is a gift that far exceeds any that I could have imagined!

Hellfire, Damnation, and Judgment

It happened every year—always at the hottest time of the summer. It was a time eagerly anticipated by many families and individuals. Schedules were carefully planned so that nothing would interfere for ten days. Weeks before the scheduled date, women sewed cotton dresses for themselves and their children. Clothes, linens, towels, food, mattresses, lightweight chairs, and cookware were packed days before the family left. Some families who participated regularly owned open trailers used for the express purpose of transporting items that would make living a bit more comfortable. It was time for Camp Meeting.

I had the opportunity during childhood and adolescence to attend two camp meetings, both of them in Mississippi. The first I attended was when my sister and I went with my aunt, uncle, and cousins. The campground was located alongside the railroad track. Trains interrupted conversations and sermons several times during the day as the engineer gave several blasts on the whistle as a way of greeting the children who ran to watch the train pass. Families who came year after year built small, roughhewn cabins, where they lived during the encampment. It was important that as many people as possible be reached and "saved" during those days, so there were frequent visitors who stayed overnight with the campers. It wasn't always comfortable, but it was a place to stay.

Aunt Nina and Uncle Dunk's (his real name was Duncan) cabin, located just behind the cook tent, consisted of two small rooms. A curtain served as a door to separate the rooms. We carried water for bathing and drinking from the well in front of the cook tent. Even though we had been taught to be very modest, we managed to bathe, dress, and sleep for ten days in that very small space. The cabin was considered headquarters, and we reported there periodically so Aunt Nina always knew where we were. We ran barefoot and played across the encampment, but when preaching began, we knew to put our

132

shoes on.

There was no bell; the sound of someone beating upon a plow sweep was the signal that the service was about to begin. As the sound from the sweep ceased, Miss Lucille Null began to play gospel songs such as "When We All Get to Heaven" or "Why Not Tonight" on the piano. Miss Lucille was a lady of ample size, and she usually wore light-colored voile dresses with a dainty floral print. She smelled of an abundance of ladies' dusting powder that was often visible around her throat and disappeared beneath her shirtwaist dress. She carried a cloth handkerchief that she frequently pressed to her forehead to catch the perspiration gathered there. Her strong, powerful arms brought her hands and fingers to the keyboard of the piano with such force that the upright piano shook from the impact. We children used to whisper among ourselves that she "beat the piano." But mind you, she never missed a note! The campers gathered, and church began under the tabernacle.

The tabernacle was a large, open pavilion covered by a tin roof. Most of one side of the covered area was dedicated to the slightly raised platform upon which the podium stood, along with the piano and a few rough pews where those who chose to sing in the choir sat. If there was a breeze blowing from any direction, it would blow through the tabernacle since all four sides were open, but it seemed that breezes seldom blew in Mississippi in the middle of the day—especially during camp meeting time. It was hot, hot, hot! Flies and gnats were always present in droves to make life miserable, in our ears or up our noses or just flying aimlessly about. Even at an early age, I became very skilled at fanning with cardboard fans provided by funeral homes. It was a matter of survival! We needed to move the hot air just to breathe, and there was always the hope that we would drive the bugs away in the process.

The benches were made of unpainted boards with spaces between the boards. The wood was rough, and sometimes we found it necessary to remove an ugly splinter if we slipped the wrong way on the bench. The dirt floor underneath the roof of the tabernacle was covered with a thick carpet of sawdust. New sawdust was added each year because of deterioration through the winter months. The deep sawdust made walking difficult for those entering the tabernacle, especially if they wore sandals.

Both the music and the singing were spirited. Sometimes there were testimonies from those moved to tell the assembled worshippers what "the Lord had done in their lives as He delivered them from their life of sin." Prayers—accompanied (and interrupted) by "amens" and "hallelujahs" from the kneeling congregants as they prayed fervently with the leader—were long and loud. Clothes became wet with sweat and worshippers were hot to the point of melting.

Preachers came from faraway places to preach the Gospel and save the sinners. For example, there was Brother Deucker, who came from California. He was a tall, gentle man with a neatly trimmed beard. When he prayed, he knelt on one knee. He wore a black suit, and his white shirt was buttoned to the top with no tie. The Pentecostal persuasion of that group taught that Christ's followers should not wear ties or yellow gold. White gold was acceptable.

The preaching was loud, convincing, frightening, and accompanied by sounds of pounding fists on the podium. There were no jokes or funny stories. These were serious times: times when men, women, youth, and children were brought face to face with God who hated sin; the God of judgment; the God who sentenced men and women who were outside the "ark of safety" to an eternal life in Hell, where they would burn in everlasting fire. It was almost possible to smell the acrid odor of smoke from the vicious flames where the damned souls from ages past burned, and the heat that shrouded us like a hot, wet blanket made the heat of that lake burning with fire even more real. Jonathan Edwards was not the preacher, but the message was the same: "It is a fearful thing to fall into the hands of an angry God!" Old Testament scriptures were quoted of a God who "poured out his wrath upon the heathen" (Ps. 79:6), and One who poured out His fury "upon the families that called not upon thy name" (Jer. 10:25)!

The crude altar, made of wooden posts driven into the ground and topped with a rough board running from one side of the platform to the other, was seldom empty. The guilt of many of those sitting in the sound of the preacher's voice had become clear to them during the powerful sermon, and they were eager to get to the altar, to confess their sins, and to beg forgiveness from God. The altar call hymn "Just as I Am" was sung over and over until finally the preacher called for a time of prayer for the souls of those who had thrown themselves upon the mercies of Almighty God. It usually was a long time until the person or persons at the altar were able to "pray through," but when they did, there was a period of great rejoicing and testimony. Nobody left the tabernacle during those times of searching and surrender for fear someone would follow and ask, "How is it with your soul? Would you be happy if Jesus came tonight?"

During the '30s, '40s, '50s, and '60s, camp meetings were a dynamic means through which countless pilgrims began their spiritual journeys. My own conversion and Christian pilgrimage began a few years later at a different camp meeting. The time between my earlier experience and the latter was filled with episodes of fearful wonderings, imagining, and dread. Countless were the nights that I lay sleepless in my bed, looking out the large windows in Grannie's big bedroom, searching as much of the horizon as I could see in an effort to determine if the world were on fire. Would this be the night when the earth would burn?

Recalling those times of such fearful anxiety causes me to be filled with gratitude as I intentionally identify and recognize the sweet peace that permeates my heart and soul. It is assuring to know that I am in touch with the God Who loves me more that I can ever know, and I am ever so content to place my future hopes and fears into His loving and capable hands—and leave them there.

Strange Among Us

To say that he was a strange man would be a gross understatement. In my effort to put names, dates, and events into some kind of order, I am uncovering both hazy and clear images; however, as I weigh both sides of the equation and attempt to make them balance, the clearer images assure me that this man stands out as one of the most unforgettable characters I have chanced to meet during my rather sheltered lifetime.

His name was James Archie (short for Archibald) Coleman. He was appointed by the Annual Conference of the Methodist Church to the Gainsville Charge in West Alabama; Emelle Methodist Church was one of the four churches he served. Scheduling called for the minister to meet with each congregation one Sunday out of the month, and Emelle's day was the third Sunday. The small Presbyterian church in our community "had preaching" on the second Sunday, while the Baptist church in Sumterville was scheduled to meet on the fourth Sunday. A person could choose to worship three Sundays out of four, even though the theology came from three different theological persuasions.

The word in the community was that Mr. Coleman and his wife owned a large, productive cotton farm in the Mississippi Delta. Mrs. Coleman ran the farm and came to visit her husband on extremely rare occasions. She was sometimes accompanied by their son. Since there was only one car in the family, Mrs. Coleman kept it, perhaps because she needed it in running the farm. The four Alabama churches served by Mr. Coleman were good distances apart, and since he had no car available to him, it was up to him and his ingenuity as to how he arrived for his preaching appointments. Different members of his congregations sometimes saw to it that he was at the proper church on the correct Sunday. He often rode the school bus from Gainsville to Livingston, where he spent the day. I do not know if he had business there or if he took those occasions to simply "get out of town."

The parsonage was one of a number of beautiful old antebellum houses in Gainsville, and was much too large for one person like Brother Coleman, as he was known to local folks. There must have been an inherent bent toward farming in this elderly gentleman, because he quickly had the back yard tilled and vegetables growing in profusion. In addition to his productivity of food, he built a pig pen and raised hogs. When it came time to butcher the hogs, Brother Coleman killed them and salted down the meat on the exquisite dining room table. It is my opinion that the women who worked so hard to make the parsonage beautiful never got over that sacrilege. That story was told and retold to ministers and their families who followed him. I do not know whether the table was ever replaced or refinished; maybe the solution was as simple as tablecloths to cover the gross abuse and mistreatment of that fine piece.

Most of the parishioners considered Brother Coleman to be a well-educated man. There were not many (if any) in our area who were adept at reading and quoting Latin, but Brother Coleman was. He also knew and quoted lots of poetry. It could have been easily construed that he was a personal acquaintance of Shakespeare and the Old Masters. He was even known, on occasion, to tease and confuse us children by using large words which we seldom, if ever, had heard, and we certainly had no idea what they meant. I recall one time in particular when he profoundly upset my youngest brother. In that brief moment he brought Howard face to face with his entire guilt as well as any potential that he had for future guilt when he asked in a voice loud enough for anybody standing nearby to hear, "Howard, did you hesitate on the doorstep this morning?" I thought the poor boy was going to cry.

The fifteen or eighteen miles of unpaved roads between Gainsville and our church were difficult to travel in bad weather; however, this did not seem to pose any problem for "James Archie," as we children used to call him when no one was listening. He always managed to get to his appointments. In typical ministerial fashion, he wore a black wool suit, white shirt, and tie. It became his custom on the Saturdays before the third Sunday to start early in the day as he set out walking to our house. He did not always walk along the road; rather, he took shortcuts through the fields and pastures. He never walked very fast but kept a steady pace. As he slowly made his way through the fields, he chewed tobacco, which was assuredly one of those habits not usually attributed to an educated "man of the cloth." But the habit that we thought was most hilarious (perhaps strange and obnoxious are better words) was that as he walked, he carried his dentures—upper and lower—in his left hand. In recalling that eccentricity, I suppose that using his left hand for that purpose was perfectly reasonable. In the event that he met someone, his right hand was free to grasp and shake the hand of the one approaching him.

Mr. Coleman usually arrived at our house from somewhere behind the barn after walking through the hog pasture—and always in time for supper. We children listened with delight to the adults' conversations until it was bedtime. Brother Coleman would then climb the first flight of thirteen steps to the landing, where he always stopped, turned, and looked down at Mother and us children. Mother usually said something like, "Call us if you should need anything during the night." His reply was always the same: "I spent the night with an old couple one time, and as we got ready to go to bed, the old lady said, 'Now if you need something that we ain't got, just ask us and we'll tell you how to git along without it!'"

There was no bathroom in our house, so we always saw that Brother Coleman's room had a fresh pitcher of water, a wash bowl, a glass, and a chamber pot. We thought it was strange that he never brought a suitcase, and there was no other indication that he brought any clean clothes for Sunday. Even though he might not have been the cleanest person at church, this preacher never allowed any foolishness during worship. My sister Wrenn and cousin Elizabeth sat in the front row one morning right in front of the pulpit. Perhaps the two girls were bored, or maybe they just had some pressing things to communicate to each other; whatever their reason, they were misbehaving according to Brother Coleman's standards. He stopped mid-sermon, looked over his glasses, and said in a tone that was heard throughout the small church and was clearly understood as correctional, "I never believed that man came from monkeys, but I am convinced there are some who are going back!" A profound silence moved across the church! Two young girls in the front pew fell completely silent. After a holy pause, the sermon continued.

One day, Miss Frances Mellen, my piano teacher, sent me to town on an errand. As I walked toward town, I met Mr. Coleman coming in the opposite direction. Upon coming closer to each other, it was obvious that he was chewing tobacco and carrying his dentures in his left hand. We greeted each other and went our separate ways. I could hardly wait to get back to school to report his bizarre behavior to Miss Frances. She loved weird stories and strange people, and she laughed easily. Besides her good sense of humor, she had the unique ability to cut directly to the heart of the matter and put things into proper perspective. Quickly I told my story and waited eagerly for her response. She shrugged her shoulders, grunted sarcastically, and said, "It would make just as much sense for me to walk down the street carrying my girdle!"

During the time that this man served as our minister, he baptized me into church membership as "Mary Ann Ferguson." The people within the church that day had all known my name since birth as Sara Ann Fuller. It still seems a little strange that he spent so many nights in our home and ate so many meals at our table, yet was totally confused as to my Christian name—even my family name of Fuller.

I do not know exactly when Brother Coleman came to our church, or when he left. I do not even know how long he stayed among us as our minister. What I do know is that he was most assuredly cut from a different pattern than most of the people I have known. Better or worse? I cannot say. Exodus 20:10 refers to "the stranger that is within thy gates." I never thought of Rev. James Archibald Coleman as a "stranger," but I am convinced beyond a shadow of a doubt that he was strange! Perhaps he was one of those special people who indeed do march to the beat of a different drummer!

Roses for a Special Lady

It may be that Christian Endeavor is still today an energetic, viable youth organization—or maybe not. For whatever reason, I have lost touch with them. This is not to say that Christian Endeavor was not important to me. It was one of the most influential forces for good in my life. The fact that it was interdenominational made it perfect for the youth in our community. The Methodist, Presbyterian, and Baptist churches all drew their membership from the sparse population residing in our rural area, and as a result, no congregation ever had packed houses from their own membership, so none of them ever had to build larger churches to accommodate overwhelming crowds. On the other hand, most of the community churchgoers attended whatever church was scheduled for worship, which was a genuine show of support for the preacher as well as the congregation. On Sunday evenings, neighborhood youth from all the churches met for Christian Endeavor at the Presbyterian church in Sumterville.

Christian Endeavor's printed materials were resources for our weekly programs, planned a month in advance. A great deal of time and energy was spent in planning, choosing hymns, and inviting those who were not "regulars" to come on Sunday evenings. Without exception, we looked forward to the monthly socials that took many forms, from ice cream socials to hayrides to moonlight picnics.

Not one of us was ever reluctant to assume personal responsibility in seeing that our youth group was a positive influence as well as a joy for each participant. Since many of our activities were limited to school and church, Christian Endeavor, which was both interdenominational and international, provided the perfect umbrella under which we all were included. It allowed us to worship together regardless of denomination, while at the same time it provided a view of what was happening outside our community. Seasons and holidays such as Christmas, Thanksgiving, New Year's, and others offered perfect settings for creativity in both programs and socials. As I look back at those shared experiences, one such program quickly surfaces and stands out as exceptional: it was Mother's Day, a long time ago.

I was at least sixteen years of age and had my driver's license, so Mother allowed me to drive our car to Sumterville to help with the preparation for that special Mother's Day program. Wrenn and Burton (both younger that I) went along with me. We had to accomplish a great deal that afternoon, so we gathered as soon after Sunday dinner as possible. Upon reaching the church, we were each assigned a part of the work to be completed. It doesn't seem important now as to what was done by whom, but the finished, completed effort was beautiful.

The Presbyterian church was a lovely little country church that had stood as a landmark in the community for a long, long time. Red carpet covered the floor in the entrance, and runners continued down the two aisles. The same faded red carpet covered the pulpit floor and stretched to the front pew. An antique table rested just below the pulpit at floor level and was used for worship centers as well as a place for offering plates. In retrospect, this wonderful little church was faded and well worn, but we loved it and saw only its beauty. The windows came to a graceful point at the top and their panes of colored glass, not very expensive, were beautiful when the sun shone through. The walls, divided by a chair rail, were a cream color, and the wainscoting below the chair rail was of bead board stained with a dark oak varnish.

The wall behind the pulpit became the perfect focal point for this Mother's Day program. Some of us went to the woods to gather smilax, a dark green, waxy vine indigenous to the area. Others of us visited neighboring yards to gather all of the red, pink, and white roses that we were allowed to cut. We met again at the church. This time, some of us hung smilax vines and covered the wall behind the pulpit. Others began making rose corsages to be pinned on every mother who would be attending as our special guests. The last huge effort came when we formed the word MOTHER across the green screen of smilax vines. It took tons of pink, white, and red roses to complete the letters, which were large enough to be read from the back of the church. Each of us children and Mother always wore a red rose on Mother's Day to honor our mothers who were alive, but I remember the sad emptiness I felt each year when Grannie wore a white rose, symbolizing that her mother was no longer alive. The red and white roses really signified something to us, and I suppose that the pink ones were thrown in as fillers. On that night, the little church in Sumterville was heavy with fragrance from countless roses that symbolized our deep love for our mothers.

I don't remember what the program was about; maybe a part of it was "'M' is for the million things you gave me…" I am thoroughly convinced, however, that the dynamics of that day were much more important than the words that were spoken. We worked feverishly that entire afternoon in an effort to pay the highest tribute we could to our mothers. Most likely, there was a dual reason that motivated our mothers and grandmothers to be present that night; their special time of recognition and honor was the obvious, but I suspect that they were also there to support us in our struggle to become good and decent folks. Many fathers were also present.

Although the program was presented by a group, and the mothers and grandmothers were honored as a group, there was no mistaking or denying the fact that every mother's heart was filled with pride as she went home wearing her handmade corsage of roses. She knew she was loved and respected! She understood that she had been honored! And she knew beyond any shadow of doubt that she was a very special lady!

Properly Embarrassed

My family was part of the pseudo-aristocracy of the Old South. We were actually poor "as Job's turkey" when it came to having a large bank account. On the other hand, we lived in a large plantation home surrounded by nearly a thousand acres of farm and pasture land left by my grandfather. A half dozen or so tenant families lived in small houses scattered across the fields where they raised crops each year. I suppose there was something about renting to families who were even poorer than we that subtly elevated us to the stratum above; after all, we had inherited wealth of sorts and we associated with the "best" people in our rural community. We had good credit with all of the merchants, and Grandmother dealt comfortably with her banker. We were truly part of the local gentry.

Being polite was one of the basic elements of becoming socially acceptable. We were taught manners from an early age. We were polite! We understood when to say "Yes, Ma'am," "No, Ma'am," "Thank you, Ma'am" (or "Sir"), and "Please." We were respectful of anybody older than we. These people were addressed by their proper names, preceded by "Mr." and "Miss." The title "Mrs." was seldom used by Southerners—it just didn't sound right! So all females were addressed as "Miss"; married or single made no difference! Special care and attention were given, without exception, to the elderly. However, elderly black folks were never called "Mr." or "Miss"; instead, they were addressed as "Aunt" or "Uncle," followed by their names.

We were reverent in church. We were expected to behave acceptably at school or else there would be dreadful and unhappy consequences when our parents learned of our bad behavior. Never was it said that any of the Fuller children acted like animals. We clearly understood that certain behavior was acceptable in good company, while other behavior was never permitted in polite society. Certain songs, like "My Bucket's Got a Hole in It…I Can't Buy Me No Beer," were not considered ladylike by Grannie; therefore, we were forbidden to sing them. We were not allowed to use slang and profanity. We did not swear! No matter how serious matters became or how much the situation called for it, we did not swear!

My mother was a lovely lady whose manners and social graces were acceptable in the best of circles. As soon as we were old enough to feed ourselves, she began to teach us how to hold our fork or spoon. As time passed, she continued the learning process with how to use our knife, how to pass dishes of food around the table, and how to use a napkin, even though we seldom had one on our table. Three years of high school home economics continued to broaden our knowledge of Emily Post's Rules of Etiquette. The classes in home economics also taught me how extremely limited our kitchen was. To describe our kitchen as "basic" was an over-exaggeration of our conveniences. We cooked on a wood stove at home, but we stirred pots on an electric range at school. We had no pastry blender in our kitchen, but we learned that two knives could be effectively used in cutting shortening into flour when making pastry or biscuits. Money was spent for edible items only, not for decorative things like parsley used only as a garnish. Wrenn and I learned that carrot tops look a great deal like parsley and worked just as well. Though I was well schooled in proper ways, I often felt inadequate, inferior, and a bit tentative in social situations. After all, I was from the country, and there seemed to be more elegance and sophistication about the girls from town.

As an officer on the State Christian Endeavor Executive Committee, I was expected to attend regularly scheduled meetings in Birmingham, Alabama. I looked forward to the three-hour bus trips to and from those occasions. Since I was always met at the Birmingham bus station by someone on the Christian Endeavor State Team, there was no concern on Mother's part that I might get lost in the big city. Before I left home, arrangements were made with a committee member and their family for me to stay overnight in their home, so Mother always knew where I was and how to contact me in case I was needed.

Warren Threadkill met me on one such trip. He, along with some of the other state officers, had visited in our home several months before, but he had since gotten married. I was invited to spend the night in the home of his wife's family. Upon arriving late that afternoon, we went directly to their home. I was shown to my room and instructed that it would not be long until dinner. I freshened up, rejoined the group, and asked if there were anything that I could do. (Mother had instructed me over and over that I must always be helpful when possible.)

As we were seated, I was impressed with the beauty of the table. A small bouquet of fresh flowers sat in the center of the white linen tablecloth spread beneath the lovely china and silver place settings. I felt ever so elegant as I spread the linen napkin across my lap. I deliberately accepted each dish of food, helped my plate, and carefully passed it to the next person. The food must have been delicious, although I do not remember what we ate. At some point in the meal, I was asked if I would like a cup of tea, to which I replied, "Yes, please." Now, I must explain that the only hot tea that I knew anything about was prepared by Grannie on cold mornings before we left for school. She stirred very hot water and milk together, then added *lots* of sugar, and *I loved it.*

Upon receiving my cup of tea, I was asked if I would like sugar, to which I replied, "Yes, please." I was then offered cream, which I accepted and poured slowly into my tea. Then I was offered lemon! I really was uncertain as to whether to take lemon or not, but I had watched others around the table add it to their tea, so I did the same. What I had obviously missed as I watched was that one person might add cream while another added lemon, *but no one was adding both!* Much to my chagrin and amazement, the acidic lemon juice curdled the sweet cream in my tea. There I sat with chunks of curdled cream floating in my cup. I was humiliated. My cheeks burned with embarrassment! I prayed that no one had noticed how ignorant I was! I wanted to die! I had tried so hard to be proper! My next thought came like a flash! I would drink that "stuff"—every single drop of it—as quickly and as quietly as possible, and I would act as though it was exactly the way I liked it. And that is what I did. However, I did graciously decline when offered a refill.

I carefully made my bed the next morning, and I politely thanked my hostess for my stay in her "lovely" home, but to this day, I still wonder if my ignorance was obvious. I was as polite and gracious as I knew how to be. When I was uncertain as to the correct fork or spoon to use, I watched those seated about the table to learn from them. What a valuable time of insight that evening became to me! I learned that regardless of how thorough the schooling, there remains the very real possibility that there is always just "one thing more" to learn. I further discovered that even though a number of people are doing different but perfectly correct things, if all of their actions are combined, the result can sometimes be disappointing or even explosive. That hot tea filled with curdled cream was almost more costly than my pride could bear; the experience itself, however, was priceless.

Fashion

Which came first: women or fashion? In about 1928, my father gave Mother a cabinet-style Edison phonograph. I loved playing her old records. One of them was called "I Haven't Got a Thing to Wear." The words went something like this:

> It's the truth as we all know,
> Eve told Adam long ago
> 'I haven't got a thing to wear!'
> Now she wore leaves throughout the spring
> But in the fall he heard her sing
> 'I haven't got a thing to wear!'
> Mr. Adam thought, 'Oh, what's the use?
> Now really, there is no excuse!
> Here's a bunch of evergreen
> That's fit for any forest queen!'
> Dressed up like a Christmas tree
> I'll bet Eve told Adam she
> Didn't have a thing to wear!

From time to time I have heard women hopelessly declare, "I haven't got a thing to wear!" I cannot recall a single time that I had to stay at home because I did not have anything to wear. I must admit in all honesty, though, that much of the time I recognized that others were better dressed than I, but that conclusion should have come as no surprise. We were poor. Mother sewed for all four of us children and Grannie, as well as herself. That alone was a demanding, time-consuming responsibility that she cheerfully assumed with never a single complaint.

During the early 1940s, World War II consumed a vast amount of our nation's natural and manufactured products. Many things like chewing gum, chocolate candy, and nylon stockings were in short supply. Canned goods, meat, sugar, gasoline, tires, and shoes were not purchased without ration stamps or coupons. Fabric was needed for military use in uniforms, tents, parachutes, sheets, towels, and other items, so it is easy to understand that cotton and nylon fabric were in great demand by the armed forces, and defense was our first priority.

Americans did not seem to mind living with less. They gladly made this effort and more for our country and the thousands of fine young men who gave themselves completely to the struggle for freedom and peace. Men and women who remained at home stepped into supportive roles for the war effort. Women for the first time were placed into jobs that had earlier been filled only by men. Swing Shift Maisies and Rosie Riveters clad in coveralls and hard hats reported by the thousands to factories and shipyards. Never was a workforce more productive. Americans were a committed people. Patriotism was at an all-time high! It clearly was not appropriate that fashion should be center stage during those days.

Many things were in short supply. This is no way implies that we were without clothes; they were just a bit coarser and more durable. The same was true with shoes. Hand-me-downs and secondhand clothes were graciously accepted and deeply appreciated. Nothing was wasted. Sugar and flour came in white cloth bags, which Mother and Grannie washed and bleached until they were snow white, then used to make our slips and underpants. Since elastic was also in short supply, if not completely unavailable, Mother made our underpants like shorts that buttoned at the waist. Of course we were embarrassed at our "homemade" underwear, even though it worked just fine. But then, we were embarrassed about a lot of things, like when we had to take biscuits instead of sliced bread in our lunch.

Cattle feed had always been sold in bland, ecru-colored cloth bags, but manufacturers began putting the same feed into brightly colored bags with lovely prints. Mother, Wrenn, and I made certain that we were with Grannie when she bought feed for the cows because we wanted to choose the colors and patterns on the bags since they would be made into beautiful broomstick skirts, dresses, and pajamas for us. The real beauty of it all was that the feed bags were *free*! Whether our clothes were made from feed sacks or from fabric purchased from the store, we were expected to take care of them. Some clothes were for school, others for Sunday, and still others for everyday use. We often had only one pair of shoes, which we wore to school as well on Sundays. Shoes that were kept clean, polished, and shined always looked nice, and they may even have lasted longer as a result of the wax protection of the polish.

Finally, the rigors of war were history. Life began to move back toward "normal," and a better economic future seemed imminent. I was fifteen years old, and like all my peers, I became very fashion-conscious like generations of women before me. I especially liked my brown-and-white–striped Gibson Girl blouse with fitted cuffs that buttoned half way to the elbow. The high collar came to long points and buttoned at the neck, where I usually wore a small matching ribbon bow or a silk flower. The mid-calf, circular ballerina skirt was the exact brown of the brown in my blouse. Poodle skirts, bobby socks, and saddle oxfords were considered essentials for every wardrobe. And so went fashion during the postwar days of boogie-woogie and jitterbugging. I still fancy that I can see those full skirts standing out as teenagers danced and whirled to the music.

Autumn days and an early winter were the signal to unpack our pleated wool plaid skirts and big, boxy sloppy-joe sweaters. We wore them with the sleeves pushed about halfway to the elbows, but keeping them up took constant attention because they constantly slipped down. Cardigan sweaters were seldom worn as cardigans; rather, they were worn backward and buttoned down the back. Pearls, a small scarf tied in a square knot, or a white Peter Pan collar were generally worn at the neck of both sloppy-joes and cardigans. Clothes were worn for a long time and then passed on to a relative or special friend.

What were the adults wearing? No well-dressed lady ever left home without hat, gloves, girdle, stockings (the term "hose" came later), and possibly the popular black-and-white or brown-and-white spectator pumps. Admittedly, we were much more *uncomfortable* then. We were hot to the melting point inside all those clothes (though proper), and there was no air conditioning! Perspiration was a way of life; however, a lady always carried a linen handkerchief to wipe away a tear or the excessive moisture that collected along her brow.

Though fashion and design have often been assigned to women, it is absolutely true that the male of the species frequently demonstrates an undeniable sense of fashion and good taste. So with that having been said, the opening question of "Which came first: women or fashion?" was not a good assumption upon which to base these ideas. It appears that both women and men live in and share the world of fashion. Oh, yes! Fashion is important—possibly more important that we want to admit. And yet, as important as it has become, fashion has found and must always find its place in the grand scheme of things—which means that *"Fashion is not the cake—it is just the icing!"*

The Last Laugh

Our morning began that day as had so many others. We never heard the loud, abrasive tones of an alarm clock at our house as it noisily announced that it was time to get up. We did not own an alarm clock. Mother and Grannie routinely rose well before they awakened us, and our breakfast was ready as soon as we dressed. Getting dressed did not take much time because we always bathed the night before, and our clothes were neatly laid out for the next day. Upon reaching the kitchen, we sat at the table with Mother and Grannie as a family, bowed our heads for the blessing, and then had breakfast.

After breakfast, Grannie washed the dishes and cleaned up the kitchen while we children brushed our teeth, put the final touches on our faces and hair, gathered our books, and climbed aboard the school bus. Mother had driven the bus since I was in the seventh grade, and I had finally reached the much-anticipated level of senior in high school. That was the same year my alcoholic father left us. The pain that Mother experienced from our family breakup was obvious. As the oldest of four children, I learned to be responsible at an early age, and I grew into a very reliable teenager. I was even the official substitute bus driver for our route, so during those difficult days, I drove to and from school with Mother sitting in the seat immediately behind me. It must have been some relief for her not to deal with the driving, and I loved it; in fact, I felt quite "grown up" and mature as I shouldered that part of her responsibility.

We had been assigned a smaller school bus since there were fewer students on our route than on most of the others, so driving to school was almost like picking up our neighbors and going someplace for the day. We grew up together and were close friends. We went to church together, and were often in each other's homes to visit or for a party. The trip to school was never long because we always had so much to talk about as well as new jokes and stories to share. Some mornings we sang choruses and spirituals all the way to school. Occasionally someone had not completed his or her homework, and there was always time to get that done on the way to school. The four people sitting in the inside seats of the four back rows often turned their knees together, placed a notebook across them for a table, and played a lively game of Rook. We liked each other, were comfortable in each other's company, and always found something fun to do on the way to school.

But that one day was special! Little did any of us know what strange and bizarre events awaited us at school. The countryside was bathed in early-morning sunshine as we made our way along those dusty dirt roads. The windows were open because it was spring, and the air that rushed into the bus was delightfully cool. Rolling hills, cleared for pasture, were blanketed with pink primroses and wild verbena interrupted by patches of bright yellow dandelions and white Dutch clover. Dew glistened like diamonds everywhere, and so far as we were concerned, we agreed with the poet: "God's in His heaven—all's right with the world."

We arrived at school safe, happy, and ready for another day of learning. As a senior, my days at Livingston High School were dwindling to a precious few, and I was experiencing bouts of deep melancholy regarding closure on this chapter of my life. All of my passengers disembarked in front of the school, and I parked the bus in the space assigned. The walk from the bus back to the school was brief, and I quickly made the trip to my locker to exchange my books in preparation for homeroom and first class. The school day had begun.

Our nation had just emerged from the Second World War, and a spirit of patriotism still filled the hearts and lives of America's people. It was customary, if the weather permitted, for our student body and faculty to begin each day by gathering at the foot of the flagpole near the front entrance of the school. We affirmed love for our country by singing a patriotic song followed by pledging our allegiance to the flag, and this day was no different. We stepped out into the early-morning sunshine. There was still enough dew on the grass to get our shoes wet. But that day, we did not sing "The Star-Spangled Banner" or "God Bless America." Neither did we pledge allegiance to the flag. As we lifted our eyes to observe the flag—Alas! Alas! There at the very top of the flagpole, fluttering gently in the breeze, was the largest pair of women's nylon panties and the biggest bra that I had ever seen! We probably all had the same kind of thoughts flying through our heads. "Who did this?" "Didn't anybody see it happen?" "But look at the size of those things! Who ever could wear them?" "Is anybody's mother that big?"

We would not have laughed out loud for anything in the world, but inside was another story. We were doing everything in our power to stifle the explosive giggles and raucous guffaws that seethed within us—even if it meant that we would burst wide open in the process. The expressions worn by Mr. Wilson, our principal, and Coach Allen convinced us beyond any doubt that we were all treading on extremely dangerous ground until the culprit turned himself in or was identified by a witness. Yet in that atmosphere of uncertainty as to what was going to happen, we simply could not take our eyes off those enormous garments that fluttered above our school. Nothing could have been funnier that day, but we dared not even smile. We just stared with open mouths.

Mr. Wilson, Coach Allen, and the other faculty members saw nothing funny about this act of sacrilege. Maybe they even thought it was time for our senior class to be graduating and leaving school because there were some who were "getting too big for their breeches." It must have been terribly embarrassing for the faculty because the entire student body was witnessing this display of utter disrespect for their authority. Perhaps the ultimate embarrassment came when they were not able to punish the guilty party. They did not have a clue as to who it was! It was a complete mystery. But surely, some time later, when the teachers were alone and had a minute to remember those enormous undergarments, they must have smiled—at least a little. We were quickly dismissed to our classes without any further ado, and for the remainder of that day, there was not a hint of any out of order behavior, even by the worst of the bad boys.

The Livingston High School Class of 1949 gathered thirty years later for their class reunion. Some of those who stood around the flagpole that day, both students and teachers, were no longer with us. We remembered and spoke of the excellent educational qualifications of our teachers, as well as their compassion. They knew and cared deeply for each of us, and I think there were times when they prayed fervently for us—not simply that we would become good, productive citizens, but that they had prepared us to meet and face the challenges we were certain to encounter.

As it turned out, both Mr. Wilson and Coach Allen were present for our reunion celebration. Each spoke in turn and expressed his delight at being included for this auspicious occasion. But it was Coach Allen who seemed to have something very special that he wanted to share. He asked Tommy Neel and Ted Smith to join him as he spoke. His request raised no suspicions because both Tommy and Ted had played football during high school; in fact, our school was so small that most of the boys had to go out for football in order to have enough players for a team.

Tommy and Ted had grown into responsible adults during the thirty years since high school. They did not feel intimidated in the least when their coach of many years ago requested that they come to the front of the room. Coach Allen was still a man of large stature, but the years had left their mark. As the result of a slight stroke or Bell's palsy, he had a noticeable facial paralysis on one side that caused his face to go grotesquely crooked when he smiled or laughed. That, coupled with a bit of rambling as he talked, made us acutely aware of his age—and our own. What a graphic reminder that time had slipped so quickly through our fingers!

Time was beginning to drag as Coach Allen's remarks grew duller and duller. He began obviously fumbling in the pocket of his suit coat, and he slowly pulled something from it. We sat up straight and suddenly became interested in every word that fell from our former teacher's lips because we sensed that something important was about to happen. Perhaps Tommy and Ted realized before the rest of us that he was pulling the same immense pair of panties and the enormous bra from his pocket that had flown with complete abandon at the top of the LHS flagpole so many years ago. Who would have guessed that Coach Allen would have kept those items for posterity?

The room exploded with peals of uncontrollable laughter—laughter that took our breath and made our sides hurt! Any words uttered by those guilty high school seniors, now adults, were completely lost in the uproar; however, the fiery color that spread from their shirt collars to the roots of their hair told us in crystal-clear tones that the blame had finally come to rest on the guilty parties. Finally, at long last, what had earlier been so much fun for the pranksters, what had fascinated an entire student body through the years as it wondered who the pranksters were, and the morning that not a single faculty member smiled—at least on the outside—had all come together in one priceless, hilarious moment.

My mother often said, "He who laughs last laughs best!" After thirty years, we finally saw and heard Coach Allen laugh loud and long about the events of that day, and even though his face was drawn by the years and a residual paralysis, I am convinced that as he drew those two enormous undergarments from his coat pocket, his laugh was the best laugh of all!

Big Ears

Even though our family had fallen into bad times, there was never any question in the mind of my mother and grandmother that we children should go to college. I loved high school. I loved my teachers, and I loved my friends. We were fortunate to have adult family members at home who were interested in what was happening at school, and they insisted that we study each evening in preparation for the next day's lessons. My school experiences were happy, and I was reluctant to let go of them at graduation. What would life be like without my friends and the teachers with whom I was familiar? Perhaps I was a bit fearful.

Surprisingly enough, it was not long after graduation day that I was completely involved in preparations for college in the fall. Rev. Paul Wood, an evangelist who had preached several revivals in our small Methodist church, encouraged me to make Asbury College my choice. He had graduated from Asbury twenty-five years earlier and was certain that I would feel at home in the religious atmosphere of the school, and that I would comply easily with the strict rules for social behavior. He sent my registration application, accompanied by a twenty-five–dollar check, to Asbury in the fall of 1948 to ensure my acceptance for the fall quarter of 1949.

Brother Wood, as he was known to us, knew that we did not have enough money for my entire education, although Mother and Grannie did have enough for my first quarter. He encouraged me to believe that God would provide for my needs, and he promised to help as he could. Often he sent a check for twenty-five dollars, which I applied without fail to my tuition bill. During my sophomore year, he confided that one of the professors at Asbury owed him some money. He contacted the gentleman, and they agreed that instead of repaying the money to Brother Wood, it would be applied to my tuition. What a Godsend that was!

I became ill during my first quarter at Asbury; I was diagnosed with rheumatic fever and was even in the school hospital for a time. It was nearing the quarter's end, and I was concerned about missing classes; however, the professors were most accommodating, and I was permitted to take at least one exam in bed in my room. Mrs. Vincent, assistant dean of women, suggested as I left for the Christmas holidays that I get in touch with "the adult part of Crippled Children" to determine if I were eligible for assistance with my education. Armed with only that scant information, Mother and I discovered Vocational Rehabilitation Service. After extensive testing and physical examinations, it was determined that I indeed was a candidate for their program. My entire tuition and book costs were covered for two quarters of each year, and I was allowed fifty dollars toward tuition costs plus books during the third quarter. A copy of my grades was sent to my counselor each quarter, just as it was to my mother.

Between my freshman and sophomore years, Vocational Rehabilitation paid for the removal of my tonsils. This was routine treatment for rheumatic fever patients since it was believed that the strep germ entered the system through the tonsils. Though I had several recurrences of rheumatic fever through the remainder of my college tenure, there was no permanent damage to my heart. I am convinced that this was "my little miracle": my college education was underwritten by Vocational Rehab, and no permanent damage was done to my heart. Mother, Grannie, and I agreed that there would have been no possible way for me to complete my college education without the help of Vocational Rehab. I am indebted to them to this day for their supportive trust in helping me to achieve my lofty goal. So this is the end of the story—but not quite!

There were so many unanswered questions at the end of my first quarter when I stepped off the Greyhound bus in Livingston, where Mother met me. I had not shared news of my illness earlier, for I knew she would worry. I learned the exact diagnosis just a few days before the Christmas holidays, and I reasoned that it would be easier to discuss these new developments face to face when I got home.

The first thing that Mother wanted me to do was to see Dr. Hill, our family doctor. He verified what Dr. Williams had told me in Kentucky. I needed to get as much bed rest as possible during my three weeks of holiday. I would not be allowed to work in the dining hall upon returning to school, and I would be limited to fewer hours of classes. Bed rest would be a requirement every day when I was not in class. I agreed to follow every single requirement to the letter. I wanted to return to school, and I was prepared to do whatever was necessary to make it happen.

That Christmas holiday was different for our family. I had always been very active physically, but I spent most of my time in bed. It seemed that every conversation was centered around money. Our family resources were exhausted following my fall quarter. We still did not know if Voc Rehab was going to accept me as a client, and if they did, what would that mean financially? When we added to the mix the fact that I was not going to be allowed to work, the picture became even more dismal. Money! Money! Money! What were we going to do about it? Was there any way for me to return to Asbury for the winter quarter?

Howard was the youngest child in our family. He was eleven years younger than I, so at that time, he was six or seven. Like most other "babies," he was always underfoot, hearing everything being discussed by the adults. Admittedly, as the baby, he was spoiled, but we thought he was adorable. He stayed at home with Grannie during the day while Mother drove the school bus and operated the school cafeteria; however, there were days before he started to school that he was allowed to ride the bus to school and spend the day with Mother. The big boys teased him unmercifully, and among other things, they called him "Jughead." To this day, some of those boys, now old men, still call him "Jug."

Living was simpler then, and it was customary for neighbors to drop in on neighbors for unannounced visits, and nobody seemed to mind. We children loved when Mr. Epes Simms stopped by. He told lots of jokes and stories—and laughed at every single one of them. Many adults who visited did not talk to us children, but Mr. Epes did. He often said to Howard, "Boy, when I ask you a question, you answer me and say, 'Half wit.'" Then he would ask, "If you had twice as much sense as you've got now, what would that make you?" Howard would grin and answer with gusto, "A half wit!" Then we all laughed—Mr. Epes most of all.

He also teased Howard about his big ears, and one day he told Howard that he looked like a taxi cab coming down the street with both back doors open. And I shall never forget when he looked at my bare feet and said, "Anything that big ought to have their own set of lungs!"

Big ears or no, Howard heard many conversations during the three weeks that I was at home—conversations that usually began and ended with money. Mother and Grannie were obviously anxious about my returning to school; however, I had some strange assurance of my own that not only would I be going back to Asbury in January, but I would also graduate in four years. And even though I was not able to explain exactly how it would all happen, I just somehow knew that it would.

When the day arrived for me to leave for school, I went. When we were saying our goodbyes, Howard hugged me and told me not to worry. He assured me that everything was going to be okay. I accepted his sweet, childish reassurance, all the while understanding that he wanted the best for his big sister. I did not think any more about his parting words until I unpacked my clothes at Asbury. Tucked away and hidden among my clothes was the well-worn billfold with which Howard played, and it was stuffed to overflowing with the money from our Monopoly game. I cried! My little brother, in his sweet, childish reasoning, believed that he had solved the problem that had caused so much consternation and discussion for three weeks. Without a word, he took matters into his own hands, and to the best of his ability he made things "all better." It is a given that my dilemma was not solved, but the love and concern displayed by Howard has never been forgotten. Would that all of life's dilemmas could be so easily solved!

When my mother-in-law thought we were discussing subjects that the child or children in the room should not hear, she used to say, "Little pitchers have big ears." This was a cautionary warning that matters could always be worse if the child listening to the conversation with "big ears" later repeated what he heard at some inappropriate time. In rethinking Mom's word, I am persuaded that it would not be fair to limit my considerations of a pitcher to "big ears" or its capacity for holding fluids. There is another equally important quality in a good pitcher: that of pouring. No pitcher is worthy of being called "pitcher" unless it pours smoothly and accurately when tipped. Would that all humanity came equipped with "big ears"—ears sensitive to the painful cries of brothers and sisters—and upon hearing, like good pitchers, would instinctively perform its function of being easily tipped to pour out its contents in an effort to relieve the ever-present emptiness and hurt.

Mushrooms and Violets

It was September 1951. Fall quarter was beginning at Asbury College. I stood on the landing between the first and second floor of Glide-Crawford Hall, crowded among the other "unclaimed blessings," otherwise known as the girls with no steady boyfriend. Customarily, the new freshman class was welcomed with a tea that took place in the lovely, spacious parlor of that building. And so we upperclassmen gathered at the windows on the landing to do our annual inspection of the "new crop of prospects." They filled the large porch and broad steps, and they wasted no time in getting acquainted with each other as they waited to enter the parlor. There below us was the entire crop—so unsuspecting, completely unaware of the countless eyes as we sized them up.

My focus fell immediately upon a dark, handsome young man with a breathtaking smile. The activity about him gave witness to the fact that he was the life of the party, the center of attention. My heart helplessly skipped a beat each time he smiled or laughed. He leaned heavily upon a walking cane, which only made him more distinguished. Oh, my! This one was handsome! Maybe, just maybe, I was looking at my "prince charming."

Days and weeks drifted into months. It registered every time I met him on campus—with me, anyway. There was never any conversation between us, and I was never really introduced to him. To a "casual" observer like me, it appeared that he always had a girlfriend, like the one who rushed into my room one day giddily expressing her undying love for "her Jerry!" This was just another indication that my dream man simply was not available. But I was busy with my schoolwork. I worked hard in all my classes. After all, I had come to Asbury to complete my college education. However, in my heart of hearts, I hoped that I would find Mr. Right sometime during those four years. I was already a junior. I truly did not want to be an old maid, but the clock was ticking!

Sometime during late winter or early spring, Mary Sanders, one of my roommates, learned that she had some scarring on her lungs according to a recent X-ray. The doctor feared tuberculosis and recommended that she drop out of school for a quarter to go home and rest. Mary's sister, Doris, was also in school. Five of us girls began to formulate a plan for getting Mary home to southern Indiana. None of the other girls could drive, so it was quickly obvious that I would be the driver of the rental car. Since I was cast in the responsible role of driver, I began to feel very necessary—maybe "important" is a better word. I was essential to accomplishing our plan.

But at the very end of our trip planning, "Mr. Handsome" himself appeared. I think that he and Mary knew each other, possibly from a class they were both taking. Upon hearing of Mary's need to go home, he offered his new Ford car, and he immediately had the trip all planned. He would drive us to Mary's home, and since we would be driving right in front of his home, he suggested that we stop and have breakfast with his family. Suddenly and without warning, I had lost my place of significance! I had been ambushed. I had literally been shot out of the saddle by this most generous offer made by Jerry Munday. After we had cleared everything with the dean of women, plans for the trip were finally complete.

The early morning of the trip found five girls and Jerry Munday driving toward northern Kentucky and southern Indiana. I sat in the back seat directly behind Jerry. I felt a bit uneasy because he kept stealing peeks and smiling at me in the rearview mirror. I prayed that he could not see the deep pit of "pouting" into which I had slipped. Oh, I was wallowing around in it, up to my eyeballs. I was feeling pretty ugly. Upon reaching his home in Florence, Kentucky, we got out of the car and trooped to the front door. Jerry opened the door with his key and invited us in, but there was no sign of life anywhere. They were all asleep.

Jerry's mother finally came sleepily into the living room. She was a pretty woman in her late thirties. Even early in the morning, just as she crawled out of bed, she was pretty. Jerry explained why we were there. She was glad that we had come, and she quickly decided to make pinwheels for breakfast. I later learned that pinwheels were made from biscuit dough rolled thin, covered with salad oil or butter, and sprinkled with sugar and cinnamon, then rolled up, sliced, and placed on a cookie sheet to bake. But alas! Mrs. Munday could not begin the baking since the sink and cabinet were piled high with dishes from the night before. She was not one bit embarrassed that Modelle Tabb and I washed and dried a ton of dishes before she could find enough room to cook. This lady was unflappable! I had never seen anybody like her, and I liked her right off.

Breakfast was wonderful! Afterward, we hastily said our goodbyes and were on the road again. After reaching the Sanderses' home and explaining to Mary's parents why we were there, we began to plan what we would do with the next few hours before our return to Wilmore. Doris asked her mother if she would cook mushrooms if we gathered them. Mrs. Sanders agreed. We drove to a spot known to Doris and made our way into some gorgeous woods still bare from the winter. I had never eaten mushrooms, and gathering them would most assuredly be a new experience for me. Everybody began picking those beauties nestled among the leaves, but I was having no luck at all spotting them. In my rather limited Southern upbringing, I was taught that mushrooms were poisonous and that anyone who picked them for eating purposes should know exactly what they were doing. What if I found and plucked a poisonous one and everybody got sick—or even died? I was not really enjoying this activity until my eyes suddenly fell upon another beauty: a violet. Quick as a flash, my search for mushrooms was ended and my pursuit of those fragile, fragrant blossoms was begun in earnest. I forgot all about pouting because I had not gotten to drive earlier on our trip. Jerry began engaging me in ongoing conversation, and I discovered that he had a wonderful sense of humor. I was surprised by his attentiveness to me after all the time that had passed since my heart first stood still when he was a guest at the freshman reception. I had all but given up on him; however, I was absolutely delighted with that turn of events. "I must be careful not to be too hopeful," I kept saying to myself.

Jerry borrowed a pair of Bud Sanders' overalls, which he slipped on with his white shirt and tie. He really was cute—this uptown boy had come to the farm! Mr. Sanders went to feed the hogs late that afternoon and we went along with him. The hogs were scattered from one side of the pasture to the other, so it was obvious that somebody was going to have to "call them up" for the corn that would be thrown to them from the back of the truck. A little earlier, Jerry had been heard to boast a bit about his days on the farm, so he asked if he could call the hogs. He stood tall on the back of the Jeep and made his best efforts at "hog calling," in response to which the hogs all ran helter-skelter in every direction, squealing loudly and finally stopping at the fence on the other side of the pasture. They slowly returned when Mr. Sanders' familiar call invited them back to eat. The process of throwing out the corn to feed the hogs gave Jerry a little time to recover from his own total embarrassment.

The day was nearly spent, and we were scheduled to return to Asbury that evening. This time we traveled without Mary. It was late when we arrived on campus, and we were tired. It had been a long day. As we gathered our things from Jerry's car, he managed to speak quietly to me. He asked if I would go to dinner with him the next evening. I agreed. There was certainly nothing romantic about having dinner with someone at Asbury. Everybody who lived on campus was there! There were no quiet little corners to sneak into! We ate in the same old dining hall with the same "old" people, and ate the same bland cuisine. It was understood that each person paid for his or her meal with his or her own meal ticket. Jerry and I had dinner together every night after that first date, except for those evenings when he was not on campus. I am compelled to add that as dull as my description sounds, every moment spent in his presence was sheer ecstasy!

Looking back, I don't really feel cheated that I didn't get to drive to Indiana that day. I was a country girl, and I am sure that the Cincinnati traffic would have been a challenge for me. I do not even feel shortchanged that I was not a success at gathering mushrooms. I did learn for the first time that day that mushrooms are delicious, and I consumed my fair share of them—maybe more. Picking violets was one of my happiest experiences, and though I was a failure at harvesting mushrooms, I was personally responsible for the centerpiece of violets on the dining room table. Jerry's pitiful efforts at hog calling helped me recognize his humanity, and I found that he was far more approachable than I could ever have imagined. His invitation to dinner was a delightful surprise that began a loving, lasting relationship that continues to grow dearer with each passing day.

If I were listing places and things dear to me, my list would most certainly include southern Indiana, northern Kentucky, Jerry's mom, good friends, mushrooms, and violets.

My One True Love

There may have been some before (though none could compare), but there has not been a single one since! And that's the truth! From the moment that I laid eyes on that handsome young man with the cane as he waited to be admitted to the freshman reception at Asbury College, my heart belonged only to him. I wondered about the cane. I wondered if there had been an injury. Did he have a degenerative or debilitating disease? But I did not know him, and likely never would, so it seemed best for me to just let it alone!

Later, I did find out why Gerald walked with a cane. He was born with hemophilia. Before coming to Asbury in the fall of 1951, he had worked as a cargo agent for Trans World Airlines in Cincinnati. While loading a plane, he slipped and fell against the propeller, bruising his leg between his knee and hip. The bleeding continued for several weeks. The only known treatment at that time was to lie perfectly still with ice packs on the injury in the hope that any clot being formed would not be broken by even a slight movement. Bleeding into the joints was extremely painful and required a long time to heal. Sometimes vitamin K was given, though there was no evidence that it did any good. Today, there are much better and more effective treatments. But back to My One True Love!

Though Asbury College was often referred to as the "Match Factory," it was also well known that the very strict social rules did not promote opportunities allowing couples to spend time together. Even my grandmother knew and often said, "Absence makes the heart grow fonder," so her conclusion on the matter likely would have been that maybe being a bit more lax would have been wiser because everybody knows that "familiarity breeds contempt." I certainly do not claim to know where the resolution to these thorny issues lies, so it may be best to deal only with facts. Couples were not permitted to be together wherever and whenever they chose. It was permissible to have dinner together, to meet at the Canteen for an hour in the evening, to go to prayer meeting together on Wednesday evenings, and to study together in the library *anytime* throughout the day when not in classes. So we met early every morning (as soon as the library opened), leaving each other's side only to go to classes. We also became regular attendees at prayer meeting. Regardless of how silly or strict the rules seemed, we were together enough to know that we wanted to spend our lives together as husband and wife.

Months spent dating, including our engagement, convinced me that my love was a first-class romantic, and that trait continues to be a part of the man I love. He was one of the few college students who owned a car, while the remainder of us walked, took a bus or train, or caught a ride with a student who had a car. He was also one of the many students who preached each weekend, so transportation was a necessity for him to get back and forth to his preaching appointments. However, this dashing young man who was so much in love (with me!) frequently used his car during the week for flower delivery.

Gerald loved to hike. On one of his outings, he came upon an old house site about five miles from the college, and in the springtime, the entire hill was covered with "a cloud of golden daffodils." On many afternoons after class, he sneaked away to that special place, and when he happily returned, his arms were filled with daffodils for me. Under Asbury's work program, I cleaned the school clinic as payment for my upstairs room in that same building. After Gerald came with arms full of daffodils, there were large bouquets in every room, not to mention that every nook and cranny in the entire place was filled with the sweet, heavy perfume of daffodils.

Gerald was a dreamer of extraordinary proportions. He consistently took what was and dreamed in glorious terms of what could be. During my senior year, I was chosen for a role in the senior play, "Icebound." I was cast as Sadie, a widow with a twelve-year-old son, Orin. Gerald was not in school that quarter. He was living with his family in Florence and working to earn enough money to come back to school the next quarter. Even though Florence was about seventy-five miles from Asbury, I got a ticket to the play for him, and he was able to come for the production.

Gerald had spoken earlier with Mrs. Hall, my house-mother at the clinic, who loved being included in secrets and surprises. She did bend a few rules, but she gave special permission for us to briefly go off campus after the play. She knew that I was getting my diamond before I did. That evening, throughout the play, I cavorted back and forth across the stage with my newly learned New England brogue, dressed in a black dress which silently affirmed my state as a grieving widow. My feet were shod with "old lady's comforts" (the name given to black lace-up shoes with sturdy heels). My face was covered with grease paint, and my powdered hair was pinned in a bun on the back of my head.

After the play, Gerald and I drove to a limestone quarry about two miles from the college. He drove right down into the bottom of that quarry—that deep pit. It was there that he proposed, and it was there that I said, "Yes!" He slipped a gorgeous diamond mounted in a platinum setting onto the fourth finger of my left hand. It was official! We were engaged and my heart sang.

I met Dr. Zack Johnson, president of Asbury College, very early the next morning as I walked across campus. Giddy with the newness of all that had happened the night before, I happily told him of our engagement as I extended my left hand to display my brilliant diamond ring. He studied my ring in silence for a moment and said all of the proper things. Then he added with a grin, "You mean that boy asked you to marry him looking like you looked last night?" Oh, yes, he did! And even then, I knew that he was somehow able to take what was (sad as it was) and dream what it could be.

It has been over fifty years since I first saw my husband. His handsome good looks still turn a lot of heads, and most of the time when that happens, I manage to tuck my hand under his arm and remember that he is my husband, the father of our children, and that he is going home with me!

One Flesh

Being born was probably the greatest event in my life, but all I know about my birth is hearsay; and as I understand it, hearsay does not stand up in any court in the land. Becoming a Christian and being baptized were certainly pivotal times in my life, even though I was baptized as Mary Ann Ferguson instead of Sara Ann Fuller. My prayer is that this case of mistaken identity has not kept my name off the celestial rolls. Graduation from high school and college were huge events, as they marked closure of one chapter in my life while announcing the beginning of another. Numerous births, illnesses, and deaths through the years have been important and have played significant roles in who I was and who I have become; however, the event that takes precedence in my mind at this moment is my wedding to Gerald Earl Munday, August 14, 1953, the occasion when Rev. C. A. Massey uttered those profound words, "… and the twain shall become one flesh!"

Mother and I began planning, researching, dreaming, and recruiting help from family and friends from the moment of my engagement in November 1952. It was going to be a church wedding. I had always dreamed of a long white bridal gown and a church beautifully decorated with candles and flowers and filled with guests because everybody would be invited. Gerald's family would need somewhere to stay since there were no motels nearby, and who could afford one anyhow? Oh, yes! What about the reception? There was no fellowship hall or family life center at our small rural church. The church where we would be married was a lovely old country church consisting of one large room with two small porches (one on each side) at the entrances. My grandfather had played a significant role in building it many years before, and it seemed right that I should be married there. It was almost like being married in his presence. Perhaps that is what the Scripture means when it talks about being "compassed about with so great a crowd of witnesses" (Heb. 12:1).

We planned carefully for the time when the reception was over and we would be leaving in our going-away attire. How could we outsmart those folks who seemed to feel it was their responsibility to "decorate" the car to be driven on our honeymoon? We hoped to avoid that part of the celebration if at all possible. We did not want to be the focal point of the curious gazes of strangers along the way. Neither did we want people following us for miles after the wedding, blowing their horns and calling out to us newlyweds. The two of us believed that our roles as young minister and wife were sacred responsibilities, and that kind of raucous behavior just did not seem proper as a conclusion to our sacred, loving commitment to each other. But first, before all of that took place, there were many other things to get done. First and foremost, we bought a book of etiquette! We had every intention of accomplishing our dream in a socially acceptable manner—one that would be perfectly correct according to the rules of etiquette.

The summer of '53 was filled with planning and hard work. Gerald worked as a carpenter's assistant in Kentucky that summer, earning money for fall tuition at Asbury College. Our large country home was surrounded by five acres of lawn, and it was my goal to have all the grounds beautifully manicured for our wedding day. That was a daunting task since we owned a small push mower that was far from new, so I worked countless long hours in the hot Alabama sunshine in order to accomplish my goal. My work attire that summer consisted of a pair of shorts and a halter, and by August, I was as "brown as a berry." I was convinced that the striking contrast between my deep tan and the white of my wedding gown would make me a lovely bride. Both of my goals became a reality: the manicured yard and my tan!

The Munday family arrived in Livingston a few days before the wedding and called from the bus station. We lived a good distance out in the country, and since I neither trusted myself to give correct directions nor the Mundays to follow them, I dressed quickly and went to Livingston to meet them. They followed me home. Gerald's father, mother, brother, sister, cousin, and aunt arrived in the first car. We had plenty of room for them to sleep.

Friends and classmates from Asbury College who were participating in the wedding began to arrive. The Sanders sisters, Mary and

Doris, came from Indiana, and Shirley Ford came from Pennsylvania. Available space at our house began to fill quickly with the arrival of out-of-town guests. Gerald's parents and little sister occupied one of the upstairs rooms. All the girls slept in the room across the hall, where the entire floor was covered with mattresses. Gerald, his brother Ron (the best man), Tom Pruitt and Tom Denham (ushers), and Mid Ransom (a longtime friend of the family) arrived the day before the wedding. Mid slept at our house while Gerald and his out-of-town men slept at a neighbor's house about two miles away.

The rehearsal dinner was an old-fashioned barbeque that took place on our front lawn under the pecan trees near the road. Sam Bradley, a black man who had worked many years for our family, built the barbeque pit that summer from old bricks that I had cleaned, and since he was going to do the cooking, he built the pit to his specifications. He later cut and hauled enough firewood for the cooking that would last through the night. He arrived late in the afternoon the day before the rehearsal dinner and began preparations. Sam was well known in the community for his barbequing skill and was often called on to cook for special occasions.

Cooking authentic Southern barbeque is a lengthy process that requires patience and many skills. At the very beginning, a large fire was built a short distance from the pit and allowed to burn until there was an abundance of red-hot embers—no flames. Sam salted the entire carcass of the hog, placed it on the pit over the coals of fire, and covered it with a large piece of tin roofing. He then began moving red-hot embers from the fire with a long-handled shovel and scattered them evenly beneath the pork. That process continued through the night. Since the hog was cooked in one large piece and placed several inches above the embers, it is understandable that the barbequing process took all night to complete.

Visitors who came for the wedding were from Kentucky or further north, and they had never met black people who possessed the charm and personality of Sam. He was truly an entertainer. All he needed was an audience. He was surrounded by a very attentive group for much of the night of August 12, 1953. He was pleased that he did not have to spend that long night alone as he cooked, but he was even more pleased to have such an attentive company who hung on his every word. As Sam conjured up and related stories of "haints" and spirits, his big eyes shone as large white circles in his black face, and his joyous, melodious laughter rang out through the dark sultry night. As he completed each story, he laughed loudly and slapped his leg. He would then reach for his shovel and walk around a bit as if to gather his wits for the next story. He filled the shovel with embers and scattered them evenly beneath the pork, which was beginning to drip fat onto the hot coals beneath it. There is nothing that compares to the aroma of barbequing pork over hot coals. Sam periodically returned to the pit to make certain that no detail was overlooked as he prepared this pork for our wedding celebration, and when he was satisfied that it was going well, he again turned his attention to his audience and his stories. Every one of us was caught in both the web of his stories and the magic of that sultry August evening.

The next day, the meat was done to a turn! It was perfection! According to plan, people from the Emelle community began to arrive in the late afternoon, each of them bringing a covered dish. Miss Margaret Simms (a longtime family friend) brought a lemon cheese cake at my request. That was one of my favorite desserts, and Miss Margaret was the local expert on that special delicacy. Many years later, I visited with her in the nursing home that had become home for her, and she asked if I remembered that she had brought the lemon cheese cake to our rehearsal dinner. Of course I did! She laughed. She continued by asking if I remembered that her daughter Alice had owned a parakeet that was allowed to fly freely about inside the house. Again, I answered that I did. Then the rest of the story came out. She said, "I had my cake finished and ready to bring to your house. Well, it was sittin' on the dining room table, when that durned old bird of Alice's flew down, landed on your cake, and walked all over it!" She paused, then continued, "Well, I didn't have time to make another cake, so I just got a knife and smoothed it out and brought it on to supper!" She could not possibly have known how special that story was to me—and how we laughed as we remembered!

As we left the tables around the barbeque pit, we were so stuffed that we were barely able to get through the rehearsal. Events and responsibilities packed into those days had taken their toll on most of us. We were dead on our feet. Since Gerald had gotten in just before dinner, we had very little time to talk about the things that two young people need to discuss before the wedding. Anna C.,

SARA F. MUNDAY

Gerald's aunt, was a firm believer that the bride and groom should not see each other on their wedding day, and so she appointed herself as a committee of one to see that such a meeting could not and would not take place.

The wedding day dawned crystal clear but scorching hot. Nobody—at least in Emelle—had air conditioning. There was one bathroom in our house, so it was necessary to place a signup sheet on the bathroom door. Each person was assigned a fifteen-minute time slot to wash, and whatever else needed to be done had to be done somewhere else. It was a true gift when a nice rain shower interrupted that sultry afternoon. While it was still not cool after the rain, it was something of a relief.

The wedding was set for four thirty P.M. Burton drove me to the church, and as we drove into the churchyard, the large number of parked cars indicated that there was a large crowd inside. The horses, mules, and wagons surrounding the church thrilled me: they were the transportation for the many black people who had known me from my birth and loved me through the years—and they were present for our wedding.

Howard (my youngest brother) and Kenny (Gerald's youngest brother) had already lit the candles when we arrived, and music was pouring through the open windows and doors of the church. My black friends could see and hear everything as they stood reverently outside in the shaded churchyard. Burton and I went up the steps onto one of the small porches, where Gerald's three-year-old sister Pam, our flower girl, was waiting for me. There were so many things that she needed to tell me, and each time she spoke to me, she raised my veil, put her head underneath, looked up into my face, and proceeded to talk. Flora Belle Roberts, my cousin, made my wedding dress, as well as the navy blue linen dress that I wore away after the reception. My dream of many years was that Miss Frances Mellen, my piano teacher, would play the piano for our wedding, but she could not. She was at the rehearsal for Gladys Tartt's wedding, which was scheduled for the next day. How could I ever forgive Gladys for that? As it turned out, Jane Ramsey, my longtime friend, played, and Mrs. Rein, the Presbyterian minister's wife, sang "One Alone," "Through the Years," and "O, Perfect Love." It was beautiful! And perfect for our wedding!

Becoming Myself: A Passage of Grace

As Burton and I entered the church, I was struck by the simple beauty of the moment. Earlier that day, Miss Mary Neely Willingham had gone to the woods in a truck with some black men who gathered loads of smilax vines that draped and filled every nook and cranny of the church. Their glossy dark green leaves were interrupted by two arrangements of giant yellow chrysanthemums. Soft yellow candles flickered from their perches in the two large candelabra. And there, in the midst of young women clad in mint green and soft yellow gowns, flanked by handsome young men attired in black-and-white tuxedoes, stood my most handsome husband-to-be in his black-and-white tuxedo. His eyes were upon me as Burton and I stepped across the threshold. His love for me was evident in his joyfully radiant smile, and my heart responded as it filled with a depth of love and gratitude that I had never before experienced.

The plan was that the reception should take place on our lawn, but at the last minute that was changed due to a mid-afternoon shower. Still people spilled over to the large front porch and onto the lawn. Dear black Sally carried a lion's share of the responsibility for the reception as well as for all of the days leading up to our special day. When Gerald and I were finally dressed and ready to begin our trip to the Smoky Mountains for our honeymoon, we left in Grannie's car. Wrenn and Ronnie, Gerald's brother and best man, were to drive us to Demopolis, where our car had been carefully hidden in the Rev. Hugh Wilson's garage for safekeeping. As we drove away from our house, several cars fell in behind us for "the chase," but we were ready. We had planned all summer for this moment, and this little detail was soon taken care of. The dirt road was narrow, and as we drove onto the wooden bridge that spanned a wide creek, a state trooper whom we had known for years pulled his car across the road in front of the cars that followed. As he did so, he turned on his blue lights. So ended the pursuit of the newlyweds, much to the chagrin of the pursuers!

Over fifty years have come and gone since our wedding day. I cherish every memory of that time, but as I have grown older and experienced some of what real life is about, I wonder how it all became a reality. Both my sister and I graduated from college in the spring of that year—not to mention that my brother was also in college. My mother was a single parent and our family lived with my grandmother. There was not an extra penny among us. My brother

Burton paid for the navy blue suit that I gave Gerald as a wedding gift. It was a practical gift, for he wore it many years as a minister. I wonder now where Mother found enough food to feed all of those visitors who came and stayed for days. How did she and Grannie afford the fabric for my wedding dress, and my sister's dress, and the linen dress with the gorgeous iridescent beading that I wore as we left after the reception? Though there were few flowers and candles from the florist, Mother paid for them over a period of time and she never mentioned that any of it was a burden. Reliving these precious moments has reaffirmed what I have always known: no one was ever surrounded by more sacrificial love and support than I was that day!

Since that day, Gerald and I have shared serious illnesses, deaths, problems of our own making, and problems over which we had no control. There have been times of joy, honor, achievement, and recognition as well—some undeserved. These shared experiences are powerful, unmistakable reminders that our life together is made of loving gifts that have come to us over an extended period of time from countless people who have been a part of the process that has carefully and slowly forged us into the one flesh of which Rev. Massey spoke so many years ago.

For Better For Worse

There were neither seatbelts nor seatbelt laws, so I sat in the middle of the front seat snuggled as close to my new husband as I could. Only a day earlier, on Friday, August 14, 1953, in the small Methodist church in Emelle, Alabama, we had nervously made our marital vows to each other "in the presence of God and these witnesses." Our wedding was now a memory, a beautiful memory. Everything had gone according to plan and we could hardly wait to see the pictures.

We were now Mr. and Mrs. Gerald E. Munday. We wore shiny new wedding rings as evidence. We were beginning to experience freedom as never before. We had cut the ties to our birth families and were now on our own. We were finally in a position to establish our own little family. However, when we thought long and hard on that fact, it became most disquieting. Gerald had two years of college and three of seminary to complete in preparation for his calling into the ministry.

There were no air conditioners in cars then. As we raced along the two-lane highways, our car windows were open wide in the hope that the simple movement of the air might bring a little coolness, even though the wind was hot from the sultry August day. We spent our wedding night in Selma, Alabama, then proceeded to Birmingham, Alabama; Chattanooga and Gatlinburg, Tennessee; and finally into Cherokee, North Carolina. After a few wonderful days there, we drove to Lexington, Kentucky, where we stayed for a few more nights in the home of Anna C. Kingcade, Gerald's aunt. When we arrived, Anna and Gerald's family were still in Alabama with my family, where they had been since the wedding.

We planned to make a daily commute from Anna's house to Richmond (about twenty-five miles from Lexington) to attend the Eastern Kentucky Annual Conference of the Methodist Church. Gerald was appointed that year as a student pastor to the Mt. Edwin Church in Nonesuch, Kentucky. By staying at Anna's, we were able to save the expense of a motel even though we had the expense of driving back and forth. We were frugal, even during our honeymoon, because we were keenly aware that our immediate future would be very costly while Gerald completed his education. We hoped to accomplish this goal without any interruptions such as his having to drop out of school for a quarter or more to earn money in order to continue.

We were still at Anna's when she returned from the south. She was filled with talk about her newfound friends and our latest venture of the Alabama wedding, and we were happy to talk about it all over again. Although we had been as thrifty as we could on our trip back to Kentucky, we were completely out of money. Dear, sweet Anna always came through for us, and she did again. She let us borrow five dollars for gas, which we later paid back. Those were surely "the best of times!"

We lived with Gerald's parents for a brief time—three weeks to be exact. Gerald continued to work as a construction helper to earn as much as he could before the fall quarter began at Asbury. I helped Mom Munday with the housework, shopping, and laundry, and I was happy! Deliriously so! We were newlyweds, and we were beginning to live our dream of a long and productive life of love and service. But for some reason quite unknown to me, I did not feel well. There was an underlying, ever-present feeling of nausea, and my boundless energy was much more limited. Gerald and I planned a trip to Wilmore to paint the apartment that was to be our home for the next two years, and that day was one of the most miserable in my life. I was as "sick as a dog." I spent the day lying on the floor with my head pillowed on a stack of newspapers. Gerald painted and tried to make me comfortable.

A few days later, we began to suspect that I might be pregnant. Oh, no! Not that! Being pregnant was not in the plan. I had never really thought about it, but I somehow unconsciously believed that the "for better" part of our wedding vows would last longer than just a few weeks! This simply could not be! I just could not be pregnant! But if I were pregnant, I was convinced that we had already entered the "for worse" phase of our marriage vows. In my young and ignorant years I believed—though apparently I was mistaken— that the "for worse" part of those vows would come in our old age when we got sick and died! Those days were quickly turning into the worst of times.

Each Sunday as we drove to the church where Gerald preached, we prayed for the congregation, for the work that we were called to do, and that we would be fully surrendered to the will of Almighty God. I especially recall one Sunday as we traveled those Kentucky roads that Gerald prayed that I indeed would not be pregnant, but if I were, then we would rely upon the divine grace of our Father God to see us through. His boyish good looks belied the inner fear with which he struggled, for not only had he taken on the responsibility of a new wife, he now quite possibly faced the arrival of a child.

We could stand it no longer! We went to see Dr. Daugherty, the Mundays' family doctor. He said that it was still very early to say positively if I was pregnant, but if he were guessing, than he would guess that I was most likely going to have a baby. Gerald's parents were delighted. Apparently they had had much the same experience when Gerald was born very soon after their wedding. My mother was happy, but I think she had hoped it would be longer than a few weeks after the wedding before we shared this kind of information with her.

We moved to Wilmore. My nausea did not subside. I was not able to go to work. I was too involved with throwing up and attempting to prepare meals for Gerald. The smell of food brought tidal waves of nausea, and to make matters worse, I knew practically nothing about cooking. I had always done the outside chores at home!

When I was alone, my imagination ran wild. I clearly imagined Miss Rosa Willingham, a very prim and proper elderly lady in our community, as she sat counting on her fingers to determine just how long it had been since our wedding. This pregnancy had happened too soon! Besides that, I had no idea what to do with an infant! It was my sister who loved babies. I did well with small children who were three or four years old. They didn't need bottles filled with formula, nor did they need their diapers changed, and I had never given one of those wiggly little things a bath! There were no two ways about it; I was paralyzed with fear! I was simply scared to death.

During my four years at Asbury as a student, Dr. Williams was my doctor, and he took very good care of me. He saw me every time that I needed to be seen, and he graciously did not charge for my office visits. He knew I was poor, and he gave me samples of whatever medications I needed. His family practice was located in Nicholasville, a nearby small town, so I continued to see him. The nausea did not stop. I became dehydrated and was admitted to Good Samaritan Hospital in Lexington for IV fluids and sedative injections. The treatment must have worked because I began not to worry about anything.

I drifted off to sleep one night with a thermometer in my mouth. I vaguely remember that it slipped from my lips and crashed to the floor. I was out of bed like a flash, feeling blindly about on the floor for it. When the nurse came into the room, she got me back into bed, hoping that I had not cut myself on the broken glass. I was most apologetic and assured her that my husband would pay for whatever the thermometer cost. We had no medical insurance, and poor Gerald was worried sick as to how we would ever pay our hospital bill, and here I was assuring the nurse that he would take care of everything, and that she did not need to worry about that broken thermometer!

I must have been more sedated during that week than I knew. One of the cleaning women asked if my husband weren't a preacher. I proudly answered in the affirmative, to which she said, "Good Lord, lady! Everybody in here thinks you're drunk!" One of the RNs, upon observing Gerald's concern about me, did not hesitate to explain to him that it was "all in my head." None of this bothered me. I was oblivious to everything—most especially to those things that could cause me to be anxious. After spending eight days in the hospital, it was good to get back to Asbury and our barracks apartment. The remainder of my pregnancy went smoothly with the exception of a flare-up of rheumatic fever. I spent several weeks in bed and on the sofa.

By the time of my birthday in November, I was much improved. Gerald surprised me by inviting several college students and my favorite religious education professor to our apartment. I was pleased by everyone's presence, but I felt especially honored to have Miss Serrott as a guest in our modest home. She was not cut from the same pattern as most of the professors at Asbury. She kept us well entertained that evening by singing some crazy, popular country western song: "I was lookin' back to see if he was lookin' back to see if I was lookin' back to see!"—or something! We had such a good time!

Our baby was well on the way by this time. I proudly dressed in maternity clothes borrowed from a young woman who lived two doors from the Mundays. The people in the church Gerald served were excited about this new little person who was coming soon. They regularly gave us milk, eggs, jams, jellies, and fresh fruit and vegetables. Their generosity got us through many times that would have otherwise been very difficult.

Since Gerald worked as a night watchman and as a painter on campus plus preaching every Sunday, there was not much time left for study—or for us. However, springtime in Kentucky is beguiling. As the sun shone upon fields of bluegrass, each blade appeared as if it were waxed and polished. The locust trees' lacy blossoms served as reminders that a late snow shower was always possible, even late into the spring. Golden clouds of daffodils covered hills where farmhouses once stood, and if one dared to walk among them, their fragrance begged the intruder to linger awhile just to breathe air heavy with their sweetness. Those days tempted and teased any soul possessed by even a small bit of wanderlust to lose themselves in the magic of the Kentucky countryside.

One of the favorite things to do on Saturday afternoons was to drive the mile or so to Glasses Mill, a favorite place where a mountain stream flowed quickly and noisily between steep limestone walls. An old stone bridge spanned the clear, cold water that ran eagerly over smooth stones washed for generations. This was a favorite place for students to wash their cars because it was free! Gerald drove right out into the water, soaped the car, and rinsed it clean with fresh water that flowed in abundance on one side, while the soap suds quickly vanished down the creek on the other side of the car. By the time we drove back to our apartment, the drops of water had all been blown away by the wind, and the car was clean and shiny to go to church on Sunday. Those outings were wonderful no matter how brief. Never once were we disappointed that we stole the time to escape from our sometimes drab routine.

May 1954 was very cool. I became heavier and heavier by the day, and I was anxious for our baby to come. I still had no idea how we would manage with a newborn. However, the nine months of conditioning and waiting had sped past. In spite of all our fears that we could not possibly survive, we were still having regular meals. We really were doing just fine. I had almost become a believer. I was almost convinced that we were going to have this baby, and that Gerald was going to complete all of the school that was needed to become the best minister he could be, and that I was going to carry my share of responsibility. Both Gerald and I had matured a lot during our time of waiting. He was eagerly looking forward to the birth of "our son." I suppose it is normal for a father to expect his firstborn to be a son. We were in the countdown stages of the arrival of "Mark Stephen."

Dr. Williams finally agreed that it was getting to be time for the baby to come. He sent me home with a recipe consisting of castor oil, vinegar, baking soda, and orange juice. He explained that it made a "fizzy" drink, and that some people really liked it. He was correct about one thing: it did make a "fizzy" drink. The first dose fizzed all over the countertop. With some effort, the second dose was completed inside the glass. From the very first swallow, I knew that I was not one who liked this "fizzy" drink—not in the least!

"The Dose" brought speedy results. The pains began fairly early in the evening, and it was not long until I announced that it was probably time to call Dr. Williams and be on our way to Good Samaritan Hospital. Gerald calmly replied that Dr. Williams had said that since this was our first child, we could probably take our time about going to the hospital. And so began our first disagreement over our child! After what seemed an eternity, Gerald was still pulling on his socks, and I was standing in the living room with my coat on, holding my suitcase that had been packed for weeks. What a relief when he finally began to get serious about this event that was just on the verge of moving into high gear.

Upon arriving at the hospital, I was whisked away in a wheelchair while the expectant father nervously checked me in. I was taken to a holding room where there were several women in various stages of labor: some were screaming their heads off while others with very rosy cheeks appeared to be heavily sedated, to the point of being unconscious or asleep. This "birthing business" was a new experience for me! I had never even seen a kitten or a puppy born, so I watched everything with great interest and curiosity.

Some discomfort in my lower abdomen caused me to feel as though I needed to go to the bathroom, so I made frequent trips back and forth, all the while paying close attention to everything going on inside that dimly lit room. Finally one of the very busy nurses came to me and said quite sternly, "I do not want you to go to that bathroom another time! If you don't watch out, you are going to have that baby in the toilet!" Her look and her tone of voice accompanied by her words got my full and complete attention! I was no longer aware of the other women in the room. My attention was suddenly centered on me! I was about to become a mother!

Sometime during my labor, I remembered Mother's saying that "Women have been having babies since the beginning of time, and all that screaming just is not necessary!" I was determined not to scream, but I must confess that I did probably groan a few times. I really believe that Mother would have been proud. I don't remember much that happened after that. I later learned that we were in the hospital for one hour and forty minutes before the actual birth. Dr. Williams said there were a lot of anxious nurses wringing their hands as he arrived. Apparently the baby was coming really fast, and they were convinced that they were going to be forced to deliver this impatient baby without him. When Dr. Williams noticed that I still had my rings on, he carefully removed them, dropped them into his pocket, and returned them to me next morning. He explained in his fatherly manner that sometimes jewelry goes missing when patients are put to sleep.

The next memory that I have is of my handsome young husband with a smile that reached from ear to ear. He was loudly exclaiming, "Honey, we've got a little girl! We've got a little girl!" Most likely I drifted in and out of consciousness several times. Each time anything registered, the smile and the words were the same: "Honey, we've got a little girl!" Funny how soon he forgot that we were supposed to be having a little boy.

Nine months and two days after we had pledged "for better…for worse," Rebecca Lynn arrived—all seven pounds, fourteen ounces of her. She was beautiful from head to toe, and measured nineteen and one half inches. She came with very little black hair, which she soon lost; it grew back blond. Her chubby pink cheeks quickly banished any ideas of malnourishment. Her almond-shaped eyes were dark blue but began to change after a few weeks to the beautiful clear blue that they are today. The space between her eyes was almost flat, which gave her an Asian look, and she had practically no nose. My mother was not at all disturbed about her nose. She said that we needed to pinch that little nose often and gently to give it shape, so we did, and it worked just fine. Gerald later admitted that he was concerned when he first saw the baby and feared that something might be wrong because of her tiny nose and the flat space between her eyes. Holding that new little bundle of humanity close to me during her visits from the nursery to my room convinced me early on that we had nothing to dread. We were going to be just fine!

I wanted to call our baby Rebecca—"Becky." *Rebecca of Sunnybrook Farm* was the title of a book I remembered from my childhood. The sound of it conjured up such happy images and I wanted this baby's name to have such a happy sound that anyone who met her or called her name would be aware of the joy we felt in her arrival and presence. Gerald felt there should be no nicknames. He insisted that she be called by her proper name, Lynn, and it was so!

Since our baby was the first grandchild on both sides of the family, she occupied a special place of honor—which can be interpreted to mean that she was genuinely spoiled. Gerald's Aunt Anna filled our hospital room on the first day with red roses from her neighbor's back yard. Gerald's mother and little sister Pam (a new aunt at four years of age) came to the hospital with Gerald for the big "going home" day. The weather was cool enough that the oil heater was called into service. We made certain that Lynn was warm. We had lunch soon after arriving at home. As Gerald and Mom Munday were finishing their meal, Pam became completely involved in something. She explained to Mom that the baby was hungry, and she was going to take her some beans and water!

My mother arrived in Lexington later that day by bus. Anna and her husband Clarence brought her to Wilmore. Our tiny apartment had never been so full of people who stayed for such a long time. Mother and Mom Munday slept on the sofa bed. If Lynn even so much as sighed or hiccoughed, one grandmother reached for her while the other grandmother went for a bottle. I wonder now why I was ever fearful that we could not care for our newborn; but I must hastily add that we felt great security in the presence of Lynn's two experienced grandmothers. Even so, it was wonderful when they all finally went home, and we were home alone with our baby.

Lynn was born just after midnight on Sunday morning. New father Gerald preached that morning with very little sleep. The wonderful people of the Mt. Edwin congregation decided that he should have Sunday evening off so he could visit his new baby. Lynn first

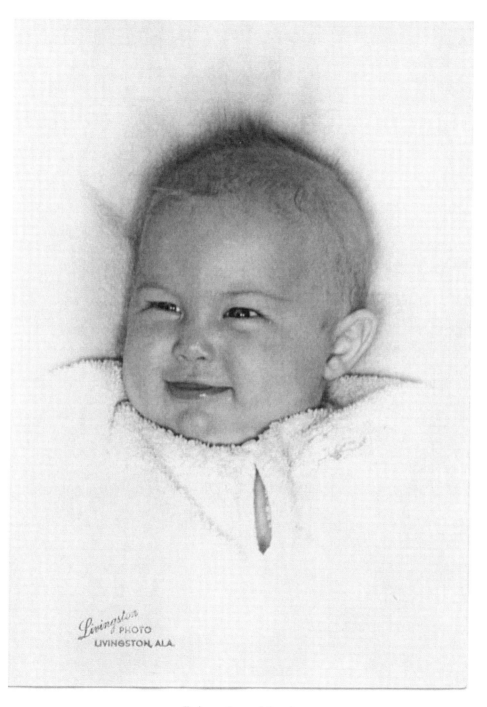

Rebecca Lynn Munday

went to church when she was two weeks old. Mother suggested that we take a pillow to place beside me on the pew for a bed. There were no church nurseries then. We sat in the back pew, and the pillow was perfect. Lynn slept through the entire worship that Sunday and many Sundays following that.

Sometimes our dreams, plans, and goals become so important that they blind us. In recreating these precious memories, I am convinced that we are among the few people who "have our cake and eat it too!" I agonized over letting Gerald down by becoming pregnant, by adding to his responsibility when he was a new husband and father, and by reneging on my responsibility to earn the money needed to accomplish our lofty goals. How stupid and limited I was in my early pregnancy to entertain the notion that we were in the "for worse" phase of our wedding vows. It is true that, on occasion, we did without some things, but we were never without anything that was essential.

In looking back half a century, I know beyond any doubt that our lives would never have been complete without Rebecca Lynn! How could that ancient, unknown poet who wrote about Monday's child and Tuesday's child have been so accurate in his description of our Lynn? He or she said:

> And a child that is born on the Sabbath day
> Is fair and wise and good and gay.

How reassuring to know that God's ways are not always our ways—as perfectly planned as we believed our ways to be! Lynn was and is a gift from God. What paupers we would have been without her unconditional love, her ever-present support, and the pure delight she brings day after day. With her coming came the best of times!

Our First Home

Maybe thirteen houses in fifty years is not a bad record. There must be people who have been married a much briefer time yet have lived in even more houses. This number includes neither my birth home nor my college home. If I had not lived in the same house in which I was born until I went away to college at almost nineteen years of age, then thirteen homes might not seem excessive. I frequently recall the opening lines from Thomas Hood's poem "I Remember, I Remember," which go like this:

> I remember, I remember,
> The house where I was born,
> The little window where the sun
> Came peeping in at morn.

The house where I grew up was not little, and the windows were far from small, but I do remember that the sun came peeping into Grannie's room through one of the big windows, and when the weather was warm, through the door that opened onto the screened-in porch. In that twenty feet by twenty feet room with a twelve-foot ceiling were three very large windows and three very tall doors. It was large enough for a number of chairs, a large desk, a beautiful antique dresser, and two lovely antique double beds. Grannie slept in one of the beds; Wrenn and I slept in the other.

Each of us who shared that room was well aware of our nightly routine, and we faithfully followed it as regularly as we went to bed. All chairs had to be pulled far enough away from the fireplace so that a stray spark could not ignite a fire during the hours that we slept. The embers and hot coals were covered with ashes, and the fire was banked to last through the night. Sometimes ashes spilled onto the hearth during this process; however, that presented no problem since a part of every night's routine was to sweep the hearth, because if any of us became ill during the night, the doctor might have to come, and under no circumstances would we ever have allowed him to find our house untidy. The broom was carefully shaken after sweeping the hearth for fear that a stray spark might have lodged in the straw. Every morning, ashes were removed from the hot embers remaining from the night and fresh wood piled on. Very soon a fire roared in the fireplace, and the darkness began to relax its grip as light from the flames began to slowly push the shadows from the room.

Sleeping in the same room with Grannie provided us with a warm sense of security in that big house with its creaks and groans. There were many nights when I didn't go right off to sleep, and as I lay in the bed, surrounded by darkness with maybe a slight glow from the fire, I could hear Grannie as she earnestly whispered to God about us children. In every instance, my unintentional eavesdropping brought assurance and reassurance—not to mention the lasting impression that Grannie's prayers made upon my life.

Each of my homes since has been special in many ways, but I suppose the first home shared by a newlywed couple always has features not common to any other. Our first house wasn't even a house. It was one of four apartments located in a condemned army barracks on Asbury College's campus in Wilmore, Kentucky. Our nation went through a period of recovering from shortages and rationing after World War II ended in 1945. Colleges experienced an increase in enrollment with the return of thousands of young servicemen and - women who began taking advantage of the GI Bill. Military bases no longer needed all the housing required by wartime personnel, thus creating a surplus. Recycling of housing began on a grand scale. Colleges obtained abandoned barracks from the military and used them as housing for returning veterans and their families. Although those abandoned, discarded buildings were ugly, they became the solution to a pressing need.

By the time Gerald and I married, ten years had passed since the war, but those old barracks were still being used as housing for married students at Asbury College. To say that they were "run down" would be putting it mildly. Though our choice of colors was limited, Asbury College provided paint that would cover the dirt and scars left by former tenants. What a fresh coat of paint did to those small, dismal rooms bordered on the miraculous. I was not at all helpful in getting our new home decorated, since I was experiencing nausea from the early stages of pregnancy. It was Gerald who worked the miracle.

We were married in August before school began in September. There was so much to do to furnish our new home, and not much time to get settled in before classes began for Gerald. There was one piece of furniture in the apartment when we arrived: a player piano. It was much too heavy for the tenants who lived it the apartment before us to move, so it was left behind. When Gerald graduated and we moved to Alabama, we also left the piano; however, we sold it for twenty-five dollars to the new tenants.

Gerald's uncle Skid worked for Clappert's Moving and Storage Company in Newport, Kentucky. There were occasions when furniture and household goods were left (for whatever reason) in the warehouse by the owners, and the employees were allowed to purchase them. As a result, Skid's basement was filled with wonderful furniture that had been picked up through the years at bargain prices. We were indeed fortunate to be allowed to shop there for our new home. We purchased an armchair for seven dollars and fifty cents and a sleeper sofa for fifteen dollars. After fifty years, both of those pieces are still being used in the house where I grew up. They have been upholstered several times but are still sturdy pieces of furniture. Our gas range for the kitchen cost twenty dollars. The Maytag wringer washer leaked transmission fluid, but it was well worth our ten-dollar investment. Our sheets, towels, and lots of diapers were always the whitest and brightest on the clotheslines.

A large oil heater occupied a big chunk of the already limited floor space in the living room. Using a five-gallon can to bring oil from the storage drum outside, Gerald refueled the heater daily. It was more than adequate for heating the apartment, but there were significant air holes around the windows, as well as along the floors where the floor and walls came together. We stuffed the spaces along the floor by using a knife to pack wet newspaper tightly into place. The windows were a different matter because the cracks were smaller. We finally discovered that if we moistened toilet tissue, it could be easily worked into the cracks. We completed the insulation process by buying adhesive tape, as we could afford it, and taped around each window. What an improvement!

The walls between the apartments were tissue paper-thin. We

could clearly hear our neighbors' conversations, or the rattling of pots and pans in their kitchen. We tenants used to joke about having to get into our cars and go somewhere if we wanted to fight or make love. We rented an area about the size of a postage stamp for a garden. We planted, weeded, and watered, but "God gave the increase." And what an increase it was! There is no way of knowing how many beets and carrots we canned from our first garden. In the spring, morning glory vines covered the old timbers around the back steps into the kitchen. The flowerbed on the street side of the house was filled with colorful blossoms during the growing season.

There were many things that we did not have. We did not have a TV, but we had a small radio. We did not have a lot of food, but we were never hungry. Gerald worked two jobs on campus, night watchman and painter, to help pay his tuition, and he preached on weekends. He worked so hard yet still carried a full load academically. Actually, I was not much of an asset that first year of our marriage. In addition to being pregnant, I had a flare of rheumatic fever during the winter. Bed rest was the prescribed treatment, so I spent a lot of time resting in bed or on the sofa. I read, wrote letters, and monogrammed the sheets and pillowcases that had been wedding gifts only a short time earlier. Gerald had lots of socks when we married, and I think they all had holes in them. I had never darned socks before, but I used a light bulb as my darning gourd, and a considerable amount of my convalescence was spent in the reconstruction of his socks. It is a real achievement to repair the hole in such a way that the sock can be worn comfortably. Those days were long and tiring, even though they were spent "resting." I waited up every night for my new husband's return from his night watchman's job. I was eager to know what was going on in his world besides work.

All in all, our first home was really not much of a house, but it provided us shelter for two years while Gerald finished school; it was warm enough for baby Lynn's first home, and we saw gorgeous sunsets from our kitchen door. The building no longer stands, and there is no marker that indicates that a surplus army barracks once stood on that spot for the purpose of housing families preparing themselves to be productive people in a wounded world that begged for healing. The only proof that any of these things occurred, or that the barracks ever stood, exists in the memories that Gerald and I treasure of our first home.

Once a Dream Maker

Wrenn and I loved the days when Grannie said, "Bring me that scrap bag in the closet." Upon emptying the contents of the bag in front of Grannie's chair, we gleefully identified colorful scraps from dresses or skirts Mother had made for us. "Ready-made clothes" (as they were called then) bought from the store were expensive. Our family simply could not afford them, so Mother made almost everything we wore. Most of the fabric came from Miss Louise Lang's country store. She bought and sold some of the most beautiful fabric anywhere. Since she sewed for Aileen, her daughter, she had a great deal of experience in buying fabric for folks in the community who sewed for their families.

There could have been any number of reasons why Grannie needed to look in the scrap bag. A worn or torn garment could have needed a patch. Or in the late summer or early fall, she might have been thinking about "piecing" a quilt. It took lots of fabric to make a quilt. We knew people who purchased beautifully coordinated new fabric to make quilts—but not us! There was too much good fabric packed into that scrap bag. What a waste it would have been not to use it!

We spent many pleasant hours in front of the fireplace helping Grannie decide what piece to use next. Making a quilt required a lot of time, and it certainly was a pleasantly productive way to pass a winter day. It occurs to me now that Grannie could have simply wanted to spend the morning with Wrenn and me, teaching us how to piece our own quilt, but her long-range goal was to teach us how to sew. Sewing was a skill that was an unwritten requirement for every girl. And though we did sew a lot of pieces together as we happily sat around the scrap bag, we never completed a real quilt.

Wrenn was the better seamstress of the two of us. I loved being outside, planting a garden, mowing the lawn, helping with work at the barn, or bringing in stove wood. I was encouraged to do those things because they had to be done, but all the while my sewing skills went woefully lacking. High school home economics classes diminished my sewing deficit only slightly. The part of home ec in which I excelled was the weeks that were focused on landscaping. And though my efforts at making a pair of pajamas did not achieve perfection, I did complete the project. I actually slept in them—with great pride, I might add.

Mother continued to sew for us through high school and college. She and a cousin made my wedding dress, but not from yards and yards of satin. We were too poor to purchase fabric of that quality, but there was lace! I thought it was gorgeous. They also made my dress to wear away after the wedding. It was navy blue linen. Braid highlighted by iridescent beads sewn on by hand trimmed the collar and sleeves. I wore it for years to come whenever I needed to be well dressed.

Our children began coming soon after our wedding, and I quickly realized that Mother and Grannie had taught me many valuable lessons that I began to recognize as extremely useful. I also understood that I needed to begin using those skills that were meant to prepare me for this time. All of us needed clothes, and they were much too expensive to purchase, especially on the meager income of a student pastor. I took seriously my responsibility as wife and mother to contribute all that I could to ease our family's financial tension. I understood that making clothes would be a huge contribution toward that goal, but my sewing skills simply did not measure up. I began to understand another lesson: "Experience is the best teacher," and even though sewing is hard work, I *had* to do it. There was so much to learn: choosing the right pattern, fabric, and matching thread, placing and pinning the pattern on the fabric, matching all the notched places, basting the pieces together, and finally, sewing the garment on the machine.

My treadle Singer sewing machine had belonged to Gerald's great-grandmother. Machines were not complicated then; they just sewed. There were no built-in fancy stitches and embroidering. Probably the worst thing that could happen was that the tension could get out of whack, and that was ever so frustrating! When Mom Munday realized that I was serious about sewing, she purchased a small electric motor to be mounted on the machine. What an upgrade! Due to my lack of experience, I often got my fingers in the wrong place, and the needle sometimes went right through a finger. Besides hurting like the dickens, blood stained the fabric I was sewing.

Recycling is not a new idea to us; we began that when our children were young. When Gerald's brown-and-white shepherd checked trousers became too worn to wear, I carefully ripped them apart and steamed each piece to remove any wrinkles and seam lines. I found enough good fabric to make Sunday jackets for both Mark and Mike. Matching brown trousers made from another pair of Gerald's worn trousers completed their Sunday suits. They were almost as proud as I every Sunday morning when they got dressed in their suits, white shirts, and ties.

When we lived near the cotton mills in Columbus, Georgia, I bought large bags of remnants of all shapes and sizes. The large amount of fabric at such a modest cost proved to be a real bargain. Not knowing what fabrics were inside was the only downside to such a purchase. Once I found in one such collection a large piece of smoke gray corduroy that looked almost like velvet. It was perfect for a winter coat for Lynn, but there was not a single piece suitable for a lining in that entire bag. Then an elderly neighbor, who was both creative and frugal, suggested that we sew numerous pieces and colors of fabric together (much like a patchwork quilt) for the lining. That's what we did, and it was beautiful. Lynn loved that coat, and she wore it until her arms hung much too far out of her sleeves to look fashionable.

I became more and more efficient with the sewing machine. One Christmas, Gerald and the children gave me a Singer Touch and Sew machine that came with three or four free lessons, which I happily accepted. I also took a class in sewing double-knit polyester, plus a class in men's tailoring. I made jackets and trousers for my husband as well as dressy pantsuits for myself. I continued to sew for the children. Even when Lynn went away to college, I made and mailed clothes to her.

However, there came a day when Lynn came home and presented me with the challenge of my sewing career. She was nineteen and much too young to be engaged. I learned that day just how difficult it is to reason with a teenager who knows beyond any doubt that she is "in love." She was clutching a *Bride's* magazine that fell open to the page at which she had looked many times, and likely had shared with all her friends. She held up the picture of a beautiful bridal gown, and without batting an eye or catching her breath, she said, "Mom, do you think that you could make this dress?"

I am not certain just how long it took before I began breathing normally again. When I was finally able to focus visually, I learned that the dress of Lynn's dreams could be seen and purchased at Brisch's Bridal Shop in Pensacola. The best suggestion I could make at the moment was that we go to Brisch's to look at the dress and try it on. I explained to Lynn that every dress is not perfect for every person, and we needed to determine if this really was "her" dress. Good suggestion! We went to town. Lynn slipped into that wedding gown— and *it was perfect!*

I seized every moment when the saleslady was out of the fitting room to study this gorgeous garment inside and out, top to bottom— the inner and outer sleeves, the lace overlay, and things that I had not had time to even think about before we got there. Upon leaving the shop, Lynn was doubly convinced that she wanted me to make her wedding gown from the picture in the magazine. I was flattered but frightened to death that my best efforts would dim in the light of the real dress that we had just seen. I found that no one pattern was what Lynn wanted, so I concluded that this dress would of necessity be made by combining pieces from a number of patterns. I purchased a pattern with a train (I had not been sewing bridal gowns), and I began a painstaking search through all the patterns that I had used for Lynn since she was a little girl. The bodice came from one pattern, an inner sleeve from another, and the outer puffed sleeve from yet another. The final creation included pieces from seven patterns.

We purchased fabric as near as we could to that in the picture and the actual dress; however, my feelings of inadequacy as a seamstress and the lessons learned from my very meager childhood would not allow me to cut such beautiful and expensive fabric. How could I be certain that the many pieces from seven patterns were going to fit together smoothly? I decided that I would first make the dress out of something that would not cost an arm and a leg. I finally decided to use well-worn colored sheets. Amazingly, that exercise was enough to give me the confidence I needed.

I was employed then by the Northwest Florida Girl Scout Council, so my dressmaking was limited to evenings and weekends, and that only after we had eaten our evening meal and carefully

Rebecca Lynn Munday

cleared away the food and dishes. Cutting and sewing were both long and tedious processes. To make matters even more difficult, for no apparent reason, my left index finger became very swollen and discolored. I could not use it to sew because the joint would not bend, so it stood at attention while all the others fingers did the work.

Gerald made several disparaging remarks about my taking on such a demanding project while working full-time...and on...and on...ad infinitum! One evening after finishing dinner, I suggested that the two of us walk to the end of the pier. I had listened to all the criticism on this matter that I wanted (or needed) to hear. I spoke very quietly (but firmly) from a heart overflowing with several emotions as I explained that I felt both honored and flattered that Lynn had asked me to make her wedding dress. Never would I allow him to verbalize any negative word that could cause Lynn to feel that I had not happily taken on this challenge. She must never think that I felt put-upon! When we reached an understanding, we returned to the house—and to the work at hand.

The dress was completed days before the wedding. Lynn was delighted. I watched as her father slowly walked her down the aisle, then stepped into the chancel and performed the wedding ceremony. She was a lovely bride in her "homemade" dress. I was proud of the dress, but prouder still as I realized how special Lynn made me feel when she believed in me enough to bring her impossible dream to me, fully convinced that I could make it happen. I suppose that generations from my past should have taught me that that's what mothers do!

And Then There Were Two

Gerald graduated from Asbury College in the spring of 1955. We had been married for twenty-one months, and we had a beautiful little girl, Lynn, who was one year old. Gerald had interviewed earlier with Dr. S. M. Baker, district superintendent of the Demopolis District in the Alabama/West Florida Conference of the Methodist Church. We were hopeful that he would be appointed to a pastorate in that district. We were looking forward to moving south.

Our first appointment was to seven churches on the Gilbertown Charge in Choctaw County. We did not have a lot of furniture, but two round trips in a rented U-Haul trailer were required to finally get all of our possessions from Wilmore, Kentucky, to Gilbertown. Even then we were not able to move the upright piano we had inherited from the renters before us; they had not been able to move it either. Fortunately, we were able to sell it to the couple who moved in as we moved out. We had lived for two years in the GI barracks at Asbury, and the prospects of living in a real house had great appeal. While serving as a student pastor of the Mount Edwin Methodist Church in Kentucky, Gerald earned $24 weekly, out of which we paid $24 each month for rent, utilities, groceries, and a tithe of $2.40 per week. For us, this appointment to the Gilbertown Charge was "the Promised Land, a land flowing with milk and honey." At the new church, Gerald would earn an annual salary of $2400 and we would not be paying rent since the parsonage was provided as payment in kind. Living within sixty miles of my family and childhood home was another positive consideration as we moved to Choctaw County.

To our horror and dismay, when we arrived at the house that was to be our new home, we discovered that it was infested with a bumper crop of fleas. The people in the church were mortified and explained that the minister who preceded us had owned a dog that lived inside the house. To make matters even worse, they opened the refrigerator door so their spoiled pet could lie in front of the opened door where the cool air tumbled forth, and sometimes, when he was not cool enough, he climbed right inside the refrigerator!

The church members quickly decided that their new minister, his wife, and their little girl would not move immediately into the parsonage. The plan was that we would stay with the Lands, an elderly couple who lived nearby. In the meantime, they would apply poison to kill the fleas. After the poisoning, it was necessary to clean thoroughly because Lynn was only a year old, and the floor was her playground! Upon finally moving into the parsonage, it did not take long to discover the big challenge: that of cleaning dog hairs from the refrigerator. I tackled the job with gusto, and when it was done, the refrigerator was squeaky clean. We were finally at home.

As I look back at our new home in Choctaw County, I must admit that it was small and plain, with an exterior covering of gray asbestos shingles. The small living room had an even smaller dining area at one end. The small dining room window was filled with an air conditioner purchased the second summer that we were there. It was the only means of cooling the house. Three very small bedrooms, a bathroom, and the kitchen completed the floor plan. A freestanding garage used mostly for storage was at the back of the house. A small floored portion was walled off at the opposite end of where the car entered, and was used to house our wringer washing machine and later, a small deep freeze. Our clothes were dried on the clothesline just outside the door of the wash room. A dilapidated chicken coop that stood in the back yard soundly affirmed that there had been little to no care paid to the appearance of the house and yard for a long time. Neglect was obvious everywhere we looked. Weeds stood head high where once there had been a vegetable garden. But we could change that—and we did!

During those years, Choctaw County was enjoying prosperity from recently developed oil fields. We frequently took visiting family and friends to watch the burning of the low-grade crude oil that was not fit for refining. The crude was pumped into holding ponds, where it was held for burning. What a fearful sight the burning oil was to those not familiar with the process as flames with smoke as black as night leaped high into the air.

Melvin was the town where the second largest church on the charge was located. The town itself and the acreage surrounding it

were essentially owned by the Land family. They also owned and operated the large sawmills that employed many of the local people. Large
forests, many of which contained virgin timber, surrounded the town,
and were the source of timber for the mills. Some of the parishioners
owned large amounts of acreage from which they sold timber, while
others raised cattle.

Since there are four Sundays in each month, and Gerald preached
at seven churches each month, our schedule was very demanding. He
preached two Sundays each month at the two largest churches. The
smaller five churches fit into a schedule that allowed each church only
one hour of worship each month. Such a schedule meant that Gerald
preached four times some Sundays: 9:30 A.M., 11:00 A.M., 3:00 P.M.,
and 6:30 or 7:00 P.M.. As a new minister's wife, I wanted *all* of the people in *every* church to love me, and I worked hard to accomplish that.
When we first arrived in Gilbertown, I went from church to church,
sitting in each congregation for an hour with a one-year-old, then off
to the next church. Since many of the churches were only one room,
there were no nurseries. Following church, more often than not, we
went to one of the members' home for Sunday dinner.

Sundays were always long for us, and Lynn was an exceptional little girl to tolerate so much torture every seven days. She was dressed
in her "Sunday best" each Sunday, but by the end of the day, it was
easy to see that the day's demands had taken most of the starch out
of her, her frills, and her ruffles. After a few months and some real
insistence from Gerald, I began attending fewer churches each week.
It is hard to tell whether it was Lynn or I who benefited more from
our new relaxed pace.

Nine months after we arrived in Gilbertown, there came another huge change in our lives: there was a second baby on the way.
Gerald was delighted! I am well aware that some women love every
single moment of pregnancy, but I was not one of them. Gerald and
I had agreed that we did not want Lynn to grow up as an only child,
and I realized that in order to spare her from such a fate, I would
have certain responsibilities in the process. So we were expecting our
second baby!

Dr. Jason Watkins, known affectionately to his patients as "Dr.
Jase," had come highly recommended by some of the people in our
congregations. Several years earlier, his father had founded Watkins

Memorial Hospital in Quitman, Mississippi. Dr. Watkins was pleasant, and as a professional courtesy to us, his treatment and medical care were given without charge. It was rumored that he had a drinking problem, and maybe he did, but we were comfortable with him as our physician. During my first pregnancy in Kentucky, Dr. Williams imposed very strict requirements regarding weight gain. Dr. Jase, on the other hand, thought that women who were expecting babies should eat all of anything or everything they wanted. To him they looked healthier when they were smooth and round. And I was just that—both smooth and round!

Since there were no dietary restraints, I ate what I chose—even the gallon of pecans that I shelled and stored in a glass jar. A member of our church suggested that we employ Mamie Lee, a black woman who lived nearby, to come one day a week to help with household chores before the new baby came. When I think about all that she did on that one day, I am still puzzled as to how she managed. She cleaned house, washed clothes, spent time with Lynn, and cooked dinner, which we ate at noon. After her first week with us, I made certain to have sweet potatoes for her to cook every Wednesday when she came. When Mamie Lee cooked sweet potatoes, so far as we were concerned, we were feasting on the nectar of the gods. Never before or since have we tasted sweet potatoes as delicious as hers. And though I have diligently tried, always using large quantities of butter as she did and sugar by the cups, I have not ever come close to producing anything like Mamie Lee did every time without a single failure! So Mamie Lee came each week, and with her wonderful cooking plus having a baby, I continued to grow...and grow...and grow!

Our church people were pleased about having a new baby. Somewhere along the way, we learned that congregations usually take real ownership of babies who are born on their turf, and this one was going to be no exception. They already loved Lynn, and they were convinced that an additional Munday baby would simply be "icing on the cake."

We kept our appointments with Dr. Watkins, and each time he told me how good I looked. All the while I knew that I was growing into a bigger person than I had ever been. The months passed in good time. Finally the time arrived when I reached full term, and I was ready to deliver! It was Wednesday, and Mamie Lee was at our house. I was not feeling well, and she pampered me till it was shameful. Mamie Lee had a house full of her own children. She knew about pregnancies and giving birth, as well as how to nurture and care for a little one after he or she arrived. I bowed to her wisdom and motherly instinct as she kept telling me that day that our baby would be coming very soon. She just knew! She was such a comforting presence that I did not want to see her leave that afternoon when Gerald took her home.

Gerald went to prayer meeting at the church that night. In reconstructing the events of that day, I believe they were in the middle of a potluck supper. Indications began to manifest themselves that alerted me to the fact that we were beginning the countdown phase of this process. In all probability, our little one would be coming soon, and I was ready! Since we were not able to determine the sex of our unborn baby then, much of his or her wardrobe consisted of shades of pastel yellows or greens. Pinks and blues could come later. I called Gerald at the church to tell him of the most recent developments. No sooner had I hung up the phone than I heard his rapidly approaching footsteps as he ran down the street from the church to the parsonage. The moment for which we had planned and waited was finally here.

Upon calling the hospital, we were told that it would most likely be some time before the baby came, but since we lived thirty miles or so from the hospital, they suggested that we start moving in the direction of Quitman and the hospital. We took Lynn to Gilmer and Sarah Doggett's house to spend the night. From the first week that we lived in Gilbertown, those two spoiled Lynn to death. They gave her anything and everything she wanted, so it was easy to say speedy good-byes and be on our way. The night was beautiful. The clear winter sky was lighted by a nearly full moon. We enjoyed the ride. It gave us an opportunity to talk and visit quietly. I was not actually in labor, so the trip was actually comfortable. Gerald was as excited as a child at Christmas. We were getting a new baby!

The hospital seemed nonchalant about our arrival. Everything was perfectly calm. We should have expected that, I suppose; after all, they delivered babies all the time. I was admitted, assigned a room, and put to bed. It was not long until labor pains began. Around midnight, as the pains intensified, the nurse suggested that we go to the delivery room, where I could scream if I wanted to! She soon learned that I was not a screamer, but I did sometimes utter deep groans.

The peace and calm at Watkins Memorial Hospital was comforting, and the fact that I was the focus of the nurse's undivided attention was ever so reassuring. Gerald went with me to the delivery room and stayed. The trip from our private room to the delivery room was as casual as if we were going to the kitchen for a cup of coffee. As a matter of fact, that is exactly what happened. Gerald and the nurse began to drink coffee while I became more and more focused on having a baby. There seems to be some kind of disparity in these arrangements as I recall them now, but I suppose we were each doing what we could to make this thing happen as quickly and as pleasantly as possible.

As the pains began getting stronger and coming much closer together, I was given a device containing gas to be worn on my wrist. The nurse explained that as each pain began, I should inhale the gas to dull the pain, and then remove it until the next pain. This was working just as it was expected to work until Gerald decided that he could at least administer the gas. In thinking about what was happening, I confess that up until that time he had not contributed much toward birthing this baby. So he positioned a stool at my head and took his seat upon it. The plan was that as each pain began, I would signal Gerald, he would place the gas gadget over my nose and mouth, I would inhale, and then he would remove the gadget until I signaled the next pain. It was wonderful news when the nurse finally announced that the baby was near enough that she was calling Dr. Watkins for the actual delivery. Gerald was asked to wait outside for the last few minutes and I was put to sleep, hoping for the baby boy that Gerald wanted so much.

As the effects of the anesthesia began to fade, I heard voices that seemed to be calling from far away as they repeated my name over and over. The real world slowly became clearer, and the most dominant image in it was that of a radiant Gerald Munday. He glowed! He beamed! He kept calling loudly, "Honey, we've got a little boy!" There was no need to discuss his name. It was Mark Stephen! This baby boy was named before his big sister was born two and a half years earlier. And he was finally here!

It was four or five A.M. on November 15, 1956. The entire night had been spent having our baby. We were both exhausted and feeling a real need for rest and sleep. It was not going to be difficult for me to slip quickly into a deep sleep because I was already in bed; but Gerald was going to drive thirty miles back to Gilbertown. I don't recall that I was concerned about his falling to sleep on his trip home, because he was on cloud nine, and sleep was far, far from his mind. He could hardly wait to tell Lynn about her new baby brother. Not much time passed before he and Lynn returned to visit me and to meet her new baby brother. There were no special hours for visitation with babies. All that was necessary was that the mother request that the baby be brought to the room. Lynn sat on the bed beside me as she happily and proudly cradled Mark in her lap. She held him so tightly in her chubby little girl arms that she almost squeezed the breath from him. Our first family time with our new baby was a little scary because Lynn immediately felt capable of caring for the baby. But it was also a precious moment.

Several days later, as Gerald and I talked about the events surrounding Mark's birth, he said, "Sara, you sure did take a lot of that gas the night Mark was born." I was curious as to how he had arrived at such a conclusion. I thought I had been conscientious in following the nurse's instructions. He explained by saying, "Well, while I just sat there waiting for the next pain, I took just a little whiff of that stuff, and I almost fell off the stool!"

Mrs. Alman, a doctor's widow from the Gilbertown church, came that afternoon after Mark's early-morning arrival. It was her custom for as long as we were in the parsonage to come by each day for a visit and to bring a gift of some kind. I loved when she brought a banana pudding with real whipped cream on top. She admired the baby with "oohs" and "ahhs." Upon learning his name, she repeated it ever so solemnly. "Mark! That sounds like the name for an old man!" I cannot explain why that one line from our conversation stands out, but I am reminded that my grandmother used to say that during a pregnancy or just following the birth of a baby, things like conversations, events, and circumstances could indeed "mark" a child. If there is one modicum of truth in that idea, the old man reference must certainly have had significant bearing on this new child of ours. He grew to be thoughtful, slow, deliberate, even-tempered, and always dependable. He was solid—our firm foundation child. Mom Munday often chastised me as I urged Mark to hurry up as he spoke. "Let him alone," she would say. "His speech is so refreshing!"

After several days in the hospital, the old man Mark and I came home to Gilbertown. Sarah Doggett came to stay with us on the first Sunday evening because Gerald went to the Melvin church to preach. True to form, Lynn expected all of Sarah's undivided attention to which she was accustomed. Somehow Sarah managed to keep Lynn happy while at the same time providing the care that this new member of the Munday family required. As she awkwardly fed Mark, she laughingly said, "I may be doing this all wrong. Lauren didn't get her milk out of a bottle, so tell me if I'm not doing it right." When she changed Mark's diaper for the first time, she reached for a dry diaper while leaving him completely uncovered. Before she knew it, Mark was sprinkling her thoroughly. She laughed as she dried her face and down the front of her dress, then added, "I *never* had a little *boy*, you know!"

Both Mom Munday and Grannie Bet came to take their shifts in welcoming and getting to know their new grandson. Mark was instantly loved. During the first few weeks he cried a lot at night, so both Gerald and I had many opportunities to become well acquainted with him. In spite of these sleepless late-night shifts, we were ever so mindful that he was a beautiful, healthy baby boy, and we were grateful beyond measure for the gift of his presence in our home. The church people adored him. After a few months, he, too, visited in some of the church members' homes with his big sister. I do not recall that we ever paid a babysitter while we were in Gilbertown. The church folks were wonderful to us and to our children beyond all expectations.

When Mark was six months old, we moved from Gilbertown to Marvyn, Alabama, where Gerald served as student pastor to three churches (Marvyn, Watoola, and Society Hill). He entered seminary at Emory University in Atlanta in the fall of 1957. I remained in the parsonage with Lynn, who was three years old, and Mark, who was nine months old. Those days demanded the best of both Gerald and me, but we clearly understood that Gerald must be educated if he were to be an effective minister. We were committed to that goal. Sarah Brasswell from the Watoola Church spent the nights with the children and me while Gerald was away at school. Lynn and Mark called her Aunt Sarah. It was little wonder that they adored her because each night when she arrived after supper, she came with presents for both of them.

Gerald was assigned to Epworth Church in Phenix City, Alabama, one year later. He left for Emory University on Monday afternoons and returned late each Friday. The children and I became good friends with the Carrolls, our next-door neighbors. Paul worked each day as an electrician and Gerald was out of town at school, so Jean and I decided to share our noon meal every day. She brought leftovers from her family's meal the night before, and I added whatever it took to complete the meal. It was usually Jean who washed the children's hands before we ate, and it never failed that as she washed Mark's soft, fat little hands, she lovingly commented that they were "like a ball of cotton." When we talk even now, she recalls how soft and fat Mark's hands were.

Mark has made his place in the hearts of countless people. As he grew physically, he developed a genuinely kind and sweet spirit. He never found it difficult to wait his turn, and while other children were pushing and clamoring to make their desires known, I cannot recall that Mark was ever demanding. While Gerald traveled for Maytag, Mark was a pillar of strength for me. When necessary, he stepped in as the man of the house. During his growing up years, Mark was the child upon whom I relied to help me complete chores that were beyond my ability to accomplish, like moving shrubs that were large and old and should have been discarded, not moved. Mark was sturdy. Mark was strong. Mark was dependable. And best of all, *Mark was always there!*

There were few similarities between Lynn's birth in the large city hospital in Lexington, Kentucky, and Mark's birth in the small Watkins Hospital in Quitman, Mississippi; however, we were keenly aware at both births that we were experiencing a profound sense of gratitude for a perfect child. We sincerely loved this special new life long before he arrived, and early that morning, we gave thanks that he was being entrusted to us. For a second time, we were aware of the miracle of birth! And with this birth on November 15, 1954, another special thread was added to the family tapestry: a second branch, Mark Stephen Munday, was added to the Gerald and Sara Munday family tree—and now, there were two.

Mark Stephen and Rebecca Lynn Munday

Notes from a Grateful Heart

Late June, July, and August was the season when farm families in Alabama enjoyed the bounty from the "good earth" as they ate fresh vegetables from gardens planted months earlier. Any surplus beyond that required for meals was carefully canned or frozen for the cold months that lay ahead. Fruits like plums, strawberries, figs, apples, and pears were made into jams, jellies, and preserves, and they truly became the "icing on the cake" when eaten with hot biscuits at breakfast.

It was a hot, humid summer day, and though it was still early, baskets of peas had already been picked and brought to my mother's kitchen. Mother, Wrenn, and I sat near the open door in order to catch any breeze that might be stirring. Shelling peas allowed time to visit while still accomplishing a task that could never be considered fun when done alone. Good conversation always makes work more pleasant—and shelling peas was really a lot of work.

My grandmother was an invalid and had been bedfast for several years. It was Mother's daily routine to bathe her and change the sheets on her bed early in the day. This had been accomplished and Grannie rested quietly in her large bedroom. All of the windows were raised, and usually there was a soft, cool breeze from some direction. The kitchen was near enough to hear her call if she needed anything.

Wrenn and I had a total of six children—Mother's grandchildren. Five of them were boys. Our Lynn had the distinction of being the only girl, as well as being the oldest. Often she felt more comfortable with the adult women rather than with "those silly boys," and this was one of those days. All six of the children loved coming to Grannie Bet's large two-story house in the country. There were ever so many places to be explored: the barn, the pasture, and even under the house, which was three to four feet above ground level in places. There had always been an element of mystery and uncertainty about the upstairs. None of the children who grew up in that house ever slept upstairs. Perhaps they did not need to because there was so much room downstairs. Or maybe it was just such a long way up those two flights of steps—especially when everything was dark. During the day was a different matter, however. There were endless things to do upstairs: dresser drawers to be rambled through, a closet or two in which to hide. Of course, it was not as scary a place when the sun was shining and the birds were singing. Lynn sat with Mother, Wrenn, and me in the kitchen as we shelled peas and talked. Grannie rested between her fresh, clean sheets as she listened to the five boys laughing and playing in the room above hers.

Suddenly, without warning, the house shook with a terrifying noise that we quickly recognized as a shotgun blast. We were frozen in place. Mother finally said, "Somebody had better go!" Wrenn had been diagnosed several years earlier with muscular dystrophy, so she could not climb the stairs. I was the one who would have to go up those steps and determine the tragedy that had taken place. As I ran past Grannie's door, she was sitting upright in her bed, calling out in a loud voice, "Oh, my Fathers! Oh, dear Lord! What has happened? Is anybody shot? Oh, Lord! What has happened?"

By this time, I was at the foot of the stairs, and I could see gun smoke billowing from the east bedroom. I raced to the top of the steps, taking two steps at a time. I met the boys one by one as they passed me on their way down the steps. I recall putting my hand on their shoulders as if to push them downstairs and propel myself up. I was scared out of my mind as to what I was about to discover as I reached the upstairs hall and burst into the bedroom. It took but a brief moment to realize that there was no body lying dead or bleeding in the room. Upon turning and going back into the hall, I discovered that I had met and passed all five boys as I literally flew up the steps past them. I was beginning to feel a deep sense of relief when our seven-year-old son, Mark, very quietly and slowly said, "I think I've been shot!"

My immediate attention went to Mark as he slowly lifted his left arm to show me where he had "been shot." Pellets from the gun had grazed the outside of his arm between the elbow and shoulder. The blast from the gun had gone through the footboard of the antique bed, through the entire length of the mattress, and through the wooden headboard, and had driven the curtain into the wall. My knees grew weak as I realized how close Mark's upper left arm was to his chest and heart. Oh, Dear God! Thank you for taking care of my little boy that day!

Piece by piece, the story began to unfold. Wrenn's son Dean, the oldest of the boys, had lined the other boys up in front of him and aimed my brother's twelve-gauge shotgun at them with the instructions, "If you move, I'm gonna' shoot you!" Dean had no idea that the gun was loaded. He was not angry. He was just playing. Also, he had not removed the gun from someplace where he should not have been. My brother had carelessly left the gun on his bed! He later explained that he had given the boys explicit instructions that the gun was *not* to be touched, and that they "knew better" than to pick it up.

Mark and I were quickly on our way to Livingston to see Dr. Hunt. Mark was calm during the entire ride as he answered questions that I could not keep myself from asking, while at the same time giving thanks that he was sitting there beside me, very much alive. Dr. Hunt was a tall, handsome man with slightly graying hair at his temples. He had served in the armed forces during World War II, and when he returned to Livingston, he brought new information and techniques for treating burns and gunshot wounds. He painstakingly cleaned the abrasion made by the shot. Mark carefully held his arm still so Dr. Hunt could see the wound and do his work. When the wound was cleaned and bandaged, Dr. Hunt walked around the table, sat down in front of Mark, and slowly removed his glasses. His eyes met and held Mark's as he quietly but firmly said, "Son, the good Lord sho' must have something special for you to do. He sho' took care of you today!"

Upon learning what had happened, my brother Howard left work and came home. He was young, impetuous, and knew absolutely nothing about child rearing. Years have taught us that it is neither responsible nor acceptable for an adult to leave a loaded gun in a child's reach with only the simple instruction of "Do not touch." There seems to be an unwritten rule that if a child is told *not* to do something, then it becomes a given that this will be the precise course of action that he or she takes—never mind the "*do not!*"

Howard proceeded to lecture Dean in loud and angry tones. Then he took him to a farm road that ran between two deep banks. He loaded the gun and instructed Dean to shoot it into the dirt bank. The target area was very near the house, so all the other boys heard the gun as it was fired again, and again, and again. I am convinced that Howard was attempting to work out his own frustrations. He must have realized how terribly careless he had been to leave a loaded gun within the reach of children, and he was unquestionably shaken at what had almost happened. He thought that this was the best way to teach Dean just how much damage a shotgun could do. He followed that painful exercise with loud admonitions that a gun should *never* be pointed at anyone! Perhaps more maturity and experience would have helped get the lesson across in a kinder and more effective way. Sadly, he was not able to shoulder the blame, thereby reinforcing in a gentler way what the children had already learned. Poor Dean was already dealing with far more trauma than a child his age should have to handle. His mother told me later that Dean had nightmares for months following that experience.

So much went wrong that day while some things were mercifully correct. Mark's life was spared! What a plus that was for Mark and Dean—yea, for us all! Possibly few people in our community ever thought of Dr. Hunt in spiritual terms, even though he attended church. He would most likely have been as shocked as the next person if he were ever referred to as "a prophet;" but today, I am remembering him as both evangelical and prophetic. Perhaps Dr. Hunt was not the lone voice on the line, but Mark's life has demonstrated that somewhere along the way, he became convinced that God had something special for him to do, and he continues to do those things day by day. Mark is admired, respected, and loved by his family, his peers, and his business associates. He is known as an honest man, a hard worker, a man who believes in and follows carefully the leadings and teachings of God. My heart is so full of gratitude to God for Mark's life—and to Dr. Hunt, who gave such gentle care seasoned with sage words of admonition to our seven-year-old boy such a long time ago.

Owned by Fear

I cannot recall a time when my grandmother was not anxious or fearful about something. When there was nothing to worry about, she looked for a reason to worry. She was afraid of not having enough money to provide for our needs! She was afraid of the weather—especially when it was stormy. Or if it was dry, she feared that the crops would not make. She was afraid of people whom she did not know as well as those whom she did know and did not trust. And though a number of black families worked as tenant farmers on our place, and could be trusted with our lives, she was mortally afraid of black people—to the point of having dreadful nightmares about them.

In addition to being a fearful person, Grannie was an inordinately convincing person. I did not recognize it at that time, but I think she was an expert in the technique of brainwashing. When she felt strongly about a principle or an idea, she badgered and nagged without ceasing until anyone in close proximity became convinced—or at least they began to believe a little. Since my family lived with Grannie, she was a powerful influence, both verbally and nonverbally, on my siblings and me. There is no question that my spirit of fear, anxiety, and dread was learned from my grandmother, who consistently exercised her skills in those areas. Her example was the most convincing nudge in that direction.

According to Grannie, one of the most important things to be concerned about was what people thought about you. We were taught that a person's reputation is what people think of you, and can be damaged or destroyed depending upon how you are perceived by those who know you. On the other hand, we were taught that character is what you actually are—observed or unobserved—and because character is who you are, it can never be damaged or changed by anyone other than yourself. I became convinced at an early age that how people felt about me was highly significant. I wanted so much to be liked and accepted, and as a result, my actions were often dictated by how I felt people would respond to them

As the child of an alcoholic father, I was possessed with deep concerns and misgivings as to how I was perceived by others—especially my peers. I worried and wondered whether Daddy might have made a public spectacle of himself. What would that cause people to think about me? What were they saying behind my back? Would my friends' parents allow them to come spend the night at our house? Or would they invite me to their homes? I made extra efforts to excel in all the ways I could – to always go beyond normal expectations. I hoped that I could somehow earn admiration, and I hoped that beyond that, I would earn love. My real objective was that I would be so perfect that it would be impossible for people not to like and respect me. That took continuous effort and hard work, and sadly, I did not learn until much later that I had set an unattainable goal for myself.

Those feelings carried over into my adult life. As a minister's wife, I was under scrutiny by church members as well as folks in the community. In retrospect, it seems likely that people were not demanding nearly as much of me as I thought—or as I demanded of myself. I was always conscious of seeing that my husband and children were cast in a favorable light. So when our youngest child, Michael, made the announcement that he was gay, it is easy to understand that my life was filled with terror and dread! What if somebody finds out? Would this news cause an uproar in the congregation? We kept Mike's secret completely guarded for nearly ten years. I justified my attitude by assuring myself that it was Mike's information and should be shared only at his discretion. I was paralyzed by the fear that somebody would find out; I was certain that if one person found out, then everybody would know! How naïve I was to think that what people knew or how they felt about Mike's being gay was the worst thing that could happen!

Then came the inevitable. Mike shared terrible news with us again: he told us that he was HIV positive and that he already had a Kaposi's sarcoma lesion on his leg. Suddenly I knew that his being gay was not the worst thing that could happen! He was now telling us that he was living under a death sentence! Our youngest child was going to die. How would we tell the congregation of the church my husband was serving? What in the world would my mother say? And did it really matter? Mike was going to die! My greatest fear then became death. My daily dread was that of facing the last moments of life with Mike, who had always been so vigorous and full of life. It had been only a year since we had faced and struggled with the high probability of Gerald's death. It had taken a year for him to regain what he could of his life and strength, and now we were facing death again. How soon? We had no idea. I was filled with terror! Everything was out of our hands. We were at the mercy of what lay ahead. We became convinced that we faced days that would hold news equally as devastating as what we already knew—or even worse!

Even Mike tried to comfort me with that oft-heard rationalization that "we are all going to die—just at different times." Those thoughts brought little comfort, though I knew them to be true. I am now persuaded that the days of our lives are lived in denial when related to our own mortality. We do not grieve daily for all of our family and friends as though we know each one is dying. I do not live my personal life as though I am dying. I never have, but there seems to always be an underlying consciousness of death. It may be that since we know neither when nor how this ultimate phase of life will occur, we feel no particular pressure to spend each day as though it is our last.

After months of dreadful suffering, Mike did die. He shared with me that he did not fear death—only the dying process! He faced death with great calm, and he died with grace. Grace and calm have been reported at the occurrence of countless other deaths. It may be that fear is associated with death because those who have experienced death firsthand were not able to leave an account of their experience with death or of the dying process. Death is and always has been a mystery. And so I suppose that we must content ourselves as much as possible with assurances from those who live and have only witnessed this process. William Cullen Bryant (1838-1915) did just that in his beautifully eloquent poem "Thanatopsis," a portion of which I learned as a teenager:

> So live, that when thy summons comes to join
> The innumerable caravan which moves
> To that mysterious realm, where each shall take

His chamber in the silent halls of death,
Thou go not, like a quarry-slave at night,
Scourged to his dungeon, but, sustained and soothed
By an unfaltering trust, approach thy grave
Like one who wraps the drapery of his couch
About him, and lies down to pleasant dreams.

"— sustained and soothed by an unfaltering trust!" Yes, my faith is intact! No, I am not at this point looking forward to death! Yes, I believe in God, my loving father! Yes, I am convinced that I can trust Him with all of my tomorrows as well as my eternity. And finally, when I come to that place and time known as death, my prayer is that I shall be calm and sustained, that I shall have a peaceful smile on my lips, and that those who are gathered near will shed a few tears as an expression of their love.

A Charge to Keep

The year was 1989; the place, Biloxi, Mississippi. For ten months I had been in Richardson, Texas, with our youngest child, Michael, who was suffering with and dying from HIV/AIDS. Everything else had been put on hold except Gerald's health. He had been infected with Hepatitis C as a result of receiving large amounts of blood products as needed to control bleeding and to provide the clotting elements missing from his blood. He had lived with hemophilia (though a mild form) since birth. In 1987, a shunt procedure was required to bypass his diseased and damaged liver. Regular follow-up visits to Emory Hospital were necessary. I made those trips to Atlanta with him before it became necessary for me to go to Texas to be with Mike. It was stressful for both of us when Gerald was put in the position of going alone for periodic hospital stays and tests. He was far from being a well man; however, he did make the trips to Emory as well as to Texas many times during Mike's illness.

Mike died on July 28, 1989. It was finally time for me to go home. Gerald had been appointed to Leggett Memorial United Methodist Church in Biloxi in June of 1988, thirteen months earlier. Since ten months of that time had been spent with Mike, I had come to feel more at home in Richardson than I did in Biloxi. I returned to Mississippi feeling completely empty and used up. I threw myself into the church in whatever capacity I could find. Gerald's health was continuing to decline, so I did much of the visiting among the members and prospective members. I sang in the choir and taught a Sunday school class of young adults.

A few months later, Karlyn Stephens, a director of the Back Bay Mission, sponsored by the United Church of Christ, came to me with a proposal. It was the challenge of a lifetime. She was hopeful that I could volunteer for at least one afternoon a week (or whatever time I felt I could give) to help organize the South Mississippi AIDS Task Force. She had met and talked with Gerald earlier and

213

knew something of my skills. My teaching experience would be most helpful in educating the public about the ever-growing pandemic—as well as in dispelling some of the myths and fears about the disease. Years spent in social work with Pensions and Security in Alabama brought another dimension to the mix. Parents, patients, and significant others needed to be contacted and their needs identified. Home visits must be made. Major networking needed to be initiated and developed among doctors, health agencies, benevolent groups, churches, and communities. The recent painful grief surrounding Mike's death gave me experiential and personal connections to HIV/AIDS. Karlyn convinced me of the dire need for such an organization because HIV/AIDS was rapidly spreading along the Mississippi Gulf Coast. Young men from more socially conservative communities were flocking to the area, only to be added to the number of infected and ill patients already living there. HIV/AIDS was growing by leaps and bounds in South Mississippi.

My decision to "sign on" with such an organization required a lot of thought. The membership of the church my husband served consisted largely of elderly people. Leggett Memorial United Methodist Church was located on the Seashore Assembly Ground, as was the Methodist retirement home next door to the church. Many of the residents from the home came faithfully every Sunday for worship. A large majority of the general population was both fearful and judgmental of HIV/AIDS patients, who were largely homosexuals or drug users. The church universal had not found a place for these "transgressors." In looking at these factors, I recognized the strong possibility that my going to work with "those people" could adversely affect my husband's ministry to his elderly congregation, although they had been very supportive in our travail with Mike. Mike had visited us, and the church people had gotten to know him. They grew to love him—even after learning that he was gay and that he had AIDS. They set up twenty-four–hour prayer vigils for our family. But I still had fears regarding how accepting they could be of my becoming a founding member of an AIDS Task Force.

On the other hand, I knew that I did have usable skills. I was knowledgeable about and sensitive to the painful process of living with and dying from this socially unacceptable disease. After all, I had been with Mike as every new stage of the disease appeared. I knew the agony of a parent and family member. I experienced the frustration and the exhaustion of a caregiver. I had seen the shock, disbelief, rejection, and denial of parents, family members, and friends as the person once loved by them fell into the relentless clutches of the dreaded HIV/AIDS virus.

My thoughts turned again to how much Mike loved us—his parents, his brother and sister, his friends—who loved him in return. I remembered how much he loved his job in crisis management with Northern Telecom and what an exceptional employee he was. I could see again his good looks and feel the warmth of his inclusive personality. Not a few girls told me about the crushes they had on him. He was talented: he played the piano, the keyboard, the oboe, and the sax, and he sang. He was in a small band and audiences loved him. There were other young people, loved and talented, who had fallen victim to and died from the virus, and there were still others whom I might be able to nurture through their last phase of life. And what of those young men who were healthy and could remain healthy if there were enough information to help them avoid the same sad plight? I made my decision. I would volunteer! I would fight this deadly disease that had snatched our child from us at far too young an age! I would work day and night for reconciliation between parents and children and friends! I would do all in my power to bring comfort to those suffering physically, emotionally, and financially! Mike would expect no less from his mom. In a far deeper vein, I kept questioning if Jesus would not heal and minister to these people. Were these the lepers of our day? Yes, yes, yes! A thousand times "yes!" I purposed to be one of the caring people whose task would be to alleviate pain and suffering wherever and whenever possible—and to bring reconciliation where there had been separation.

Becoming the first executive director (volunteer) of the South Mississippi AIDS Task Force, I quickly found myself reporting to work at one P.M. Monday through Friday. As in all new job assignments, I began reading everything that was available at Back Bay Mission about AIDS. One of the first things I learned was that the Task Force office was a storage room behind the mission thrift store. The AIDS hotline listed in the telephone directory rang into a phone that sat on an empty desk in that small, empty office. An answering machine picked up the call and responded with a long, informative, impersonal message of five minutes' duration. This was the first thing that had to change. HIV/AIDS patients were treated impersonally and as second-class citizens too many times in too many places; but it must never again happen on the AIDS hotline in south Mississippi.

In staffing the empty office with dedicated volunteers, I discovered in the process that there were people who had been waiting to learn what they could do. It was vital that the twenty-four–hour hotline be answered by a real person, so "call forwarding" was placed on the phone. This allowed volunteers to take calls in their homes from five P.M. until eight the next morning, when the Back Bay Mission opened and calls were forwarded there. The phone began to ring, and people made a path to our door. In a brief time, the office was moved into a building of our own. The daily presence of volunteers from one to five P.M. allowed me the freedom to visit homes, hospitals, and individuals, and attend funerals.

I became convinced with the passage of time that I was exactly where I should be. Each day brought new information about the disease and the heartache that accompanied it. South Mississippi was ultraconservative, a place where homosexuality was sin, sin, sin! People were highly uncomfortable or even angry if they thought they were in a room with a gay or lesbian person, and they were frightened to death if they considered for a single moment that the person might have AIDS. Many churches, groups, and clubs did not allow or accept gays and lesbians, and as a result they made their own way as best they could.

However, I cannot recall ever being turned away from a single church or group as I sought opportunities to speak. I was accepted as an advocate for a controversial cause where gays or lesbians could never have gone in southern Mississippi. I was white, a middle-aged minister's wife, and a mother whose son had died of AIDS. I was still grieving. Who would think of turning me away? And I was equally accepted by the gay community. They understood that we loved our son deeply and cared for him until his death. They learned quickly that I was not judgmental, and that I saw AIDS not as a moral issue but as a health crisis!

Thankfully, I had some previous speaking experience. When I spoke, I took Mike's picture, billfold, and a few other items. I introduced him as the reason for my being in their midst. His picture was in plain view throughout my presentation. Nine months after Mike's death, the Task Force arranged a seminar and workshop for area ministers of all faiths. Gerald spoke early in the day in an introductory address. Beverly Ernst, RN, addressed medical and physical elements of the disease. We were still learning so much in 1989–90 and the workshop proved to be an excellent way to educate. Psychologist Dr. Edward Graham discussed HIV/AIDS in terms of the psychological, emotional, financial, and spiritual. I was the last person to speak. My reason for speaking was obvious: Our youngest son had died of AIDS at the age of twenty-nine. I told our story as best I could—sometimes amidst tears.

When the presentation was over, Steve Brunsman, staff writer for the *Biloxi Sun Herald*, approached me apologetically. He asked, "Do you have a manuscript for your presentation?" I did. By way of explanation he said, "This has never happened to me before, but I was so touched by what you said that I was not able to take notes." He asked if he might be allowed to print the speech in its entirety. As I gave my permission, he quickly warned that "there are a lot of mean people out there, and there might be some mean, harassing phone calls." I was willing to risk it. I never received the first mean call. Instead, there were only supportive calls from well-wishers, calls from people who wanted to help by working with the Task Force, calls from people who invited me to be the speaker for their groups, and calls for help from AIDS patients and their parents. Possibly the most memorable call came from an anonymous young man who had AIDS. He had not been able to tell his mother of his illness and impending death. He kept the newspaper article for months, and called to ask what I thought of his sharing my story with his mother. He wondered, too, if I would mind talking to her if she wanted to talk. I answered, "Of course, share the story with my blessings! Have your mom call me when she wants to talk!" Another benefit from that day came in the form of ministers who made themselves available to bury young people who had no church, and no minister.

A gay couple came to my office one day. One was a robust, healthy-looking, tanned man with silver hair. His partner was young, handsome, brunette, and HIV positive. Both were frightened; the younger especially so. He had a purplish-colored spot on his leg. His primary doctor had recommended that he see a dermatologist. I thought I recognized it as Kaposi's sarcoma, one of the opportunistic diseases associated with HIV/AIDS. Mike had experienced the same AIDS-related condition. I shared this with the two men, and suggested that they circumvent the dermatologist and go directly to the area physician who handled most of the AIDS patients. There was nothing that the dermatologist could do except diagnose. They followed my suggestion only to learn that my suspicion was correct. They were grateful that I had referred them to the best doctor in the area for problems related to the virus. The younger of the two died many years ago, but his partner and I continue to exchange Christmas cards each year.

Often, I made late-night trips to pick up patients who had been dropped off along the road. I then found lodging for them. After breakfast the next morning, I drove them to the destination of their choosing. There was so much work that needed to be done. I did what I could. Administrative duties were difficult for me because I am and always have been a hands-on person, a caregiver. Warming soup for a patient who was much too weak and feverish to prepare his food, washing sheets and pajamas wet from night sweats, or sitting on the sofa with the patient's feet in my lap as I rubbed them were times and places when I felt needed.

Some things have changed since 1989–90; but not enough. We continue to hope and pray for a cure or a vaccine. To date, there is none. We still struggle with and work for reconciliation, and to this very moment, our churches continue to ask, "What shall we do with the homosexuals?" The excruciating pain of rejection learned and felt with such force as I cared for Mike was later reinforced as I worked with HIV/AIDS patients along the Mississippi Gulf Coast. Deep scars remain as reminders of those days. I realize now that rejection, isolation, pain, and fear exist apart from the HIV/AIDS pandemic. I am convinced that those of us who consider ourselves to be human—and certainly, we who name the name of Christ and consider ourselves to be Christian—are troubled by what we see reflected in our fellow man, and we know all over again that we still have a charge to keep.

Mike's Best Friend, Rudy

It was easy for me to understand the excitement we heard in Mike's voice when he called to share with us that he had purchased a baby grand piano. His further explanation that it was secondhand in no way diminished the joy of possessing such an elegant instrument. And we rejoiced with him, even though we remembered that the years of his practice discipline had not always been pleasant for Mike or for us. It dawned upon us that maybe the time and money invested in his piano lessons had not been wasted. After all, we were delighted that he had missed the piano enough to invest in purchasing his own.

The phone connection between our home in Meridian, Mississippi, and Dallas, Texas, carried as much joyful excitement (if not more) when our youngest child called again to tell us of another purchase. This time he had bought a thoroughbred black-and-white Springer spaniel. Not only had he paid for this new acquisition, but he had purchased a cage in which to transport him. He flew to Houston to pick him up then flew him back to Dallas. At no time in my life had I ever been allowed the indulgence of such lavish spending. It simply made no sense! For several weeks, I thought of this entire matter as a foolish waste of hard-earned money! And to make matters worse, Mike explained that this dog was the runt of the litter and probably would never make a show dog because he was not aggressive enough. But Mike liked this pup's sweet, gentle spirit, and one of his first acts as a new dog owner was to change his dog's name from "Rowdy" to "Rudy"—it seemed to fit better.

The huge change that came as a result of taking Rudy from his mother and placing him in new surroundings went fairly smoothly, and Rudy was finally "at home" with Mike. The next big thing deter-mined by Mike was that Rudy should be enrolled in obedience school. Rudy did well and finished his course. He was well behaved and always a "perfect gentleman"—a man with class. He had all of his shots and treatments as scheduled, and he dined only on the amount and brand of food recommended by his veterinarian. The two became great friends—Mike and Rudy. When Mike was at home, they were together. Rudy slept in Mike's room every night in his travel cage, the floor covered and well padded with several layers of blankets.

Mike worked for Bell Northern Research in crisis management, and his work hours were often long and irregular. He liked to put Rudy outside when he was at work, so Rudy had the run of the fenced-in back yard when the weather was nice! But Dallas weather is not always predictable, nor is it always fair and warm. One long day when Mike left Rudy outside, the day turned freezing cold, accompanied by rain. All day and into the early hours of the dark, cold night, Rudy was outside. I have come to the conclusion that it must be instinct that causes a dog to run...and run...and run—or maybe Rudy was just trying to keep warm enough to keep from freezing and all of the rounds that he ran around the margin of the yard were his effort at survival. At any rate, Mike came home after his long day at work, and after Rudy's long day of running round and round the yard, to find a dog worn out from running, his long coat soaked by the rain and frozen all over into little icicles. Rudy was delighted that Mike was finally home. He eagerly danced about as he gleefully twisted his body from side to side, almost as if his short tail were wagging him. He jumped up on Mike's chest, licking as much of him as he could, all the while barking loudly and happily as if to say, "I'm glad you're home!" As they crawled into a warm shower together, the trials of a difficult day and the icicles all melted and washed down the drain.

As Mike became sicker and sicker from the deadly HIV virus, our telephone conversations became more and more frequent. I hated the fact that Mike was alone, but there was a bit of comfort as he talked of Rudy's presence. The tone of his voice revealed his feelings and love for his sweet-spirited black-and-white Springer. However, it finally became necessary for me to go to Dallas to care for Mike. I liked Rudy all right—Mike adored him—and he was a beautiful dog. The intense gaze from his gorgeous brown eyes was the means by which he gained lots and lots of attention and numerous treats. Caring for Rudy began to require more and more of my time. He quite politely requested to go outside by sitting at the door and staring at me until the door was opened. It seemed to me that he made such requests much too frequently. Mike felt badly when I responded so quickly to Rudy's requests rather than have him make the effort. I began taking more and more responsibility for Rudy, feeding him and, on occasion, giving him a bath. Mike often called a mobile pet-grooming unit, and Rudy was shampooed inside a self-contained unit right in our own driveway. Speaking of luxury…

Mike spent only five days in the hospital during his lengthy illness. While he was there, my favorite cousin Vivian came from Meridian, Mississippi, to be with me as well as to visit with Mike. We spent the entire day at the hospital, arriving home well after dark. It had rained all day, and Rudy was outside again for the entire time. Dallas mud is black and very sticky, and Rudy was covered with it. He greeted us from the patio with his usual exuberance. Vivian and I instantly saw through the sliding glass doors that we had a problem with a wiggling dog covered in black Texas mud who was busting the door down to get inside the house! We were smart, we thought. We devised the perfect plan! One towel was placed around his back end, while another towel was placed around his front. Vivian took one end, I took the other, and we made our way as quickly as possible to the bathtub. We all three needed a warm bath that night.

Rudy was most attentive to Mike during his illness and death. He lay in his cage-bed with his head resting on his paws, which were crossed in front of him. His eyes were sad beyond anything I had ever seen. Much of Mike's conversation was garbled and unintelligible as he was dying, but he clearly and loudly called Rudy's name, to which Rudy quickly and quietly responded by approaching his bed. For days after Mike's death, Rudy grieved. It was obvious that his loss was almost more than he could bear. He made countless trips to Mike's room, looked inside, then turned away. He stayed closer to us than usual, almost as if he were saying, "Please don't you go, too!"

Before Mike died, he placed Rudy into our care with explicit instructions that we were to care for Rudy in the same loving way that he had. So Rudy moved to Mississippi with his new family. He was an important part of our family when Gerald was so sick with end-stage liver disease. I cannot describe the comfort that he brought the two of us. He was always quietly sympathetic, yet there were times when he was so clever that he was able to bring a smile or perhaps a laugh into our anxious days. After Gerald recovered sufficiently from his liver transplant, he served as minister to a small church in rural Santa Rosa County, Florida. Rudy became my constant companion. Since Gerald lived at the church parsonage many nights during the week, I was left alone at home in Gulf Breeze, except for Rudy. Hearing Rudy's breathing as he slept beside my bed brought all the assurance I needed to sleep well.

With Rudy, as with us all, the years began to take their toll. His last few months were painful as he suffered with arthritis in his hips, to the point finally that he was unable to stand as he ate. Gerald took him to be put to sleep and held him while he died. We had him cremated, and his ashes were scattered on the beach in the area where our family had placed Mike's ashes years earlier.

It was a wonderful and special gift that Mike gave us in the person of Rudy. Though a dog, he possessed and demonstrated the genuine qualities and characteristics of a tried and true friend. He was ever faithful; he never held a grudge; he was quick to forgive; he was always nearby but seemed to understand when we needed our space; he grieved when death came, but after awhile he grew to know that life had not ended for him; he found other lives and other loves; and until the last of his life, the trust that he and Mike shared seemed to be reflected in his kind and knowing brown eyes.

Dearest Mike

Dearest Mike,

Today is your forty-seventh birthday. Happy Birthday! You were our baby, the last in the line of our children. Each of you was such a delight, yet you were so different from each other. Adulthood only made your uniqueness more apparent.

My thoughts of you are always accompanied with the pain of how much I miss you. We hardly had the chance to know you since you died so young at only twenty-nine. We speak of you often and wonder if you would still have a mustache or if you would have gray hair. You had one or two gray hairs before you died, and in Lynn's language, "They made you crazy!" Maybe you were going to be like me

John Michael (Mike) Munday and his mom

and gray at an early age. Perhaps Mark is going to be like Daddy in that he has very little gray. The likeness between Mark and Daddy ends there, however, because Mark is beginning to bald slightly, and your dad has the same abundance of hair that he always did. Lynn has colored her hair for so long that I have no idea if she is graying, but if I were asked, I would have to say, "Yes, I think she does have some gray hair."

When you were born on September 1, 1959, we lived next door to the Carrolls in Phenix City, Alabama. That summer was unbearably hot—for me, anyway. The parsonage did not have a central cooling system, but it did have a large attic fan that was very powerful. And even though it was hot air that it brought into the house, I spent much of the summer on our bed right in front of the window to catch as much of the breeze as I could—but I was still hot. When I went for my checkup on the last day of August, I asked Dr. Munn if I could please take castor oil to induce labor. I was so tired and hot, and this pregnancy seemed to drag on and on. He replied that I really was not a long time overdue, but since everything appeared to be in readiness for your arrival, he saw no reason that I should not take oil if I chose to do so.

Your dad was playing golf when I got home from the doctor's visit. This just somehow did not sit well with me. Why should he be having so much fun when I was "head over heels" in the process of giving birth to his third child while caring for the two that we already had? I went next door to the Carrolls' house and shared my "poor me" feelings with Jean. She always listened. Then she did a noble thing! She volunteered to go get a bottle of castor oil and "prepare" it for me. She seemed quite happy about her new and unexpected responsibility. According to her, she knew the best possible way to keep that less-than-delicious dose down, and she could make it happen on the very first attempt. I always had to take at least two doses to get castor oil to stay, so I agreed. Since I was committed to taking the oil, there was one thing that troubled me: What if Gerald did not get home in time to take me to the hospital? Jean assured me that she would be sure to see that I got to the hospital, so I began to hope that this baby would come before his father even got home. Wouldn't that just embarrass him to death?

Jean was such a good friend. She carefully measured and warmed the castor oil. She poured about an inch of very cold Coca-Cola into a glass; on top of that came the warm castor oil, and the last layer was another inch or so of the very cold Coke. Her instructions were, "Drink this fast!" I did, and as the last drop went down, Jean simultaneously popped a peppermint into my mouth and applied a cold bath cloth to my throat while rubbing with a downward motion. The dose was down—all of it—and it stayed! Now all we had to do was to wait on you.

Your dad did get home, and at the proper time that night, everybody went to sleep—except you and me! We were quite restless. About midnight, you began to signal that it was time to go to the hospital in Columbus, Georgia. Dad quickly awakened Lynn and Mark. The three of them went rapidly through our carport, the few steps through the Carrolls' carport, and up their steps, and knocked on their kitchen door. Jean met them. Even in the middle of the night, there was no fuss about leaving them with the Carrolls, whom they adored. Besides, they knew they were going to "get a new baby," and going to the Carrolls' was part of the plan.

My prior history of giving birth convinced us that we had no time to waste. It was not a long distance to the hospital, and there was no traffic at that time of night. I still hurt when remember how painful it was when we crossed the railroad tracks. We arrived at the hospital in a very short time. Your dad went to check me in while the attending staff began to prep me. The women on duty did not seem nearly as convinced as I was that you were coming soon—very soon. Though I was not screaming, I expressed sincere urgency as I told the lady who was methodically shaving me, "The baby is coming!" Finally, in desperation, I said a bit more convincingly, "I think my water broke!" and I most certainly did not want to have you right there in the bed with no doctor or nurse present. It is true that I had given birth to two babies, but I had been anesthetized, so I did not have a clue how to deliver this one. After what seemed to be an eternity, a second woman came to check me. She exclaimed rather excitedly, "Get back! This woman is crowning!" I was not certain what that meant, but to my relief, I was quickly on a gurney and on my way to the delivery room.

The lady shaving me in preparation for delivery did not give up easily. She finished her job while we were moving full speed ahead

225

down the hall. We were in the hospital only forty minutes before you arrived; in fact, your dad had not even finished admitting me. You were our second son, our third child! What a proud day—and what an unknown challenge you were as you came!

I later learned that the nurse's announcement "She's crowning!" meant that your little head was visible. You were truly "on the way!" We learned in your first year that you had an eye problem diagnosed as "amblyopia." Your depth perception was not good, and your eyes crossed easily. Your eyes worked separately due to a lack of muscular coordination. On occasion, I laughingly said that I, too, would probably have been born cross-eyed if the first thing I saw as I entered the world was a razor!

You dealt with more than your share of difficulties after your birth. Over a period of time, it took four procedures on your left eye plus one on your right to get your eyes cosmetically corrected. You were wearing glasses at the age of eighteen months. You hated them, and it was quite difficult to keep them on you. You had countless places where you hid them—the toy box, between the mattresses on your bed, in Daddy's shoes—and when I asked where they were, you always said, "Dey gone home!" But you never got away with that answer—cute as it was. Your eyes were a dead giveaway. When you strayed from the truth, even just a little bit, your eyes crossed in spite of the fact that you were looking as directly at me as you could.

In addition to your eye difficulties, your naval leaked! The umbilical cord apparently did not close completely at birth, which resulted in a slight seepage of urine for several months. It finally corrected itself. I must confess that there were times when I wanted to hide you from curious eyes as you sucked your thumb, picked at your naval, and your eyes crossed. People who did not know you might well have suspected that you were not "quite right." You had bilateral hernia surgery at an early age, and you broke your arm soon after we moved to Eight Mile. Lynn was holding you up in the air on her feet, and you were supposed to be a plane. And as luck would have it, you broke your arm when you "crashed."

But those were not the only things I remember about you, Mike. There was a delightfully happy side about you. Mentally, you were as bright as a new penny. You loved learning new and complicated words like "Constantinople," "su-per-cal-i-fra-gi-lis-tic-ex-pi-al-i-do-sious," "equilibrium," and "Chattahoochee," which always came out "Hatta-choo-chee" when you said it. One night we were at a football game in Columbus, Georgia. Judge Shannon Burch (judge of the Muscogee County juvenile court) and his wife were seated in front of us. You and Mrs. Burch had quite a conversation, and she was impressed with how intelligent you were at such an early age. She commented to us that you were simply adorable. After the conversation ended and things were relatively quiet (probably boring to you), you quite unexpectedly reached around Mrs. Burch so that your crossed eyes were almost in her face, and you asked rather loudly, "Where is your equilibrium?" Oh, how she did laugh! You were a genuine con artist—a real charmer, but a con artist nonetheless. I have saved a note that you wrote in 1972. Though it has grown dim with age, I cherish it. Like your father, you consistently made a production of everything. The note was addressed in your childish scrawl: "To a mother who is totally incapable of being nice to her son who cuts her grass, takes out her garbage, buys her presents, and cleans her bathroom. And who loves her dearly."

The note itself was on the other side of the three-ringed, lined paper:

Dear Mrs. Munday,
Wife of Gerald,
Mother of Lynn,
Mother of Mark,
Mother of the famous, great genius Mike,

I cannot find the trash bag.

Mike

As you grew, your talents became more numerous. For instance, you and Kelly Mix danced your way to stardom when you played the lead role in "It's Cool in the Furnace" at the Presbyterian church in Gulf Breeze. You loved taking tests at school because you always did so well. But there were a few things you did not master easily. Remember how difficult it was for you to learn to break an egg? Without fail, you managed to squash it on whatever you struck to break the shell. Even Peggy Hinman, a home economics teacher, was not able to teach you that skill. You did eventually become proficient in the fine art of egg breaking—a lot of practice and countless eggs later.

To our chagrin, you were never reluctant to call any of your teachers' attention to the fact that they were in error, or worse, that they had just screwed up. You usually were correct, but you were rude and sometimes cruel about it. I remember well the night when Mr. Levantino called me in tears. You had corrected him earlier that day at school—in front of the entire class! He quit teaching at the end of the year. You had no patience with incompetent and inept people. Your dad and I made several trips to school to apologize for your disruptive manner, and we always left with a prayer that some day you would grow into a kind, sensitive, and compassionate person. And there was an additional prayer: that somewhere in the mix, you would find it possible to tolerate the gross imperfections of your teachers and associates until that time. Those prayers were answered, Mike. You did become kind, sensitive, and tolerant while retaining all of the attributes that were a part of the package when you came.

Have you noticed that I have not dwelt on how much we still miss you? That will always be a given! This birthday was somehow a good time for me to remember our special baby who grew into a precocious child, a restless teenager, and a young man of whom we are so proud—whose memories we shall always cherish.

Happy birthday, Michael!

I love you,

Mom

—September 1, 2006

When Silver Linings Are Tarnished

"Into each life, some rain must fall—but too much is falling in mine." This line comes from one of the Ink Spots' hit songs of several decades ago. Most people experience times when it seems that the floodgates open and a deluge pours forth—not the "Showers of Blessings" of which we sing at church, but an outpouring of the "too much" kind of rain with thunder, lightning, wind, and hail that for my purposes here translate into heartbreak, loss, loneliness, fear, distress, and separation.

Our family, like so many others, has known serious illness, loss, and death, but as I focus on those times of grief, I can see that every experience, without exception, has been balanced with God's grace and enough faith to sustain us. A line from yet another song suggests that "Every cloud must have a silver lining," which leads me to say that during those times of grief, we worked diligently at believing there would somewhere be a silver lining—and at times we even came close enough to catch a glimpse of it—but the lining was tarnished, and we wondered if it could ever be silvery bright again.

Gerald and I are a part of the generation between the one when thousands of young men announced to a shocked world that they were "gay," and the generation of their stoic grandparents who cut them no slack. This is where we found ourselves in 1988, when from one generation Mike shared the terrifying news that he was HIV positive, while from her generation, Mother vehemently declared, "Sin is sin." A Kaposi's sarcoma lesion on Mike's leg gave evidence to the fact that the disease was advanced. I did not want to talk to my mother, but I knew what I had to do for Mother's sake as well as Mike's—and for my own.

That fateful day that Mother and I talked, I explained everything I knew about HIV/AIDS—which actually was not very much. There was so much that I would learn as Mike's caregiver. Mother sat like stone while I wept through the story of our tragedy, arms crossed over her chest, her eyes a steely gray. When I finished all that I knew and understood about the disease and Mike's present state, and I asked Mother if she wanted to ask me anything, she replied, "Well! Sin is sin!" If only she could have heard my heart as it broke; how I was helplessly drowning in unshed tears—in "too much rain." Our youngest child was dying, and I was filled with nothing but emptiness. How was it possible that my own mother did not understand the desperation I felt? Did she have no idea of my yearning for just a bit of reassurance from her?

Nothing will be gained by belaboring the fact of Mother's rigid, unyielding attitude except to say (whether intentionally or accidentally) she never spoke to Mike again. Though her refusal to maintain a relationship with her grandson was heartbreaking, there were other families whose lots were much worse than ours. In the early days of the AIDS tragedy, undertakers were actually afraid to embalm the bodies of those dying of the disease. Mean-spirited men and women picketed the funerals of AIDS victims. Those were terrible days; stormy, turbulent days; days when "too much rain" fell into too many lives. Mike died July 28, 1989.

Gerald's father, Lyman Butner Munday, died the following January. My stepfather, John Knox Elliott, died ten days later. Gerald's nephew, Tommy Haines, died on March 28, 1990, eights month after Mike. Gerald was growing progressively worse with liver disease. There were too many funerals too close together, and too much serious illness. Rain was falling into our lives in such proportions that we were helplessly being sucked into the rushing floodwaters and fearfully facing the swirling rapids that threatened our complete destruction.

Gerald was the recipient of a liver transplant in 1995. Mother became critically ill in 1998. She was dismissed from the hospital to a nursing home, where she lived for almost three years. She adjusted as well as or maybe better than most patients. She met old friends there and reestablished good and meaningful friendships. When we took her for outings, she soon became eager to return to the home and to her room. While the last months and weeks of her life were not easy for her, she did not complain. Giving up was very difficult for her. She pushed herself to do as much as she could. She even walked (with assistance) to the bathroom three days before she died.

Going to see Mother was a four-hour trip, but I drove those miles back and forth for a number of weeks. Mother loved having me with her, and that feeling was mutual. She often said she would be happy as long as she could see her children. We talked during her wakeful times, then she drifted off into peaceful, relaxed naps. I spent long days in her room from early morning till almost dark each day. I cross-stitched while she napped. Each time she awakened, she asked to see the progress I had made on the sampler I was stitching.

Time spent with Mother during those months was good for us both—especially for me. We talked about the good times as well as those that had been a bit more tedious. We talked about family, about expectations and failures. Trusting, bonding, and understanding were byproducts of the conversations that grew out of those days. Then, as we expected, those peaceful times of sharing were gone. Mother's condition worsened. It was clear that her days were numbered.

As Mother's death became imminent, I thought of all she had taught me from my earliest childhood. The position of the oldest child in the family brought with it certain responsibilities. I must always be watchful of my younger brothers and sister. That was never troublesome for me. With an alcoholic father, it was only natural that I was also protective of Mother. So in my role as her oldest child, I felt responsible to express the love and appreciation that we all had for her, and to assure her that we did not want her to struggle to live. It was my intent to give Mother our blessings and also our permission to die. We had the conversation—the two of us. I was doing the talking (difficult as it was), and Mother was listening—without comment.

Through my tears I managed to say, "Mother, you are ninety-three years old. You have had a good and rich life, even though there have been some really tough times. You worked hard to see that all four of your children were educated, and grew to adulthood [I was seventy], and that all of us were living independently with families of our own. We are grown now, Mama. Our families are doing well, and we owe it primarily to you and Grannie. Mother, please be assured that Burton, Howard, and I will take as good care of Wrenn as she will permit." I made a special point to talk about taking care of Wrenn, who was diagnosed with muscular dystrophy while in her thirties and had been confined to a wheelchair for more than thirty-five years. Wrenn was a genuine concern for Mother from the day of her diagnosis.

I also gently reminded Mother that her entire life had been invest-

231

ed in preparation for this day, and that just the simple chore of living had become an impossible effort for her. With some joy, I began to talk of our special people who had already made the journey to that land beyond the river. We were taught to believe that it was a given that those special folks would be waiting with outstretched arms to welcome her: Grannie, Granddaddy, Daddy, John Pa (my stepfather)—and Mike. I told Mother again how much Mike loved her, and of how proud she had been of him and his accomplishments. Then we waited.

Mother died about five A.M. on February 14, 2001 (Valentine's Day). It was another rainy day for me. This time the rain fell as a soft shower, and this time I believed there was a silver lining off somewhere in the distance. Yes, it was tarnished a bit because of the separation between Mike and Mother, but I am trusting that the One Who makes all things new will apply His healing grace—and will polish this special silver lining to a warm glow!

ADDENDUM: My good friend Annice Webb has encouraged me since her first reading of these stories to get them into some kind of readable order. One day as we worked on doing just that, I kept returning to and picking at this story. Something in my telling of it simply did not ring true. I knew that something important was wrong and I was not able to pinpoint the problem. Finally, in a moment of revelation, Annice blurted out in a firm voice, "You have not forgiven your mother!" Then in a much softer voice, she calmly asked, "Have you forgiven your mother?"

I was speechless. I was not sure. It had never been a subject of any of our conversations. But I was unable to make any kind of a declaration to the effect that I had forgiven Mother. Annice and I continued to talk. I slowly became more objective. I began to recognize the pain that I had clutched to myself for nineteen years. It had been gathering there constantly, like a storm brewing with lightning and thunder somewhere off in the distance. With great clarity and one piece at a time, I began to see the impossible position that had been mine, both as a daughter and as a mother. I was between both sides, with each of them so very dear to me. I was being squeezed. On the one hand, Mother was not aware that she had done anything wrong because "Sin is sin" and that is how to deal with it! But Mike, on the other hand, stood staring at the "great gulf fixed" between him and his beloved Grannie Bet.

Finally I was owning the hurt of Mother's not being there for Mike or me—the hurt that had lain dormant for nearly twenty years, unnoticed and unrecognized. As painful as Mike's illness and death had been, the ache did not end with his memorial. As a result of that tragic grief, I became one of the "walking wounded"—one of the casualties of the dreadful stories and events surrounding the HIV/AIDS era. My illness was both undetected and undiagnosed until Annice courageously placed her finger on the excruciatingly painful sore place.

The remaining part of that day was spent in deep and tearful soul searching. Mother had never asked forgiveness because she never knew that she had done anything wrong. I never forgave her the hurt that she caused because she never asked; I just buried it! Now, finally, the conclusion to this painful matter is this:

I have forgiven Mother a thousand times over.

I am asking forgiveness for my failure to forgive her so many years ago.

I don't know if those who have moved from their earthly dwelling to the "place prepared for them" have any consciousness of what is happening with us who continue to strive to "fight the good fight," but if Mother is where she can know anything of my heart, then she will surely hear it say, "Mother, I forgive! And I love you with all my heart!"

• • •

A few years after Mike's death, Sally Anne Fuller Richard, my niece, designed and made a memorial quilt in his memory. She made it according to the specifications of the AIDS Quilt. It was quilted by Marydean Fuller, Sally's mother (my sister-in-law). I am including a copy of the letter in which Sally interpreted the symbolism in the quilt as well as my letter in response to her, followed by my letter of deep appreciation to Marydean.

19 Nov. 2000
Dear Aunt Sis:
I'm not sure where to begin. Mama and I have wanted

to make a memorial quilt for Mike for a long time. I guess the time was finally right. I designed and pieced; Mama consulted and quilted. The final design is nothing like we initially intended. I have to say that from the first of going to buy fabric, something or someone else guided my actions. It may be presumptuous of me, but I feel this quilt isn't my design. I feel that it's Mr. John Michael's. I think I was just his hands. I hope this represents his voice.

My interpretation of the design is this:

Obviously, it had to have Mike's name and "pertinent" dates. The stars are of a traditional piecing pattern; the background is rather contemporary—much like Mike, a blending of traditional and modern. I'm not sure if the sky is meant to be a night sky or a day sky. Probably that time that is just in between. I heard someone say that stars are like love (or maybe that should be love is like stars). Just because we do not see the stars all the time, it does not mean they are not there. I think this applies to people we love. Even after they are gone from our sight, there is a part of them that is always with us.

The landscape had to be the beach. Maybe there is a certain serenity found there. Or maybe because it is a reminder that this world moves with or without us; the waves tide in and out, and have for an eternity before us and will for an eternity after us. We are just a small part of this creation.

In the borders are quilted some of who Mike was to so many people. It is also a reminder that AIDS is not discriminating. It chooses anyone. The sailboat says to me something of a journey. Again, I think Mike may be gone from us, but that is not something final; he has just moved on to another part of the journey.

The quote on the sail I found in a quilt magazine featuring a quilt made for the Marian Residence for homeless and mentally disabled women in the San Francisco area. (The quote is this: "The great activity of our life is to love. I see God as one act—just loving, like the sun is always shining." Fr. A. Boeddeker, DFM.) Once I read it, I could not forget it. We wander through this life trying to discover the "great mystery." I think this sums it up fairly well. Whether it is AIDS or some other crisis, it is not up to us to solve or to fix or to judge. It is just up to us to love. Always.

We were blessed to have enjoyed John Michael for nearly thirty years. I cannot claim to have actually known him that well, but my memories are of a beautiful young man with a smile as bright as the sun and a laugh of music. I know he touched so many lives. I hope that through this quilt, he might touch a few more. The quilt is designed to the specifications of the AIDS Memorial Quilt, but it is yours to do with as you choose. I have included the forms required for submittal if it is what you choose. If you donate it, I believe that you can request that it be sent to a specific chapter, such as the Dallas chapter or one in Florida. Whenever the quilt panels tour in certain areas, you can request that Mike's panel be included for that area. There is no limit to the panels a person can be represented with, so if someone else wants to do a panel for Mike, they can. But again, it is yours to do with as you choose.

You and Uncle Jerry have always been special to me. You've always done such sweet things, and have made me feel special. I so enjoyed making this quilt for you. It was an experience I cannot explain, but one I'll always remember.

I think that quilt panels were a perfect choice to create a memorial for so many people. A quilt has always represented comfort and warmth and love. I hope you find all of these in this quilt.

I love you!
Sally

• • •

February 22, 2001
Sally, my dear,

This letter should have come to you much sooner. It has been difficult to write, however, because the contents are so precious to my heart, and I have been taken back in a bittersweet kind of experience when I have relived days which I shall always cherish. So forgive the long and tearful delay—I'll try to get back on track.

So much has transpired since you and your mom

bestowed upon us your memorial quilt for Mike.

Uncle Jerry and I participated in our local World AIDS Day that very next Friday (12/01/2000). I am enclosing the order of worship. At the very beginning of worship, the organ ceased playing, and a number of representatives of those who had died walked in silence down the center aisle of that beautiful old church bearing our banners/quilts. Those who were seated in the pews stood in silent reverence as we placed our symbols of love and memories on the altar. Your quilt was viewed and discussed by many of those present—recognizing the love and sensitivity of the creators and artists of such a special piece.

There have been other viewings, private and personal, with very special people who have deep appreciation of your sensitive love and skills, and some who knew Mike and who still express their own sense of love and loss of that very special young man.

Grannie Bet died on Valentine's Day. How grateful I am that our love for our special lady and our love for each other made that bearable—in some ways gratefully joyful.

Since putting the stamp on the envelope when I thought I could write this letter, postage has increased! Let's try again to get on with it.

I agree with the opening thought of your letter: "I'm not sure where to begin." I simply do not have the words to express the gratitude and love that Uncle Jerry and I feel for you, as well as for the beauty of your gorgeous interpretation. Maybe the best plan is to listen to my heart; while at the same time I know full well that these heart trips often take us down little traveled and possibly even unexplored paths. Let's start!

Uncle Jerry and I were deeply touched by the love revealed and reflected through your gift of Mike's memorial quilt, your very personal presentation of it to us, and also your interpretation of the symbolism that it contains. Your view of who Mike was and of who Mike continues to be was amazingly accurate. Your being in our home and your brief encounters were not enough to give you such insight. Perhaps you are correct when you said: "I feel this quilt isn't my design.

I feel that it's Mr. John Michael's. I think I was just his hands."
It is uncanny how tuned in you were/are to him, and I believe
that somehow you have felt Mike's heart.

Mike loved the beach—the sun—the days—the nights!
You were not sure if the sky was day sky or a night sky. The
sky is perfect! Daytime sky? Nighttime sky? Both were loved
by Mike. He was filled with excitement and enthusiasm about
any time—all time, and he packed each second with eagerness
and expectation until the very end of his earthly life. He
requested over and over that he not be sedated or given a
morphine drip because in his words: "I want to know everything to the end." And he did!

By the way! After Mike died, the summer clouds held such
an attraction for me! I caught myself wondering if Mike were
hop-scotching among them—playing hide-and-seek with me
just as he had done so many times when he was "my baby."
And the sunsets! Some days I seemed to know that the exquisite display of colors in the western sky was especially for
me—a special request by Mike. He always received great joy
from giving me gifts, and he loved giving to lots of people. He
was a true giver! Christmas was his special time, and there
were no lengths to which he would not go.

I really never thought about it, but I think that you are
correct in that Mike was a blend of traditional and modern.
He was somehow able to discard any of the past that had no
relevance; however, he tenaciously held on to the good, solid,
useful principles and precepts of his past as he leapfrogged
into all the new and challenging information with which he
was bombarded daily as a professional researcher. Through
this process, he discovered much real truth, and the older he
grew, the more honest he became—both with himself and
others. He had little or no time for pretense. He finally
reached the place that he did not have to be someone whom
he clearly was not. He was comfortable with the man he
became!

During Mike's last weeks, it was not unusual to find him
completely absorbed while listening to classical music—the
music of the masters—melodies and harmonies that had

withstood the years and the critics. He seemed to leave himself and the pain of his frail body, and his seeking spirit moved into a peaceful, calm soul almost as if he were preparing for his life that was yet to come.

I loved what you said about the star being traditional piecing patterns. And you added: "I heard someone say that the stars are like love (or maybe that's love is like stars). Just because we do not see them does not mean that they are not there." That sounds very much like the words found inscribed on the prison wall at Auschwitz. One of the wretched souls imprisoned there, even though facing the furnaces, spoke of his/her unshakable faith in these terms:

"I believe in the sun even when it is not shining.

I believe in love even when it is not shown.

I believe in God even when He does not speak."

Let me share another reason for the stars—one which you could not possibly know because it happened before you were born.

Your dad and mom owned a little blue Sprite convertible—one that anybody would have loved to drive. We were living in Mobile, and your Uncle Jerry, "horse trader" that he was, was able to negotiate with your dad to borrow his car for a week. We left our car, maybe as security, but more likely as a means of transportation. As I recall, Lynn and Mark were spending that week with Grannie Bet.

We enjoyed riding down Mobile's streets lined with huge live oaks whose great branches grew together across the streets and formed a canopy. At the end of the week we were returning the little blue convertible, as agreed. Uncle Jerry was driving; I was seated on the passenger side with Mike on my lap. The top was back. The warm wind blew our hair with reckless abandon as we rode through the countryside filled with the evening sounds of crickets and June bugs. It was easy to become convinced that "God was in His Heaven—and all was right with the world!" We were wrapped in a warm blanket of His summer evening beneath His sky crowded with "a million" stars. More stars crept into view as the evening settled around us and they became increasingly radiant as the velvet sky became darker.

Mike's face was turned toward the heavens and the stars, and his head rested on my shoulder. My knowledge of astronomy is extremely limited, and so it did not take very long to point out what I knew—the Big Dipper, the Little Dipper, the North Star, the Milky Way.

When we finally reached Mother's house, following the customary greetings and hugs, I said, "Mike, why don't you tell Grannie Bet what we saw on the way?" His look of complete bewilderment caused me to add, "You know—up in the sky!" He knew immediately what I was asking and he gave this very interesting but highly convincing answer: "I saw God pouring chocolate on the Milky Way!"

Mike loved chocolate. I recall instances during his last illness when Uncle Jerry drove to the farthest point in Dallas to get him chocolate truffles and chocolate milkshakes from places that were special to him.

And who knows? Maybe God is allowing Mike to pour chocolate on the Milky Way as other children behold its beauty! Maybe Mike is singing, laughing, and excitedly skipping from star to brilliant star. Yes, Sally. I do know that the stars are there even when I cannot see them shining! And I shall forever know that Mike loves us and cares for us even when we cannot put our arms around him and pull him close.

There is no way for me to express the joy we feel in hearing Mike's name spoken, or at seeing it written. Your gift of time and creative talent along with your uncanny insights and intuitions are far and away more than anything we could ever have imagined. We are grateful that you are "ours." You are a special young woman—one who makes a significant impact and difference in the people whom you touch—the kind who clearly sees the chocolate on the Milky Way.

I love you!
Aunt Sis

• • •

2-24-2008
Dear Marydean, my soul sister!

239

As usual, I do not know just how much of you went into the creation of Mike's memorial quilt. I'll only be able to guess. There were some spaces of age and geography between Mike and Sally, and yet, there is an unexplainable complete-ness in the interpretation of the quilt! I strongly suspect that much of it could have come only from you and God. There is a little poem (poor as it is) that says:

"Bring to God your gift, my brother.
He'll not need to ask another
You will do!
He will add his blessing to it
And the two of you will do it—
God and you!"

So many of us have stood for a long time and watched you and God in action. What an example you are to the rest of us who struggle with the true meaning of self-giving love and service! I talk a lot about "mission," and I see you doing mission with no fanfare. Thank you for the beauty of your life and for all that you give me.

I can never thank you enough for the gorgeous quilt. I somehow get the feeling that every single stitch is a love note from you to Mike—as well as to Gerald and me.

And thank you for being a real daughter to my mother! I recall all of those times when she was with you and Burton—and you patiently fed her good food and bandaged her wounds. Mother knew that she was welcomed by you both—as well as that she was loved! Again, I can only guess how many times you were there for her—sometimes in my place!

And for the times that you saw that Mother got to church and that she didn't eat Sunday dinner alone, I thank you! All of the alterations to make her dresses "fit"—the piles of laun-dry that went to your washer and dryer and always came back to her so beautifully clean and "ready to wear"—even to her beautiful pink dress, which you had ready and hanging long before she needed it for her last public appearance. She looked beautiful!

You were the glue that held us all together during those last days with good hot meals and a quiet, clean place to rest. Only my Father, the King of Glory, can pay you just recompense for those gifts of yourself—so I leave that to Him in His great wisdom. Just accept my love, admiration, and appreciation for who you are and for all that you have brought to so many—and I am not the least of these. Thank you for being my soul sister!

I love you!
Sister

P.S. I am enclosing a copy of the letter which I addressed to Sally. It is partially addressed to you, you know!

As I See It

"Beauty is in the eye of the beholder" is a much used and well-worn cliché. Not only have we heard it said, but we have often spoken it with our own lips. It was a long time before I realized that every person actually perceives beauty differently. What is perfectly lovely for one person might be extremely dull or plain to another. I am thinking that perceptions and perspective are born out of personal background, experiences, relationships, likes, dislikes, etc., thus causing one person to see beauty, and another to see ugliness; one beholds riches while another sees poverty.

If the above conjecture is true—that "beauty is in the eye of the beholder"—then I submit the possibility that Utopia is also in the eye (or the mind's eye) of the beholder, and that it differs from person to person. In dictionary terms, Utopia can be any idealized place, state, or situation of perfection; any visionary scheme or system for an ideally perfect society. Like countless men and women from the beginning of time, I have reached and struggled toward that point where I would know that I had arrived and was experiencing Utopia. But it has been an elusive quest. I have actually known several Utopias—at least for a brief time. They have each in turn ultimately escaped me, while others (equally alluring and intriguing) have replaced them. It has been a veritable kaleidoscope, constantly changing both in pattern and in color.

For years, I dreamed of being sixteen; I truly expected perfection upon reaching that magic age. I do not recall that perfection was actually achieved, and even if it was realized, it must have been for a fleeting moment, because I quickly turned seventeen and the sixteen-year illusion was gone. I thought that if I ever left home, went to college and earned a degree, fell in love, became engaged, married the man of my dreams, became a mother (once, twice, or three times), achieved a state of love and respect from those whom I called friends (and the list goes on), each in turn would be Utopia. As each event came and went, it was Utopia. The fascinating thing is that as each state of perfection was realized, it became a steppingstone to the next Utopia. I must hasten to add that in recounting my Utopias and relegating them to the position of steppingstones, their luster as visionary schemes of perfection has in no way dimmed, even though they might have been fleeting.

My being married to Gerald, the love of my life, fulfilled a dream of long standing. His being a minister made a place of Christian service for me, and that was a call that my heart had felt for years. I knew and understood that the minister's family lived in a parsonage, but I had no idea what living in a parsonage was really like until we moved in. The parsonage was the home provided and inconsistently furnished by each local congregation. By "inconsistent" I mean that one parsonage might have a washer and dryer, while another would not. Some parsonages came complete with bed linens and pillows while others did not. Some were furnished with cookware while others came with empty kitchen cabinets. If I used "their" things along with my own, and if we stayed for a number of years, it became difficult to remember what was "theirs" and what was "ours." As a matter of confession, we may have picked up a few items along the way—even though I tried very hard not to have that happen.

There were various ways to go about furnishing a parsonage. Some churches purchased new items of furniture and decorated the minister's home in good taste with basic pieces, using as many neutral shades as possible in order that a minister could move personal items in and possibly match (or at least not clash with) the existing scheme. Then other congregations furnished the parsonage with pieces that had been used by their members for many years, and when it was time to replace them with new pieces, they donated them to the parsonage; after all, those items had been used and loved by their family for years.

When Lynn was three years old and Mark was a baby, we were assigned to a charge in east Alabama known as the Marvyn/Society Hill/Watoola charge. The house was a typical country home with a screened-in porch across the front with a swing on it. It was located on Federal Highway 80, which ran from the East Coast to the West Coast. The house was nestled beneath huge pecan trees with a dirt drive running from the highway back along the side of it. A large storage room with a shed used as a garage stood at the end of the drive.

The building was quite old and rustic. There was a quiet peacefulness about the place, and sometimes I still long for its serenity.

There was no air conditioning then, and the hot, sultry days of summer were almost unbearable at times. The summer that we moved in, we decided to move our bed out onto the large screened-in back porch in hopes that we could catch any breath of air that might be stirring. The well, the source of water for our household, was located in the part of the porch that formed an "L" off the main porch area. Lots and lots of snails, probably attracted by the damp-ness from the well, made their home on the porch. They made slimy trails everywhere, but it didn't matter; we were going to enjoy that back porch. There was enough space to accommodate a few chairs, and it was much more comfortable than trying to sit or sleep inside the hot house.

Our new space was coming together beautifully when I was struck with a moment of pure inspiration. There was an old braided straw rug (probably nine by twelve feet) beneath the dining room table that would fit perfectly into our summer escape. The rug was in a heavily trafficked area and was actually a safety hazard due to the fact that it was so worn. There was a hole in it and one of the edges was very ragged, but those places were on the side of the room where people seldom walked for fear someone might trip and fall. With all that in mind, we decided that the rug would be fine on the back porch.

This parsonage belonged to one of those churches I mentioned earlier that gave their loved and worn pieces to the parsonage. I did not know at the time that the tired old rug had been a gift from a member of the Society Hill Methodist Church. She was a widow, a wealthy landowner, and she lived in an antebellum home. She grew cotton on her thousands of acres that were cultivated by tenant farm-ers. She owned the cotton gin where she ginned her cotton, as well as the cotton of other cotton farmers in the surrounding area. She did a thriving business. Both of her sons worked for her, and at no time did anyone question who "the boss" was. She was one of the top con-tributors to her church in Society Hill. Her influence and clout were felt throughout the entire community. Clearly, in her eyes, I had trans-gressed one of those unwritten laws governing the parsonage: I had taken the rug given by her from the inside protection of the house to the outside back porch.

Becoming Myself: A Passage of Grace

I do not recall putting that dangerous floor covering back under the dining room table. I really don't think I did. Perhaps I did not make the change because I learned of the donor's displeasure so near the time that we moved from there to the lovely new parsonage at the Epworth Church in Phenix City. Living in a personage was always like living in a fishbowl—after all, the people in the congregation owned everything. The pastor and his family (there were very few female pastors then) were allowed to live in the house rent-free as payment in kind. The expectation was that the preacher's wife would keep it clean and orderly, thus making a good impression at all times on anyone who passed through its doors—or anyone who just happened to drive down the street. Intentional or not, this arrangement was actually a powerful means of control by the church.

During those years of parsonage living, I began to dream and look toward another Utopia: a time and place when our family could have our own house and yard. What a day of celebration it was when we finally moved into a small concrete block beach house on the inter-coastal waterway east of Gulf Breeze. Words cannot describe the freedom I experienced as I drove a nail into "our" wall or chose what color paint to use in our living room—and I didn't have to wait for the Parsonage Committee's approval! I had arrived at another Utopia—this time in our family's very small house. My Utopia kaleidoscope still changes in design and color when new goals and dreams are born. But one very bright piece in the kaleidoscope seems to be caught in place: the piece that represents "home"; the Utopia that has housed the love that Gerald and I share as good friends and lovers; our mutual love for our children; our love for the ministry; our deep and sincere love for the good and gracious God who made us.

In looking over my shoulder at these countless, personal Utopias, I feel compelled to address this question: "Who of us achieving our heart's desire will then be satisfied?" I think that my answer lies in the concluding words of the Lost Chord, which profoundly declare, "It may be that only in Heaven I shall hear that grand AMEN!"

Now Who's In Charge?

One experience I never had before going away to college was that of spending a night alone. In fact, when I graduated from college, I still had never spent a night alone. After marrying at the age of twenty-two, several more years passed, and I had spent no night alone.

Growing up in the country, having one or more family members home at all times, and being the eldest grandchild of Sallie Lillian Roberts Burton (a self-proclaimed coward when it came to staying alone) were three good reasons for my inordinate and unfounded terror of being alone. After the passage of many years, the time finally did arrive when I would be spending nights at home alone. Gerald was entering the seminary, and that meant that he would be away from Monday afternoon until Friday night. I really was not prepared to spend all of those hours alone in the dark. Actually, I would not be completely alone because Lynn, who was three years old, and Mark, who was six months old, would be with me.

Seminary students were usually assigned churches or charges (a grouping of several churches) as near the school as possible. Gerald was to be a student at the Candler School of Theology, Emory University, in Atlanta, Georgia, so we were appointed to the Marvyn Charge, consisting of the Marvyn, Watoola, and Society Hill churches in east Alabama. It was not long before the people in each of the congregations learned that their preacher's wife was scared to death at the prospect of staying alone, and they tried to be as helpful as they could.

The parsonage sat alongside Federal Highway 80. There were no close neighbors except for a small country store and filling station located just beyond some pecan trees to the west of the house. While working outside, I discovered that the store was the hub of activity for the Marvyn community. There were always people coming or going for grocery items that they had failed to pick up in Opelika at the larger chain groceries. The gas pumps drew even more customers, and when it was not convenient for the buyer to pay, he or she simply charged the purchase to a running account to be paid at a later date. Local men gathered every afternoon to sit and talk or play dominoes under the front shelter that covered the gas tanks.

Sarah Brasswell, a member of the Watoola Methodist Church and a divorcee, lived nearby with her mother. She was employed as an office manager by the Pepperell Mills in Opelika, Alabama. Sarah was a delightful lady who went out of her way to do everything that she could for her preacher, and for his family. She decided early on that she would stay with the children and me when Gerald was away. I cannot express the comfort I felt every night just as it was getting dark, when we saw the headlights from Sarah's Jeep as it slowly made its way down the drive. She brought presents for the children every single day, so seeing Aunt Sarah was almost as joyful for them as waiting up for Santa.

There was always much to do during the daytime hours: two small children, laundry, housecleaning, cooking, and those other chores that came simply as a part of everyday life. I looked forward to the time after lunch when both children napped, because it gave me an opportunity to get some of the chores done that I could not accomplish while they were awake. However, a boisterous woodpecker invaded that routinely quiet time to which I had become accustomed. Sometimes I had the feeling that he waited just outside the window to be certain that the children were asleep. Then with the ferocity and clamor of a jackhammer, he attacked the rafters in the attic. The house trembled under his assault.

This burst of loud noise always brought screams from Mark as he was awakened from his peaceful slumber. Sometimes Lynn managed to sleep through the storm. When Gerald came home each weekend, I complained of the woodpecker's intrusion into the peace and tranquility of our days. I insisted that he kill that bird! So, with gun in hand, he faithfully took his seat on a tree stump where he was able to observe the woodpecker stick his bright red head from high in the gable just below the roof. It was almost as though he were teasing Gerald as he sat turning from side to side—almost like he knew the gun would not be fired until he left the attic and was "on the wing." When he finally did fly, it was with great speed, and he dove at Gerald's head. Of course, Gerald ducked, and the woodpecker escaped again.

With Gerald away in seminary, my days were long and filled with responsibilities that would have been easier if they had been shared by the two of us. But we had agreed, and even though we knew that it would be difficult, we decided that Gerald must complete his seminary work. There are no two ways about it: I was tired physically, and I was especially tired of having that flying critter waking Mark from his nap every single day.

So when I could not take any more, I loaded the shotgun and positioned myself on the stump outside the end of the house where Mr. Woody had such fun playing peek-a-boo—and then, with such braggadocio, in diving at the person who sat in wait. My mind was made up! I had not come to play! I had come for blood! I waited, and there he came, head outside the hole, ready for his game. I didn't give him an opportunity to dive at me! I looked him dead in the eye, took aim, and just as he was leaving his perch high in the gable just under the roof, I fired! My aim was true! My prey was dead at my feet! I was the conquering hero! At long last, I had overcome! And as a permanent reminder of that day, there in the gabled end of the Marvyn parsonage were countless little holes made by multiple shots from the blast of a .410 shotgun.

It became a joyous celebration to put the children down for their naps and have them sleep! But there was another benefit to this episode that I did not know until just before we moved to Phenix City. The local men were gathered at the country store the day that I shot the woodpecker, talking or playing dominoes, and they observed the entire action from "front row seats." Word soon got out in the community that it wouldn't be wise for anybody to go to the parsonage unannounced after dark, because the preacher's wife could "sho' shoot a shotgun!"

In looking back at those days, I know now that I was safe—if for no other reason, the word was out that I could take care of myself. I suppose that many of our fears are unfounded, and that much of our anxiety is without cause. My mother often said when she was trying to drive home a point, "The wicked flee when no man pursueth" (Prov. 28:1)! Perhaps I am beginning to understand that Scripture.

Life on Long Street

The year was 1957. Gerald had just been appointed by the Alabama/West Florida Conference of the Methodist Church to the Marvyn charge in east Alabama. A short time after we moved in, we began to explore our new surroundings. We had worked at unpacking one day for about as long as we could endure, so we decided to take Lynn, who was about three years of age, and Mark, who was six months, and drive away from all of the mess—just for a little while! After driving for a time, we found ourselves in Phenix City, Alabama. We knew very little about that small town except that it was located along the west bank of the Chattahoochee River across from Columbus, Georgia, and Fort Benning. One other thing we knew was that Phenix City was known far and wide as "sin city" because of political corruption fueled by greed and graft that held nothing sacred—even human life.

We drove along Seale Road, which we later came to know as Long Street. As we continued driving south through a residential community, we detected no evidence of wealth or prosperity anywhere. Small businesses such as family-owned groceries or motor repair shops were sprinkled among the small homes, which, for the most part, were owned or rented by the folks who were employed by cotton mills just across the river in Columbus, Georgia. At the crest of the hill, which we later came to know as Flea-hop Hill, we discovered the Epworth Methodist Church on the left side of the street. A sidewalk ran at street level from the city sidewalk directly into the second floor of the church where the sanctuary was located. The large basement was below street level since there was a significant drop from the street's edge. The ground level dropped sharply on the left side of the street, while rising equally as sharply on the right side. One of us, I think possibly I, said, "I sure hope we never are sent to this church!" The very next year, Mr. Capps from the Watoola church moved us in his large farm truck from the Marvyn community parsonage to the

Epworth Methodist parsonage, located on South Seale Road. We lived there for the next five years, during which time Gerald completed his seminary work at Candler School of Theology in Atlanta.

Those five years were difficult years because Gerald left each week on Monday afternoon for Atlanta and returned late Friday, usually in time for dinner. I taught school for three years during that time. I was also called on during the week to keep the church moving along as smoothly as possible. The people who were a part of our flock were some of the most loving, dedicated, interesting (though sometimes strange) folks we have ever been privileged to know. Many of them had spent their lifetime working in the cotton mills in Columbus. They were not highly educated; in fact, some of them were not able to read.

Mary Henderson lived four or five houses from the church toward town. She was the single mother of three sons. The husband/father had been out of the home since the children were small. She worked long, hard hours at the Schwobilt Men's Suit Factory for as long as we knew her—as well as for many years before. Her sons became fine young men, and I can only hope that they gave Mary the love and honor that she so richly deserved.

Most of the streets off Long Street were not paved, and Miss Carrie Griggs lived on one of those dirt streets behind the church. She often played the piano at the church. Miss Carrie was a middle-aged woman with lots of children of her own. She knew all the children up and down her street. They knew and loved her as well. One day as she sat on the front porch of her small house, she greeted a few children as they walked barefoot along the dusty street. In reply to her question as to how they felt, one little girl answered, "I ain't doin' too well, Miss Carrie." Miss Carrie responded in a most concerned manner, "What do you think is wrong, honey?" The little girl said, "I don't know—unless I'm goin' through the change." Little pitchers have big ears!

Charles and Ione Rice lived up a long flight of concrete steps directly across the street in front of the church. They had a handsome young son named Ronnie. Charles was a laid-back, pleasant, happy, helpful person. Ione was frail and "sickly," and as a result, she could not always be counted upon. They all sang in the choir: Charles sang tenor, Ronnie sang bass, and Ione sang soprano with a lot of vibrato and sad, sad eyes which I thought were meant to convey a spirit of devotion and worship.

Mr. Johnny and Miss Sacie Harris lived next door to the Rices. Mr. Johnny was Ione's uncle. He was such a good man, while Miss Sacie could sometimes be right sharp. It was easy to conclude that the old adage about opposites attracting was absolutely true when thinking about those two folks. Mr. Johnny was deeply loved and respected by the people in the congregation; however, they simply could not help giggling when he prayed almost every Sunday evening and asked God "to help us in our falling shorts."

Miss Linner Franklin was Mr. Johnny's sister and Ione's mother. She lived just a few doors from the church. There was never any question as to whether she would be present for any of the activities at the church. She was always there, and she knew everybody in the neighborhood. She was also a member of the ladies' group that met each week to quilt. They always brought food, cooked, and ate their noon meal together. Times spent around their quilting frames were perfect opportunities to catch up on the latest news, both true and untrue—and to dip snuff. When we first arrived at the church, Gerald had no way of knowing that he should not know about their snuff-dipping vice. He walked in quite innocently one day, only to discover those poor ladies with their lips filled with sweet, dusty lumps of brown ground tobacco. He quickly learned that they were highly embarrassed that they had been "caught" by their new preacher. There was a mad effort to hide the tin cans that they were using as spittoons, and they rushed quickly to the bathroom to empty and wash their lips and mouths. From that time on, he solved the problem by walking very loudly through the sanctuary that was located directly above where they were quilting. Upon hearing him enter the church, they sent their tin can spittoons singing across the floor to an out-of-sight location, and by the time he came into the room, most of them had their mouths in presentable conditions.

We owned a blue Mercury Comet station wagon during those years, and Clara Murphy, who lived just across the street from Miss Linner, owned a blue Ford station wagon. The two cars were almost identical in appearance, and it would have been easy for a casual observer to mistake one automobile for the other. One winter afternoon, Miss Linner called Clara. The conversation went something like this:

"Clara, hon, is the preacher over there?"

"No, Miss Linner, he's not here."

"Well, has he been there today?"

"No, Miss Linner, he hasn't been here today at all."

"Well, whose car is that in front of your house?"

"That's my car, Miss Linner. The preacher is not here. He hasn't been here."

Miss Linner chuckled to herself, then said to Clara by way of explanation, "Lord God, Clara! I thought the preacher was over there, and I just knowed he was coming to see me next. I ain't had a dip of snuff all day!"

This grandmotherly old lady knew and loved every baby and young child in the congregation. It was her custom upon meeting a mother with her baby or small child in her arms to walk right up to them and plant a kiss on the child, all the while vigorously beating the child on the back and asking questions.

One Sunday evening, I was walking along the sidewalk toward the church door. Mike was in my arms. He saw Miss Linner coming. I could feel him bracing himself and drawing his knees up and his arms in as much as he could against the onslaught on this sweet little old lady's love attack. She was headed straight toward us, and she did not miss. Mike got his big kiss, and all of the patting that came with it. Then she said rather loudly between clenched teeth, all the while still slapping Mike on the back, "Mike, who is your daddy, hon?" Mike looked as directly as his little crossed eyes would allow and replied, "Paul Carroll! Dat's who my daddy is!" Miss Linner laughed robustly and said, "Lord, God! Mike said Paul Carroll is his daddy." Let me quickly explain that Paul Carroll was our next-door neighbor and an electrician. Finally, at long last, Miss Linner stopped beating the breath out of Mike. She paused a minute, then asked, "Mike, what does Paul Carroll do?" Without blinking, Mike said, "Paul Carroll turns on the moon."

Paul Carroll died in December of 2005. The Carroll family and we were very close friends. When I told our daughter Lynn of Paul's death, her immediate response was, "Oh, no! Now who's going to turn on the moon?"

I would never want to go back to Long Street to live, but I shall forever cherish the days spent there, the people who became very dear to us, and the priceless lessons we learned.

A Car of My Own

It wasn't much of a car, I suppose, but Mr. Johnnie said, "It runs good." I had just gotten a job teaching seventh grade math, and it was vital that I have reliable transportation to get back and forth to school. Gerald was still in seminary at Emory and was one of the carpool regulars, so he was expected to take his turn driving. He also needed our car to go to hospitals and call on parishioners when he was home on weekends. So a second car for us was no longer a luxury; it had become a necessity while we lived in Phenix City.

Mr. Johnnie Harris was retired and a faithful member of the Epworth Methodist Church. In searching for reliable and cheap transportation, we learned that Mr. Johnnie had a 1946 Fleetline two-door Chevrolet sedan for sale. From all indications, it had been well cared for. The interior was in good condition, but the paint job was far from beautiful. By that, I mean it appeared to be neither a factory finish nor a professionally baked-on job. If I were guessing, I would suppose that Mr. Johnnie had cleaned the car himself, maybe sanded it some, and then spray-painted it. But no matter! Mr. Johnnie said that it didn't use any oil to speak of, and the tires looked pretty good, so we bought the car for me for fifty dollars.

I had never owned a car, and I was proud as could be of my newly acquired mode of transportation. It was hard to believe—a car of my very own! I took good care of it! I cleaned it often, inside and out. Every time I washed it, I was reminded again that the paint job was really not the best. The rusty-looking tan color on the top of the car always came off on the sponge as I washed with soapy water. The awful chartreuse color on the lower part of the car had not faded nearly as badly as had the tan on the top. Because the color on the lower part of the car was the original finish, it really didn't look too bad.

Lynn was in the first grade at Girard Elementary that year. Since it was on my way to Central Middle School, where I would be teach-

253

ing, it was convenient for me to drop her off at her school. Paul and Jean Carroll, who lived next door, had three children enrolled in a private Catholic school that was also on my way to school. Jean and I agreed that I would take our children to school in the morning, and she would pick them up in the afternoon. That arrangement worked well for both of us.

The morning route to school took us down a long hill on Seale Road. When we reached the bottom of the hill, we had to make a ninety-degree left turn to go up the hill to Girard School. Since there was no traffic light at that busy corner, a policeman stood in the center of the street directing traffic during the morning rush. We recognized his presence at that place, and were certainly glad he was there. We took his presence for granted—feeling that it was just his job.

One cold morning on our way to our respective schools, as I made the left turn to go up the hill to Girard School, suddenly, the horn blew loudly—without warning or any direction from me! The policeman quickly turned and looked at us as if demanding an explanation for what he most likely interpreted to be a rude blast from my horn. I was embarrassed that my old car was "acting up." Without even thinking, I quickly said to the children, "Wave to the policeman!" They did—and he waved back.

The next morning was cold again. The same strange thing occurred at the same corner: the horn blew for no reason. The policeman looked at us again; we all waved again, and the policeman again returned our morning greeting—this time with a hint of a smile. We got to be pretty good friends before the winter was over. As time went on, we learned that when the weather was cold, we could expect the horn to sound when I made a turn to the left; we also learned to laugh and wave to accompany the honk.

Some time after school started, I added another passenger. I began going by a teacher's home to give her a ride to school. It was not out of our way since she taught ninth grade English at the same school where I taught. She had three small children and was going through some difficult times financially. Her husband was irresponsible and often in absentia, so a ride to school seemed the least I could do to help. We also shared our food with her and her children when she was without. We grew to be good friends.

One day, Mrs. Smith asked if she could borrow my car to go

home briefly for some kind of an emergency. I was happy for her to use the car, and as I was giving her the keys, I reminded her that the transmission was a "stick shift." She assured me that she knew how to operate a manual transmission, and with that, off she went.

My class was outside in the park in front of the school when she returned. I was not aware that she was back, but the children certainly were. One of them finally asked why Mrs. Smith kept driving around the block in my car. On the next trip around, she drove as slowly as she could—all the while beckoning me to the street. I moved toward the curb, but she was already making another trip around the block. Upon her next approach, she called to me, "How do you make this car stop?" We finally coached her to a stop, and I parked the car. My seventh grade class watched with glee as Mrs. Smith, a ninth grade teacher, found herself in a position where she was not in control, and it was necessary for her to ask for help. Later, I could not help wondering how she stopped the car at her house—or if she did.

I was driving in the second lane one day when the children and I were in town doing errands. A car ahead of us was stopped in the first lane for a red light. As I approached the traffic light, it turned green, and though I slowed, I did not have to stop, and as a result, I seemed to speed past the car that was stopped. The children cheered and yelled in chorus, "Wheeeeee! We passed a car!"

That dear car's name began as "Leaping Lena," which was not an original name with us. Lots of old cars were called "Leaping Lena." But when the radiator began to leak, the children appropriately changed her name to "Leaking Lena." Repairing my old car would have been a financial hardship for us; however, there were two wonderful mechanics in our church, A. J. Carroll and Herman Head. As a favor to us, they maintained my car at barely any expense to us. So when the leak began, they agreed that the best thing to do was to a shave a bar of Octagon laundry soap into the radiator, and that is exactly what they did. I had no faith that such a "cure" stood a ghost of a chance in stopping the leak, but it did! When it leaked again, we shaved more soap.

"Leaking Lena" was old and not pretty to most people, but there seldom was a time when her motor refused to start. Many cold mornings, she pushed Gerald's new baby blue Comet station wagon up and down the dirt streets behind our house to coax it to start. Jean Carroll used to say that when Gerald started his Comet, it sounded like some-body flushing the toilet. So it made her day when dependable old "Leaking Lena" was called into service behind that new and shiny car because it wouldn't start.

Some of the precocious boys at school stole a number of gas tank caps from Lena, leaving her tank open to public stares and allowing gasoline to evaporate. Gas tank caps cost five or six dollars, so after buying two or three, it made no sense to keep replacing them. After all, the whole car had cost only fifty dollars. I borrowed an idea that I had seen other people use: I squeezed a doubled thickness of alu-minum foil to fit over the top of the tank that protruded from the back fender. The foil needed changing periodically, and it didn't look so good, but the boys never bothered it again.

No, she wasn't pretty! And she was old! But she was dependable. She was affordable, and she rose to the occasion when it came to transporting the children and me. When we moved from the area to our next appointment in Eight Mile, Alabama (near Mobile), we were not certain that she could make the trip, so we sold her for fifty dol-lars, our original investment. Though she is no longer a part of our family, there are times, even now, when we think of her, and we speak in affectionate, grateful, almost reverent tones as we relive the happy times spent inside dear old "Leaking Lena."

I Played Bass

Is it my imagination, or do we really work at making good impressions? I do not recall that I was specifically taught to act in such a way as to make a good or lasting impression on my associates or casual observers, but on my own, I recognized the subliminal concept that I could expect favor in the eyes of others in direct proportion to the efforts I invested to impress them. Is this concept one of those traits that is a part of my DNA? Is it genetic?

As a child, I expected, anticipated, and bathed in the praise Grannie lavished on me each time I filled the stove wood box. On the other hand, I worked as hard as I could to impress my father, but I never got his attention, let alone his approval. Studying hard and being prepared during class and test times certainly made a good impression on my teachers. Honesty and dependability were the traits that impressed Miss Louise Lang when she hired me to work in her country store on Saturday afternoons. I didn't have a large wardrobe of expensive clothes, but I dressed as cute as I could, curled my hair, and made myself as charming as possible for that certain cute boy that I worked so hard to impress. I am left to conclude, then, that at an early age I began working very hard to impress everyone who was impressionable!

However, this idea of impressing others did not end with my teens. It followed me through college and into my marriage. When I applied for a job, I made the best impression that I could because I wanted the job. In listing references, I did not necessarily list those who knew me inside and out, but I listed names of those who were well known for their achievements or their standing in the community. In all honesty, I must confess that I still get something of a superior feeling when I gracefully practice the fine art of namedropping. Whether consciously or subconsciously I do not know, but I believe that I somehow implanted within each of our children this same drive to impress others.

That same sense of impressing others was alive and well each time our family moved from one church to another. From the day that we moved in, it was easy to learn the things—every single one of them— that had not been accomplished by the minister who preceded us. I wanted so much for Gerald to be the best minister/pastor any of our churches ever had, so it became easy for me to take on far more responsibility in the churches than was prudent. Not only did I just naturally want to make a good impression, but when I heard members of the congregation talk about ministers' wives who were not "supportive" of their husbands, I was even more motivated to surpass them all.

After five years in Phenix City at the Epworth United Methodist Church, Gerald was appointed to the church in Eight Mile. As I shared our forwarding address, it became more and more hick-sounding: PO Drawer H, Eight Mile, Alabama.

"Hicks" or no, we found wonderful people in that congregation: people who were devoutly Methodist and who practiced their faith and supported their church. To name a few of those great people, Claudia Bleasdale lived across the church from the parsonage in which we lived. She taught both Mark and Mike in the first grade. The fact that there was a rocking chair in her classroom where she frequently rocked children on her lap impressed me. Ed Fitzgerald, a fireman, came countless times to the parsonage to start the Yazoo mower that was almost past going, and Mr. Smith, whose heart was not healthy, still came to help me pull the honeysuckle vines out of the large azalea bushes. I taught a Sunday school class of young people who met in the parsonage because there was no space available in the church. The class members had completed high school but did not feel that they were quite grown up, so we called ourselves the Misfits. Three young men entered the ministry while Gerald was pastor of that small congregation in Eight Mile, Alabama.

When Gerald arrived as the new minister, he wanted to make a good impression. He preached his best sermons, of course. He became the gregarious life of every party—and there were lots of those; not "parties" per se, but fellowship suppers. It became apparent that the time was right for this new minister to take on the huge project of remodeling and updating the existing facilities. The work began, and as with most such projects, things began to surface that were not part of the original plan but were nonetheless deemed necessary. It became quite obvious that the Eight Mile Methodist Church was in dire need of a new organ—and it was certainly not difficult to convince the organist.

Harry McDavid was the Lay Leader of the church. His wife Betty played the organ, and had for years. Harry's brother Joel had grown up in that congregation and became known to Methodism as Bishop Joel McDavid. Harry and Betty's son Neil answered the call to preach during Gerald's ministry there. One of the new responsibilities that fell to me as the new minister's wife was that of choir director. Betty and I worked well together, she at the organ and I directing the choir. It was a known fact that the old organ had served its time, and it really was time for it to go. A committee was organized, and the search began to find and purchase the best instrument for the church. This was serious business. Good Methodists were under a strong obligation to practice good stewardship of God's money, and so the committee prepared themselves to work hard at their assigned task.

The day came when the decision was made: a wonderful Baldwin organ was purchased and installed in the chancel of the church. This new organ was not a pipe organ; it was electronic and part of its insides contained tubes. I would be hard pressed to scientifically explain what happened, but on several Sunday mornings, a loud, commanding voice from the local radio station broke into worship, and was broadcast through the organ. Without a doubt, that was an unexpected interruption to worship. In fact, it was really frightening. Was God speaking? Was this some message that was being given as a divine directive? The mystery did not last long, however; some of the men understood what was happening, and with the help of the technician from the Baldwin Company, the problem was soon corrected.

The hard work Betty and I were doing began to pay dividends. The choir was growing in number and improving in quality—that is, if we forget that Easter sunrise service when the Baptist congregation joined our congregation for worship. The choir was rehearsed and ready! Betty was seated at the new organ. I rose, stood before the choir, and gave the down beat; Betty struck the first chord, and the choir with Easter fervor began to sing the Call to Worship. But there was a problem. The choir was singing and the organ was playing, but we were singing and playing two different songs—"Oh, worship the

Lord in the beauty of holiness …" and "The lord is in His holy temple…"—both at the same time. Upon hearing what was happening, the Easter "mezzo forte" faded rapidly into "pianissimo." We began at the same time, but while some continued to sing, others just stopped singing. Betty continued to play whatever she had begun, and when the sound ceased, I weakly motioned the choir to be seated and gladly collapsed into my chair. Not a single Baptist asked for a copy of our newly arranged call to worship.

Three free lessons came with the purchase of our new organ. Finally, Betty was able to arrange her schedule to take advantage of this special offer, but even though she went for the lessons, she still was not comfortable playing the bass pedals. She had played the keyboard of the old organ for years—much like playing the piano except with an organ sound. I kept feeling that this noble new instrument was not being represented in its best light when the bass pedals were silenced. I wanted our church people to be impressed with the complete harmonies that I knew were locked within. Then came a time when Betty and I talked about how we could make this happen. She understood that playing the bass pedals would add a great deal to her already good playing—so we worked out a plan.

Sunday evening worship was well attended in the '60s, and the Eight Mile Church was no exception. The congregation arrived. The "song service," which consisted of several spirited hymns—sometimes hymns that were requested by members in the congregation, and an appropriate hymn before the evening prayer—was well underway. I do not know if I was missed by the folks who came to worship that evening, but I was there—just not in my regular pew. A low wall separated the congregation from the chancel, where the organ resided. It served as a blind for the choir and others seated in that area. Betty was at her regular post on the organ bench, but what the congregation did not know was that I was on the floor, on the left side of the organ; I was holding a Cokesbury Hymnal on my lap, and I was playing the bass pedals! We were good!

Were those members within the walls of the church that night impressed that finally the organ music was complete with deep bass richness? Oh, I don't know. Betty and I thought they should have been. This was a once-in-a-lifetime experience, and I am convinced that no other organist or minister's wife can tell this same story. We were quite a team!

Betty is ninety-six now, still drives her car, and still plays the organ at the Eight Mile United Methodist Church. I very seldom see her, but I do occasionally see her daughter, and when I do, we always remember the night when Betty played treble and I played bass!

Bright Blessings from Grace

"If you tell what you are, you'll lose your power!" This was the response to my question, "Are you a witch?" Her black hair was pulled smoothly to the back of her head and fastened there. Her black eyes observed even the smallest detail. The smile that played about her lips gave me the distinct impression that she was toying with me as she sat cross-legged in the chair facing me across my desk. Her classic Greek beauty and features were a dead giveaway as to her nationality and roots.

It was the early 1970s, and I was Program Director of the Pensacola YWCA. New classes were beginning. Those interested and wishing to be assured a place in various classes had called earlier to pre-register. And though I knew who was coming, it was necessary for me to go back to the Y whenever night classes began. That evening, I was at my official post of duty to register the ladies for the newly formed yoga class. All of the ladies had arrived except Grace Efstathiou, so the class began without her. She finally did arrive, though tardy, and I suggested that she go directly into the class. I promised to wait to take care of her registration when the class ended. Mrs. Efstathiou went happily into her group, where class members were already assuming beginning yoga positions.

Upon completion of the class, Mrs. Efstathiou came to my office to pay her registration fee, as well as to complete information required on the membership card. She wore a black leotard and a white sweatshirt. She sat cross- legged as she pulled both legs into the large chair beneath her. She was perfectly content to sit there while I quickly read the information on her card. Everything appeared to be correct and in order until I got to the line that read: "In case of emergency, please notify _____." She had written the words "Yahweh, God" into the blank. I had never seen that very unusual answer given before, so I laughingly turned to her and said, "You know, I had always thought (and hoped) that if I had an emergency, God would already know—

262

and I wouldn't have to wait for somebody to notify him!"

From that point, the conversation began. Though I do not recall the exact progression of our discussion, I do recall that there were times during our conversation when I wondered what in the world Mrs. Efstathiou was talking about because what she said sometimes seemed to have no relevance to what was being discussed. Then things began to get really strange. Right out of the blue she said, "I see somebody who loves you very much!" That comment was followed by "She has a wonderful sense of humor!" followed by "You are surrounded by a large number of people who love and support you!" Suddenly it all became clear. I got it. She was some kind of a fortuneteller or palm reader or one of those people who had "supernatural" powers! I determined at that point that I would say nothing at all that would give her any information about my family or me. I was convinced that all those people were fakes anyway, even though it was common knowledge that my grandfather's sister possessed the power of divination. I was also told that, like Aunt Lou, Granddaddy Burton had "special" powers; but he never practiced or pursued them because he did not believe it to be compatible with his ministry.

All the while, Mrs. Efstathiou continued to verbally offer information about some person who I thought could well have been my grandmother. She continued, "She has a knot on the back of her head." I assumed that this statement was referring to the fact that Grannie combed her hair back and fastened it in a large bun at the back of her head. "She is a strong-willed person!" "She has crossed over to the other side now!" I became aware that this person sitting across the desk from me was looking at me as well as the wall behind my head. Then she made a statement that made it impossible for me to remain silent. She placed her fingers on the outside corner of each of her eyes as she said, "There's something funny about her eyes!" I slapped the desktop with the palms of both hands as I stood to my feet. I am certain that my voice betrayed the calm façade that I had so carefully put into place as I blurted out, "How did you know that?" Mrs. Efstathiou's calm response was, "I see her on the wall behind you!"

There was good reason that the statement about the eyes had gotten my undivided attention. Grannie was an invalid for the last five years of her life; she was bedfast. Each morning at bath time, we went

263

through the same routine with her eyes. As a part of the aging process, her lower eyelids had begun to roll in, thus causing the eyelashes to scratch and irritate her eyeballs. A simple surgical procedure could have corrected the problem, but Grannie was mortally afraid of surgery of any kind, so the surgery never happened. Instead, we carefully pulled her lower lid toward her temple and placed a small piece of Scotch tape at the outside edge of each eye, and it worked just fine.

Grannie had been dead for ten to twelve years when this conversation between Grace and me took place. I had completely forgotten about the eye problem, which had been insignificant to us even when she was alive. When I later reported this conversation to Lynn, our teenaged daughter, she asked, "Mom, did you look at the wall to see if Grannie was really there?" My reply? "Are you kidding? I did not take my eyes off that woman!"

Things had, by then, gotten to a place in our conversation where I was so curious about this person that I could hardly stand it. Who was she really? Did she possess some strange and unusual powers that made her capable of knowing personal things about my family and me? Was this experience authentic? She was not freely providing me with any information about herself. It was a given that I was going to have to ask pointed questions in order to learn what I wanted to know, so I began by apologizing, then asking forthrightly, "Are you a witch?" She ignored my question and spoke of other things. Now I must confess, at this point I was really confused. This whole conversation was maddening—she was playing with me. My curiosity had reached fever pitch! So I took a deep breath and tried again as I apologetically asked, "Mrs. Efstathiou, are you a witch?" She laughed at my uncomfortable awkwardness, and she said, "If you tell what you are, you'll lose your powers!" I had my answer!

We talked a lot that night about my father, who was also deceased. She told me that she knew that he was an alcoholic and that there was great tension between him and my grandmother. She made brief mention of my mother also. From that time I could hardly wait until the next yoga class, because Grace stayed afterward and we talked. I always had a million questions, and she patiently dealt with each one. I asked her during one of our visits why she had these special powers and I didn't! Her response was, "How do you know that you don't?" She continued, "If you are interested…" at which point, I quickly interrupted and said, "Not interested—just curious!"

We developed a friendship, Grace and I. I learned that she was a member of the Wicca religion and considered herself to be a white witch, which meant that she did only good things for people—never bad. Truthfully, she was strange. She talked strangely. She saw and interpreted things differently. She was employed by a local, well-established furniture company when she came to the YWCA that first night. It was not long until she lost her job, and a lawsuit ensued. She was fired for practicing her religion. Her family had long ago disassociated themselves from her. She had no money and no visible means of income. Sometimes she was able to tell a fortune, do a spiritual portrait or read the tarot cards for a few dollars. Her health began to fail and she was on dialysis for an extended period of time. She drove a small Ford station wagon whose floor was rusted through, and more often than not, she had no money to buy gas to drive herself to dialysis.

She told me once in a phone conversation that she had been to the grocery earlier, and had seen some perfectly beautiful strawberries that she could not afford. She was bitter as she asked why she could not have simple things like other people were able to afford, like strawberries. I slipped some money into an envelope and marked it "For Strawberries." I occasionally took her out to dinner, or would drop by her home with something that I thought she could use. I was instrumental in getting the youth from the Gulf Breeze United Methodist Church to spend one Saturday cleaning and raking her yard. She loved having our young people there, and she laughed as she described how curious they were as they tried to catch glimpses of her—this strange person. She told them lots of stories that I'm sure are remembered by some to this day.

Grace told me stories about an old monk living in her house who was several centuries old. According to her, he sometimes got a "bit rowdy" and made a lot of noise. Once lightning struck her house. The police and fire department responded, and she thought that it was the old monk causing the disturbance. The sheriff's deputies came on numerous occasions to issue a citation to court, and she did not answer the door—even though she was inside. She reported that she had not heard them, and she explained her behavior by saying, "That must have been when I was out of my body."

For some reason Grace felt indebted to me. She wrote lots of letters and notes, and usually somewhere on the letter or the envelope she wrote the words "Bright Blessings." She sent me small gifts; once it was a pair of monogrammed hand towels. I wondered if she also had skills in shoplifting, because I knew that she had no money to purchase them. Grace offered, almost pressed, to do a tarot card reading for me as well as a spiritual portrait, but I refused. I explained that she was my friend and that I would never take advantage of her by allowing her to do free services for me. Sometimes now I wish that I had accepted the offer of a spiritual portrait, though I don't actually know what that is.

Grace and I often discussed our faith. Recently, I have remembered her saying, "If you tell what you are, you'll lose your powers!" Through the years, Gerald and I have known church members, or others, who for whatever reason felt it necessary to tell aloud as often as any would listen how Christian they were. For whatever reason, we have sometimes been skeptical as to the depth of the commitment of these folks. If they were, in fact, as Christian as they said, would it not be evident to all who observed? Say what you will about my friend Grace, the white witch. Perhaps she was right on target about people in general, and though she was referring to her own state of being, I am becoming convinced that when we who call ourselves "Christians" feel the necessity to tell what or who we are, we lose our power.

Grace has "crossed over" now, and I miss her! My prayer for her is that she has found peace, good health, friends who love her for the eccentric person that she is—and strawberries.

Somewhere Between Dumb and Dumber

It was a cold, rainy afternoon in Pensacola, Florida. The day was nearly dark because of a thick cloud cover, even though the sun had not actually set according to the almanac. The streetlights were beginning to come on. If people working in the city looked outside before they glanced at the clock, they might well have thought it was time to leave their places of employment and return to their homes for the night. It was truly a dark, cold, and rainy afternoon.

As program director for the Pensacola YWCA during the early 1970s, I initiated several significant inner-city programs. It was my great privilege to work with General Lane, Escambia County Commissioner, as well as Rev. B. J. Brooks, the local NAACP president. We were on the cutting edge as we identified and confronted some very explosive issues in Pensacola and Escambia County brought about by racism. Those years marked a time of real growth in our area.

New classes were quickly added to the few that existed when I began my work at the Y. The building became a beehive of activity as a result of the addition of yoga, sewing, tailoring, exercise (after the purchase of exercise equipment), upholstering, powder-puff mechanics, and others.

The Y was housed in a beautiful home that had belonged to a physician and his family many years earlier. It sat in the center of an entire city block and was bordered by a wrought iron fence. Huge oak and magnolia trees shaded the yard and provided a lovely backdrop for the building. The top portions of the tall double doors at the front of the house were gorgeous leaded glass. I loved watching the light play on their beveled edges, casting rainbows of colors as it was strained through their prisms. Those front doors opened into a large hall with hardwood floors. Within the vast expanse of the hall, there were tables, lamps, and comfortable chairs that beckoned visitors to "come in and linger awhile."

Pocket doors separated the three very large rooms on each side of the hall. In addition to those rooms, the first floor included a kitchen, office spaces, an exercise room, and baths. The second floor was designated as a residence for young women who were away from their homes and were either in school or working for the first time. Their parents felt a sense of security regarding their young person's safety if they were living in the Y. Besides, housing there was much less expensive than living in an apartment in town. I do not recall how many rooms there were upstairs, but there were always a number of girls and young women living there, and they were constantly coming and going. Seldom was the building empty. Daytime hours were filled with activities and classes; even newly formed night classes were bringing in good attendance.

I am not certain what day of the week it was, but I am guessing that it most likely was Friday. Activity had slowed to a near halt. Mrs. Woody and I were the only people in the building. There was not even a resident upstairs. Mrs. Woody was nearly seventy years old—maybe older. I thought of her as a very old lady, but I was also much younger then. She had worked many years as a receptionist in a doctor's office before she retired. She had good typing skills, and she answered the phone graciously, so she was an excellent "fill-in" staff person, particularly if and when the limited number of staff needed to be out of the office for any number of reasons. Mrs. Woody was diabetic, and as a result, she was extremely careful about her diet. She brought frozen lunches and cooked them at the Y on the days that she worked. Her feet gave her a great deal of trouble, so she always brought a pair of bedroom slippers to wear throughout the day.

That afternoon, Mrs. Woody and I sat working in the same office since there was no one else in the building when suddenly a young black man stood in the doorway beside Mrs. Woody's desk. I became aware of his presence about the same time that she did. I asked if we could help him, and he explained that he was looking for work. I responded that we had all of the employees that were needed at that time. He continued to stand in silence. Long silences have always made me uncomfortable, so I asked if he had been to the grocery store down the street to inquire about work. He answered that he had. In fact, he said that he had been every place about which I asked. I finally asked his name and phone number and offered to call him in the event that I should hear of any job openings. He gave me "a" name and "a" phone number; both proved to be erroneous when, out of curiosity, I later tried to reach him.

By this time, I was beginning to feel a bit uneasy; no, to be more accurate, I was feeling very uneasy and quite vulnerable. Mrs. Woody was the only other person in the building, and only a slight glance in her direction revealed how frightened she had become. During my conversation with the man, as well as when things became very quiet, his eyes constantly moved about the large, unoccupied building—first up the stairs that led to the residence, then to the other large rooms, always returning to the office and the old-fashioned safe with its door standing wide open. There was never a great deal of money inside, but I knew that this young man did not know that.

I looked away from Mrs. Woody as much as possible because I was personally frightened enough without observing her panic. In my assessment of this young man, I considered him to be a school dropout, possibly unemployable because of his rather slow mental acuity. I was convinced, however, that he had a plan, and that he had every intention of carrying it out.

I felt completely unprepared to handle the situation in which poor old Mrs. Woody and I were caught. I was convinced that I had to do something, and that I must do it quickly. I don't know if I actually prayed, but suddenly my moment of insight and inspiration came. This was going to be a battle of the wits, and though I felt dumb and ill-equipped, I knew I was going to have to try something—prepared or not. I quickly assessed where we were.

It was late in the afternoon, and it was nearly dark.

We were inside a very large building that was located in the center of a city block. We would not be heard if we screamed our heads off.

My husband, then minister of the Gulf Breeze United Methodist Church, was probably visiting members of the congregation or those in the hospital. I actually hoped that he might have gone home to be with the children since the day was so gloomy.

My plan was beginning to form, and it just might work if I could carry out my part! As casually as possible, I picked up the phone and dialed the minister's office at the Gulf Breeze United Methodist Church: 932-3594. The phone rang once…twice…and I began my conversation while the ringing continued on the other end: "Hello!

This is Sara Munday at the Y. I was just wondering if your group is still planning to come today since the weather is so terrible. [long pause] You must be kidding! [pause] Oh, great! So a whole busload will be arriving here in about three minutes? I'll get the lights turned on and meet them at the front door!"

I quickly replaced the telephone receiver and started around the desk to "get the lights turned on." The young black man, who was still standing in the office doorway listening carefully to my telephone conversation, turned on his heel and made a mad dash for the back door of the building. He did not bother to close the door behind him. He jumped down the six or seven concrete steps to the sidewalk, and as he jumped, another youth hiding in the shrubbery just outside the door joined him in fleeing from the building. They were quickly lost in the darkness of the rainy afternoon.

I did not mind one bit closing the back door behind him. In fact, I hastily closed and *locked it*, along with all the other doors in the building. Poor old Mrs. Woody padded along behind me in her bedroom slippers, wringing her hands all the while. Her face was ashen and reflected the terror we had just experienced. It was amazing to see her recovery level move up a notch as each additional door was locked and secured. While we walked from door to door, she kept chattering about how brave I was; that I was a real hero; and how did I ever think to make that fake phone call? When all the doors were finally locked, and the police were called, Mrs. Woody and I sat down and breathed a deep sigh of relief!

Mrs. Woody's initial report of the incident, as well as any later conversation, reported me as courageous, brave, smart, brilliant—a hero! The dictionary definition of brave is "willing to face danger, pain, or trouble; not afraid." I must admit that I enjoyed hearing Mrs. Woody's account of my fearlessness. However, as I recall that experience, I would never have been "willing" to face that young man on that winter afternoon, and I was literally scared to death. I think that "brave" was a much-too-extravagant description of what happened. Perhaps "survival" should somehow be thrown into the mix. Or who knows? As ill-prepared and uninformed as I was to face that young man, maybe in that incident I was a bit "smarter than the average bear." Maybe I did believe that I could outwit him! At least, I surely did have to try! Perhaps the real truth was that a battle was waged that afternoon between Dumb and Dumber—and for the life of me, I do not know which I was!

The Ugly Green Blanket

Our nights had gotten cooler, and as is my custom at this time each year, I put an additional blanket on our bed. In the process, I was reminded of how often a single simple act triggers a veritable flood of memories. This time, I was overwhelmed by memories of Christmases from my past.

Some years ago a songwriter convinced everyone who paused long enough to listen to his words that "There's no place like home for the holidays!" My heart knows that to be an undeniable fact, even though I am conversely persuaded that "you can't go home again!" I am convinced that there is no season in the calendar that can vaguely compare to Christmas—Christmas, that season that holds us captive, not only with thoughts and activities centered on "the things that Santa Claus will bring," but by an enlarged, exaggerated focus on love, hope, joy, and peace that somehow magically comes with the season.

I was about twelve years old when Mother and Grannie took us children to Meridian, Mississippi, to do our modest Christmas shopping. It seems quite possible to me now that they perhaps had some shopping of their own to do. We were allowed to shop alone and at our own pace as long as we stayed inside Kress's or Newberry's, two five-and-ten–cent stores located next door to each other. Though many years have passed, I can still see the dazzling radiance of the large display of glassware beneath brilliant counter lights. I was immediately drawn to a small pitcher and eight glasses. Every piece of the set was trimmed with a gold band and a graceful design of grapes and leaves that sparkled like diamonds. The price tag read $1.29 or $1.39 for the set; but I could afford it. I had worked hard to earn money for Christmas. From my first sight of that gorgeous set, my childish heart knew that it was going to be my grandmother's gift. She had lots of other pitchers and glasses, but I never gave that a thought. I proudly placed Grannie's gift beneath our huge Christmas tree. The tree, a cedar cut from our pasture, was decorated with paper chains and snow whipped from Ivory Snow soap flakes, along with icicles and tinsel garlands that had been used for many Christmases before. I waited impatiently through the days that remained until Christmas Day, the time when Grannie would open her gift and I would hear her say how beautiful it was.

Years passed. I was grown, married, and the mother of three wonderful children. Our family was caught in the pre-Christmas hustle and bustle, and we found ourselves trying to remember if we had all bases covered. It was daughter Lynn's custom to spend long hours in her room as she made special preparations for this much-anticipated season. She loved keeping her surprises in her room, which was strictly "off limits" to "all creatures great or small." On the other hand, our middle child, Mark, was quiet, unassuming, and always available to lend a hand. His preparations never seemed to take on frantic dimensions; rather, he was deliberate and methodical at carrying out his plans. It wasn't that he did not enjoy Christmas and all that it entailed, for I cannot recall a single time when he was not prepared with thoughtful, special gifts. The sweetness of his spirit and his ready availability to bring in wood or take out ashes or any other chore that needed doing gave us the feeling that underneath were his very strong arms.

Wonderful aromas floated from the kitchen, indicating that Christmas baking had begun. The fire in the living room snapped and crackled as it cast a tranquil spell that reached to the farthest and darkest corner of the room. Gifts were mounding up beneath the tree, and I was of the impression that everything had been accomplished. At long last, the Munday family was prepared and waiting for the arrival of Christmas.

During all of the busyness, I had failed to observe that our youngest child, Mike, was carefully taking stock of every gift beneath the tree. Upon completion of his inventory, he concluded that there were not enough gifts under the tree for "his mom" (me). Mike was not at all pleased with that fact, but that was something that could be solved. He always had a plan; it just needed to be worked out. He was too young to drive, but Lynn agreed to take him to town so he could purchase all the things needed to fill my stocking to overflowing. Early Christmas morning, I happily opened my gifts to find a singing teakettle with a copper bottom and a *Better Homes and Gardens Cookbook* from a very proud and smiling Mike. It did not matter one bit that I already had a cookbook just like the new one.

These gifts are still a part of our household and are so precious to me, though one gift I *gave* to my grandmother and the other gift I *received* from Mike. I look forward to a quiet time each Christmas when I can dredge up those same deep, compelling emotions that shrouded each piece as a newly given gift.

My family lived in Grannie's house as we grew up. She loved us, disciplined us, and provided most of our financial support. Without exception, she expected the very best from each of us children. Grannie's death in 1964 left an enormous hole in our hearts, but half a century later, her admonitions and expectations are still compelling directives. My Mother was ninety-two years of age and living in a nursing home in 1999. In the spring of that year, she divided her belongings among her four children. One of the things that came to me was a small glass pitcher and eight glasses, each with a gold band around the top and a design of grapes and leaves that sparkled like little diamonds when the light struck them just right.

I am filled with nostalgia each time I look at that gift which I chose with such love. Grandmother always had time to read to us. She often had molasses bread ready for us when we came home from school, and it was always warm enough to melt homemade butter. During World War II, when sugar was rationed, Grannie never seemed to mind sweetening her coffee with honey or molasses in order to save the sugar for "the children." In looking at that gift from so many years ago, my sincere prayer is that I may touch the lives of my own grandchildren with the same depth of love and expectation with which Grannie touched us; and when they grow to be grandparents like me, that they still feel my genuine love and inspiration even though my audible voice may have been silenced for a long, long while.

Today I remember Mike, who probably loved Christmas more than the other children—Mike, whose joy was in giving, and whose list of people to whom he gave grew ever longer and longer. It was not unusual to have him call at very strange hours, day or night, with a request for a little help with his Christmas shopping: a size, perhaps? Maybe a color? He never talked a long time because he was always in a hurry to get on with his shopping, but he never failed to end his hurried calls with "Merry Christmas, Mom! I love you!" Mike died in 1989, twenty years ago—what a long time—and yet his little teakettle still sings and I can see his happy face on every page of my cookbook. Mike's call from the mall has become a tradition—a part of every Christmas since he died. Lynn calls now from some unexpected place at some unpredicted time. So whether I am making pie crust or the singing teakettle is signaling that the water is hot or it is Lynn calling to say, "Hi, Mom! This is your call from the mall!"—I can still hear Mike saying, "Merry Christmas, Mom! I love you." And at that moment, I breathe a prayer that all mothers everywhere will hear those same cherished words: "Merry Christmas, Mom! I love you!"

What was it about adding a blanket to our bed that triggered all of these memories? The answer to that is easy: it was the blanket itself. It was a Christmas gift from my mother many years ago. Like other mothers, my mother had her own personal collection of tailor-made eccentricities. For some unknown reason, she thought that she should show absolutely no partiality to any one of her children, and so on numerous occasions that philosophy translated to mean that we each got exactly the same gift. In the Year of the Blankets, there were four large, soft, gift-wrapped packages under the tree: one for Gerald and me, another for Wrenn and Jack, one for Burton and Marydean, and the fourth for Howard and Janice. Each of us received a blanket that year. I do not remember if they were the same color, but ours was chartreuse, that terrible bilious green that matched nothing. The color has neither dimmed nor faded with the passage of time. Grannie used to say, "Beauty is skin deep, but ugly is to the bone." I had the feeling that those words were spoken of our blanket. Actually, I suspect that even Mother did not like the glaring shade of the fabric from which our blanket was made, but it was a bargain.

We still have that blanket, even though we could have given it away any number of times to people who would have been so grateful to have it. It is on our bed again this year, where it has been every year since it was given to us. A strange thing happened to me as I tucked it in around the corners of the mattress. I realized that I was having a mental conversation with Mother, who died on Valentine's Day 2001. I wondered if she had known how much I disliked that shade of green. In something of an apologetic attitude, I began to search for all the redeeming features of that blanket. I observed that the ribbon with which it is bound is neither frayed nor worn. It is still intact. The fabric does not have the first hole in it. That in itself seems quite unusual after all these years. Mother never had much to spend on anything other than necessities, so her frugality stood her in good stead. It seemed to me that her dollars always went much further than most of the people I knew. She often purchased one big gift for each family— a gift that included everybody. I laughed quietly to myself as I realized that Mother had probably come upon a bargain. Maybe she found at least four blankets on sale, and she bought them all (regardless of color), and they became Christmas gifts for each of her children.

As I smoothed the wrinkles from the blanket, I suddenly felt deeply grateful for such a practical and durable gift. As I continued in my awkward way to make amends for my ungrateful attitude, the good qualities of this chartreuse blanket continued to surface. I became aware for the first time that this is the one blanket we reach for each year as cooler days arrive. It is large enough to amply cover the bed as well as those who rest beneath its protection—and it still keeps "Mama's children" warm.

Christmas is the special time and season when a magic chain forged from collected memories anchors us to our roots and binds us again to the stuff from which we came.

Christmas Is...

There was a time when we were young
When we, too, dreamed of sugarplums.
And in our dream, so very clear
Were Santa's sleigh and his reindeer;
And gifts piled high beneath the tree
Would bring surprise and fill with glee.
The tinsel gleamed in firelight's glow
And lovers kissed 'neath mistletoe.
And o'er it all there beamed a star
Which spoke of God—so near—so far—
Christmas was a wondrous time!
The years slipped past. And there came to be
Children beneath our family tree;
It became our turn to bring surprise
With gifts and trees and pecan pies.
As life has led us door to door
We've gathered friendships by the score.
And we saw manger, shepherds, kings,
And mankind hearing angels sing—
And baby Jesus, meek and mild
Who came to dwell with men awhile.
Christmas was a joyous time!
Now countless memories crowd our mind
Of those we've loved—and left behind—
Of cherished friends we'll ne'er forget
Of joyous days; yet—some regret.
Though time has passed, some things remain
Like trees and gifts and candy canes;
And children's eyes still dance with glee
As they love, and laugh, and play carefree.
Today we pray *the Prince of Peace*
To come again that strife will cease!
To bless our children where they are
To embrace our friends both near and far—
To bring to all *love, health,* and *peace*
Abundant *joy, hope,* and *release.*
Christmas is a holy time!

Speaking of Angels

Angels are perceived as heavenly beings with greater-than-human powers attributed to them. The Psalmist said that "man has been made a little lower than the angels," thus making angels superior to humankind in God's pecking order (Ps. 8:5). We sometimes forget that there are also supernatural beings with greater-than-human powers that are bad as opposed to good. Numerous stories and accounts of angelic creatures contained in the pages of Holy Writ seem to point to the fact that angels have a specific task or mission. They never appear to be wandering about looking for something to do. It would seem safe to conclude, then, that they were messengers of God—or messengers of the Powers of Evil.

An occurring and reoccurring question in my own mind is why we do not speak as naturally and literally of angels today as those folks who lived generations before us. When I focus on these thoughts for any extended time, I begin to feel cheated in that I have not known and shared in the presence, songs, inspiration, and divine intervention of angels. Actually, I do not know of anyone who has literally witnessed the presence of an angel or angels. Still, many of us, during times of deep need and spiritual depravity, have experienced reassuring peace or perhaps a warm feeling that we have attributed to "the presence of angels." I have come to grips with both my limitations and my depravity, and many times I seek and rely upon the presence of the supernatural to accomplish those things that I cannot. Since we are not able to see angels ascending to and descending from Heaven, have we in our own minds relegated them to the pages of the Old and New Testaments? I think not. There seems to be too much evidence to the contrary.

Our lives, our theology, our romance are filled with angels, but I believe there are other angels: those angels who live among us that we never recognize as angels. Dale Evan's little book entitled *Angel Unaware* was written about her severely handicapped daughter Robin, who lived a brief two years, and though most of us would not have thought of Robin as an angel, Dale Evan and Roy Rogers did.

"Be not forgetful to entertain strangers: for thereby some have entertained angels unawares" (Heb. 13:2).

There have been many people in my life who have done the work of angels. They have brought me messages of good will and good cheer! They have helped me discover security and foundation when my whole world was shaking! They have brought music and singing into my life! They have brought light to my darkened path and inspiration to my seeking heart! They have brought hope when there seemed to be no way! They have given love and support when I was not able to stand on my own! I cannot begin to name them, and I will not even try, but I do want to describe one special event in my life for which I have no explanation.

The year was 1987. We were at Emory Hospital in Atlanta, Georgia, where Gerald had survived an extremely tedious and difficult shunt procedure in the hope that his badly diseased liver would sustain his life for a while longer. After leaving the intensive care unit, he spent one sleepless, fear-filled night in a private room. He was not at all aware of what he was doing or saying. He was agitated and restless. All the while he was attempting to get out of the bed to go who knows where.

When the nurse who spent much of that night in our room came on duty the next afternoon, she came by Gerald's room to check on him, even though she was not going to be his nurse. She quickly observed his agitated state, assessed his vital signs, and calmly asked, "Where are your children?" She added that I needed to have them with me. I explained that Gerald had been so restless that I was not able to leave his bedside. She promised to stay with him until I could make the call.

As I was leaving the room, the surgeon came in. He wrapped the blood pressure cuff around Gerald's arm, but never took his pressure. His sensitive, skilled fingers were upon the pulse in Gerald's elbow. After just a touch, he hurriedly left the room. Before I realized what was happening, the room was filled with young doctors and nurses. One of them quickly inserted a breathing bag into Gerald's mouth and began pumping air into his lungs while another unplugged his bed.

We were suddenly out of the room, and I was running to keep up with those dedicated young people who were taking my husband (bed and all) down the hall. We reached the nurses' station. The surgeon was at the desk, and he tossed Gerald's chart onto the bed as we passed. One of the nurses held the elevator by the Coke machine. The elevator trip was not long, and we were again running down the hall. This time it was into the Intensive Care Unit. I was stopped at the door. I suddenly was alone. It was obvious that Gerald needed all of the attention at that moment.

William, a young black man, was a nurse in the ICU. He came outside and sat with me a few minutes. He learned that I had not eaten, so he quickly got a Coke and some cheese crackers for me. He made a call to the chaplain on duty to let him know about our crisis situation. William was gay—but he ministered to me. Surely God had sent him. Was he an angel?

As I sat outside the window of my husband's ICU room, I listened to the doctors and nurses working feverishly with him. I heard them as they ripped off rubber gloves, or pushed the bed around, or called out orders to each other as they were putting my husband on a respirator. I suddenly realized that I was alone, and I began to pray. It was not long until I was aware of others who were present. They were very near me. I do not know where they came from. I was only aware of three or four beautiful ladies with dark hair. They hugged me, assured me of their prayers, and said that if I should need them, they would be near. They gathered at the end of the corridor, talked softly, and were there for most of the night. When morning came, they were gone. I did not see them again. Surely God had sent them. Were they angels?

Are there angels among us? There must be! Are there angels in human form? There seems to be evidence to support that. Are we all angels? Well, maybe each of us is an angel to somebody. I hope so. However, as we explore the possibility that we may be an angel to someone, we are forced to remember our own humanity and to accept our imperfection and incompleteness. I love Leo Buscaglia's statement regarding this. He said, "Each of us is an angel with one wing, and we can fly only as we embrace each other."

Recycled—Restored

March 14 and 15 will forever be days of thanksgiving for our family. As I write today, we are gratefully celebrating the tenth anniversary of Gerald's liver transplant. During those difficult yet exciting days, I kept a journal that continues to serve as an accurate account of all I felt and experienced, as well as what actually took place with Gerald as a patient. As I read and reread the words I wrote then, I experience again the heights and depths of such emotions as fear, gratitude, joy, hope, and sympathy that packed every hour of every day.

Gerald and I had dreamed, hoped, and prayed for a liver transplant since we received the grave news that his liver was severely damaged by hepatitis C. We came to understand in 1987 how critical his condition was when he experienced an esophageal bleed. We learned that the cirrhosis (or scarring) that had occurred and was continuing to occur in his liver would shorten his life. It became clear that he would ultimately need a liver transplant.

In August 1994, we went from Gulf Breeze, Florida, to Emory Hospital in Atlanta, Georgia, for the thorough and comprehensive workup to determine whether or not Gerald would be a viable candidate for transplant. We feared that he would not be accepted because he was too old (sixty-two years) and he was a hemophiliac.

Hemophilia had been a terrifying shadow under which Gerald had lived and functioned since birth. Any injury or surgery was handled with extreme care and utmost caution. In 1970 it became apparent that his gallbladder needed to be removed, and only one surgeon in Pensacola agreed to do the surgery. However, after a night of study in the medical library at Sacred Heart Hospital, that last local doctor decided that he could not go up against Gerald's bleeding disorder—even though it was a mild form. Three hospitals were suggested to us as possibilities for surgery: Emory in Atlanta; Oschners in New Orleans; and Duke in Raleigh, North Carolina. The local medical staff provided pertinent medical information and made necessary contacts and arrangements.

Emory Hospital accepted Gerald as a patient. The first step toward making surgery less risky was to raise his blood clotting to a level considered to be safe enough to attempt surgery. That level was maintained through surgery and for an extended time following surgery in order that healing could occur. This was accomplished by administering "factor eight" extracted from hundreds of units of blood donated by countless donors. From some of those donors came hepatitis C (then referred to as non-A non-B hepatitis). For seventeen years the hepatitis ate away at Gerald's once-healthy liver. His esophageal bleed in 1987 served as a wakeup call to the grim fact that his liver was in a very unhealthy state. The hemophilia again became "a force to be reckoned with." If they attempted to inject the bleeding varix with a clotting medicine, there could possibly be additional bleeding from the needle puncture. There was no hands-on control to stop the bleeding if that should occur.

According to the doctors in Meridian, Mississippi, there was little to no hope! Maybe he had five minutes to live, maybe five days—who could say? I asked for help in getting a second opinion. After twenty-four hours, the only thing the attending physician told us was, "My nurse called the Hemophilia Foundation and their line was busy." Gerald, the children, and I were filled with nothing but emptiness! It became obvious that we had a lot of work to do if we were going to find help for Gerald. We had to find a hospital and staff who would accept him as a patient, and the medical professionals in Meridian offered no help at all in that endeavor. Our lives and times had suddenly become very uncertain. I knew that whatever we did must be done quickly. Lynn remained at the hospital with her father; Mark and Mike got on the phone to find a hospital, and I set about closing the Maytag appliance store that we owned.

The Warren shunt, or the splenal renal shunt, was the procedure needed to save my husband's life. Dr. Dean Warren, who had developed this procedure, was Chief of Surgery at Emory Hospital, and it was he who ultimately did the surgery on Gerald in May 1987. There actually were two very difficult surgeries during that hospitalization. Gerald became septic following the first procedure, and it became necessary to reopen him. After fifty days (thirty-five of which were spent in the ICU), Dr Warren readily admitted that Gerald had presented a significant challenge, and that even as he was discharged, there still remained many unanswered questions.

Dr. Warren's skilled hands and brilliant mind carefully made the essential realignment of Gerald's spleen and kidneys in order to bypass the liver and take pressure off the portal vein. He explained that the life expectancy of the shunt was probably about five years, after which Gerald would need a liver transplant. His life had been extended. We gladly accepted a five-year outlook with the hope that procedures and techniques would be much improved by that time. His recovery from that procedure required a year, and all the while the scarring and deterioration of his liver continued. Extensive workups requiring several days at Emory were done approximately every six months. Finally, in August of 1994, seven and a half years after the shunt procedure, Gerald was evaluated and accepted as a viable candidate for a liver transplant.

On September 6, 1994, Gerald's name was placed on the national registry for a liver transplant. I secured a pager on that date and was never without it for the next 189 days. There were numerous false "beeps" during that time. Even though we were warned that this frequently happened with pagers, each "false beep" was quite emotional. With each "beep" I called Emory with great expectations, only to have them tell me that it had been an erroneous ring. Each time they assured me that they were working diligently for us, and that they would call as soon as there was an organ available. Every ring of the phone intensified our already fevered pitch of expectation. Days came and went, and I repacked our luggage as the weather changed from hot to cold and back again.

The transplant coordinator at Emory helped us finalize plans so that we could leave quickly if and when the time ever came. We made arrangements for our dog Rudy to stay with Shonna Shanahan. I set up telephone trees so our friends and relatives would know within minutes that we were on our way. They had been and were continuing to pray for us, so we wanted them to know before we ever reached Atlanta and Emory Hospital that the moment for which we had waited had finally arrived.

On March 14, 1995, I called transplant coordinator Rebecca Butler with questions. She was wonderful at keeping us calm throughout those turbulent days. During that call, she encouraged us to make an appointment with Dr. Orth, a local internist. She thought that we needed to see a doctor rather than limiting our medical information to lab reports and living with numbers only. I agreed to call his office that afternoon. In the meantime, Rebecca would also call him to provide initial medical information. I was in touch with Emory that day because Gerald's condition was rapidly deteriorating. Toxins from his liver were causing a great deal of mental confusion. He looked dreadful—as though life were slipping quietly away. His eyes were yellow. His face was so jaundiced that he appeared to have a deep tan. His movements were slow. His strength was ebbing away. Though he had been in physical therapy for months, he had become so weak that it was necessary to lower him into the pool by means of a lift. He was determined that his body should be in the best shape possible when (and if) the opportunity came to go for his transplant.

I never made the appointment with Dr. Orth. About three and a half hours after Rebecca and I talked, she called again. This time she said, "Mrs. Munday, this is Rebecca. We have a liver for Mr. Munday." Somehow I think I had not really expected this time to ever arrive! I was in a complete state of shock. I could not believe the words I was hearing. I stupidly asked, "Are you sure? Tell me again." Then I asked, "What shall I do next?" She quietly responded, "Since you are going to fly, call the airport to be sure that the plane is ready." I was back on track!

It was about three P.M. I quickly turned to my list of things to do that had been outlined months before. I knew that time was of the essence, and that we must move swiftly. Mark came from work in Fort Walton Beach. He drove us to the airport and kept our car overnight. In addition to the luggage that we took with us, the car was packed for an extended stay. The next day, Mark drove our car to Atlanta and left it as transportation for me while we were there. We would also need it when it was time to go home. Lynn came from Crestview to meet us at the airport. Her bags had also been packed for months, since the plan was for her to go to Atlanta with Gerald and me. It was almost too perfect that Lynn was at home when I called. It was not her usual custom to pick Ashley up at school and take her home, but on March 14, 1995, she did just that. Aaron and Ashley helped in her final preparations to leave. Aaron drove her car as he and Ashley returned to Crestview. Craig was caught in traffic as he left Eglin Air Force Base, and was fearful that he would delay our departure if he tried to get to the airport; so he called and said that he was not going to try to make it. Kay was transporting children from place to place, so it was impossible to get everybody to the airport for the big sendoff.

Mark, Gerald, and I arrived at the airport about four thirty P.M.— just briefly before Lynn, Aaron, and Ashley. The plane that was scheduled to take us to Atlanta "where the liver and Mr. Munday are supposed to meet" (according to the Medicare representative) had developed a mechanical problem. Black smoke was pouring from one of the engines. But Judy Roach, who had known our plans for a long time and was responsible for scheduling the plane, was not going to allow anything to keep us from our destination if there were any way possible. She quickly had a Leer jet on the way from Marianna, Florida. The change in our transportation meant that our flying time would be reduced—which was just fine with us.

We departed Pensacola at five twenty P.M. under cloudy skies with gusty winds. After a relatively smooth flight of forty minutes, we

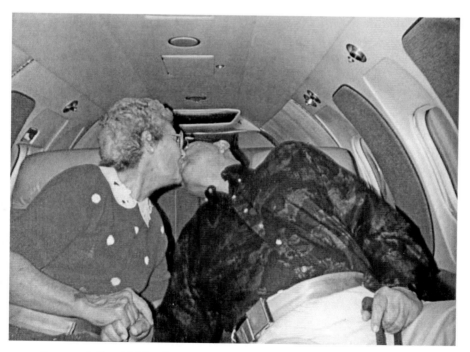

Sara and Gerald Munday in flight to Emory Hospital for liver transplant.

arrived at Cobb Peachtree Airport in Atlanta at seven P.M. The pilot radioed ahead, and to our great delight, a taxi awaited us on the tarmac. When the driver learned what was happening, he was almost as excited as we were. It was dusk as we rode through the streets of Decatur. The radio played soft jazz as Gerald and the driver conversed pleasantly. Lynn and I held hands in the back seat. By seven thirty or seven forty, we were on the ninth floor of Emory Hospital. We had arrived about two hours before we were expected. Were we anxious? Without a doubt!

It was finally happening. A nurse took Gerald's medical history; an aide checked his blood pressure and temperature. Though weak, Gerald was in high spirits. His sense of humor was responsible for a lot of shared smiles that eased some of the tension as the process continued. We were fast becoming a team! Two young doctors came to get Gerald's medical history updated. As they left the room, it was with the promise that they would return to do a physical exam. They had earlier ridden up the elevator with us, and had recognized Gerald as the patient who would have their full attention that night. One of them said, "Mr. Munday, we were looking for you—but not so soon!"

A doctor from the anesthesia department was with us when two men and a woman entered the room with a gurney. They had come to wheel the patient away to a new liver and a better life. Lynn and I walked beside the gurney as far as we were allowed to go. We kissed our smiling Gerald, and the doors to the elevator closed. It was then about eleven thirty P.M. We went to wait in the 5E ICU waiting room.

Around midnight, a handsome young man approached us and identified himself as Dr. Steiber. He informed us that he would be doing Gerald's surgery. His eyes were bright as diamonds as he eagerly faced this new challenge with all of its possibility. I felt that he was much too young to carry such heavy responsibility, but through the course of the next weeks, I gained a deep respect—almost a reverence—for his depth, commitment, devotion, and skills.

Dr. Steiber explained that the first part of the surgery would be spent searching for a blood supply for the new liver. We had learned from an arteriogram seven months earlier that the portal vein was blocked. It had most likely closed due to lack of use since it had been bypassed with the shunt procedure. Since Gerald had had four previous abdominal surgeries (gallbladder, appendectomy, Warren shunt,

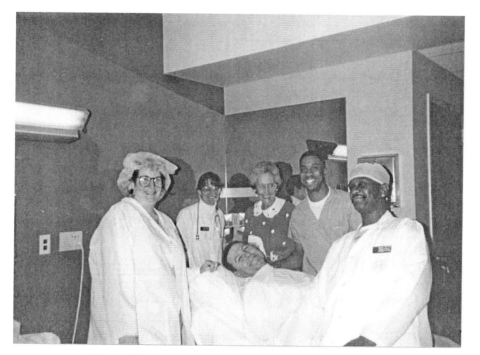

Emory Hospital staff as they transport Gerald to surgery

and reopening for sepsis), Dr. Steiber felt that it would be a lengthy process to locate a blood source due to the large number of adhesions. He agreed to let us know when he had accomplished that first hurdle—and we would then know if a transplant were an option.

Lynn and I began to refer to ourselves as "bag women" since all of our luggage was loaded into a wheelchair and we rolled it from place to place as needed .We had pillows and blankets, so we settled into chairs and sofas as we made at least some effort to sleep—or at least to be quiet. At 3:10 A.M., an ICU nurse came to tell us that Dr. Steiber just called from surgery to tell us that they had found a blood supply, and they were going to proceed with the transplant! What good news!

We were warned that this would be a long surgery, but Lynn and I had not realized how extremely long an hour could be. We literally noted every single minute as the hands of the clock on the wall pushed slowly past each one! The staff and personnel were extremely mindful and considerate of us. We were immediately taken into the circle of caregivers who waited anxiously but patiently near the ICU room where the ones they loved were confined as they fought to live.

Kathy McDonald, a psychiatric social worker, checked on us about eleven A.M. the following day. When she learned that we had had no word since 3:10 A.M., she went in search of information. She soon returned to inform us that at that very time, the *new liver* was being sewed into place! What a special time to receive word from surgery! They estimated that surgery would require another four to five hours. Mark arrived at 11:45 A.M. He probably had not slept well the night before and had driven the seven-hour drive from Gulf Breeze. Though he was very tired, he was fully restored and thrilled upon hearing the wonderful news from surgery that had just come to Lynn and me. The three of us went to lunch in the hospital cafeteria.

It was about three P.M. when a very tired Dr. Steiber came to where we waited outside Room 518 of the 5E ICU. This was to be Gerald's room as he came from surgery. Dr. Steiber was completely exhausted, so he chose to sit on the floor as we talked. The surgery had taken fourteen hours. Though the portal vein had been very difficult to locate, it was open and flowing. Dr. Steiber felt that although it was small, it would provide an adequate source of blood. Were the earlier reports of a closed or blocked portal vein incorrect? Had it been open all along? Correct or incorrect, no matter! I choose to believe that God in His great mercy had been and was continuing to be at work in our lives. Suddenly, we all felt drained!

Lynn and I went to the University Inn located on Emory's campus. It became our home away from home for the next few weeks. Mark decided to stay that night with his dad, who, by the way, looked good! His cheeks were pink instead of yellow. It had been a long but wonderful day! The work was done! It was over! We fell exhausted into bed, and as we slept we dreamed about a life recently restored—made possible by another life that had gracefully been recycled!

Letter to Our Donor's Family

August 1, 1995

To Our Donor's Family:

This is the most difficult letter by far that we have ever written. No doubt it will be equally difficult for you to receive and read. Nevertheless, we are compelled by our deep sense of gratitude to contact you via this letter to express our profound indebtedness to you. We regret that we are not adequately skilled to verbally express our deep appreciation and admiration for the generous and brave gift which you have given.

Only on extremely rare occasions are human beings placed in positions where, briefly, they are allowed to perform acts which are attributed only to God. We are referring specifically to your generous act of the unconditional gift of life to one whose days were numbered—and you gave when you were not able to hold on to life for one who was so precious to your family. What a magnanimous gift of life and courage!

Countless people are daily finding themselves in positions where they are literally watching the sands pour from the hourglass of their lives. And as the hourglass is nearly empty, it is only on extremely rare and special occasions that those same people are able to experience the reversal of the dying process. The reversal comes about when a courageous, loving, compassionate family makes a life-giving donation of a vital organ to replace the non-functioning organ in one who was realizing that he or she was nearing or even entering into the shadow of death.

March 14, 1995 will be a day which both of our families shall always remember. Both your family and ours grieve the loss of life for a very special twenty-five–year–old man. As parents, we understand such grief because our youngest son died when he was twenty-nine. As the liver transplant for my hus-

289

band was completed and healing was beginning for us, we were daily aware of the sorrow that you had experienced on March 14, 1995. We continue to be aware that you have faced and continue to struggle with grief every single day since that time.

We shall continue to pray for healing for your family as you cope with the pain of loss. We shall continue to be grateful to you for not allowing death to cheat you of the opportunity of giving life. In a strange and unique sense we feel that our family circle has been extended to include you. We shall never cease to be grateful to you for extending life to us when ours was virtually gone. Thank you.

We pray God's richest blessings for you...and for us...as we face tomorrow!

A Grateful Family

What a Day

It was only two days until the "big" day! When I thought about it, my stomach automatically flip-flopped and concurrently became the landing strip where millions of butterflies were practicing takeoffs and landings. The same haunting question kept flying through my mind: "What if nobody comes?" The question sounded a little like a slogan I had heard years before: "What if somebody gave a war and nobody came?" The conclusion to that matter was, of course, that people would not come and participate in war efforts because they had found something profoundly more productive to do with their time and energy—and there would be no war!

As a child, I somehow came to believe that I needed to earn love, respect, and approval, and that nobody could love me simply for the person that I was. There was, therefore, a residual fear that I might not be able to please my friends enough, and as a result they would withhold themselves from me. Couple that with the quote about someone's giving a war and it only reinforced my anxious question: "What if nobody comes?"

Despite the anxiety and trepidation regarding attendance of our special celebration, the invited guests did come!—from Florida, Georgia, Alabama, and Mississippi. Lynn, Craig, Mark, and Kay had worked tirelessly, day and night, to ensure that this day would be perfect. Printed invitations containing a warm personal message had been sent to our friends. In preparing the guest list, Gerald and I discovered that it was necessary to limit the list since God in His infinite love and generosity has allowed us to gather countless wonderful people whom we have been privileged to call "our friends" through the years. Even so, the list was long—and they did respond to our invitation! Thank goodness!

The special occasion being celebrated on this perfect day was that of our golden wedding anniversary. Fifty years of marriage! Where had the time gone? How could we possibly be at this time in our lives?

Answers to these questions became perfectly clear as we proudly looked around the room at our adult children, Lynn and Craig, and Mark and Kay, who so lovingly planned and became busily engaged in the process of seeing that their carefully laid plans became a living reality. Lynn's lovely daughter, Ashley, was the epitome of hospitality as she balanced her time between her boyfriend Bill and our invited guests. Mark and Kay's handsome sons, Ben, Philip, and Keith, were polite and attentive far beyond their teenage years. Ben felt comfortable enough to bring Michele, his girlfriend.

Gilmore Fellowship Hall at the United Methodist Church in Gulf Breeze, Florida, lent itself beautifully to the afternoon activities of October 5, 2003. That morning, the hall was filled with children and Sunday school teachers until about 12:15 P.M. Our party was set to begin at three P.M.; therefore an efficient use of time was essential. The setup process went so smoothly that one might have thought the work was being done by professionals who were well trained at their job.

A guest registry and pen rested upon a table located just inside the door. Beside the book was a black-and-white picture of a much younger version of Rev. and Mrs. Gerald Munday that had been taken as they exited the Emelle Methodist Church after having pledged their troth to one another on August 14, 1953. Miss Mary Neely Willingham grew up as a friend and peer of my mother. She watched me grow from infancy to a young, blushing bride. Mother and I asked her to decorate the church where my Grandfather had been a member, and where our family had belonged for at least three generations. Her creativity and hard work were evident on the day of our wedding. The small country church was resplendent with smilax that had come from local woods and large yellow chrysanthemums from the florist. Miss Mary Neely still found time to crochet a pair of white gloves, which I wore as we left on our honeymoon. The gloves, though a bit yellowed, were placed on the table along with the picture.

Pictures of our wedding, together with an assortment of family pictures, were scattered throughout the room. Numerous cards from well-wishers were shared. Our dear friend Lucia Pepper sent an arrangement of beautiful yellow roses (a dozen and a half long stems) that were a gorgeous part of the celebration. Bill and Barbara Hocutt, hindered by health reasons, were not able to come from North

Carolina, but a peace lily reminded us of their love and good wishes.

The book of Bridal Memories was placed so that any who wished could share the collected thoughts and treasures contained between its covers A yellowed news clipping of the wedding announcement was slipped between the pages. The garter that represented "something blue" was also there with the notation: "Something blue—the blue was on a garter in the form of a blue ribbon rosette. It had been worn first by Elizabeth Roberts Swarthout, then by her sister Vivian Roberts Valentine—then came my turn—after that, it was reserved for Wrenn." Wrenn, my sister, never wore the blue garter because she and Jack Weston eloped four days after our wedding.

Perhaps the dearest thing in the Bride's Book was a handwritten note from Josephine H. Swetnam that read as follows:

> Covington, Kentucky
> Dear little Girl:
> Would you carry this hanky for something old on your wedding day—I did 47 years ago last June; and I want you to have it. I dearly love Jerry; he was born next door to me, and his lovely Mother you also will love.
> I only wish I might be with you on the happy day. So much love.
> Fondly,
> Josephine H. Swetnam

I carried the hanky with a great deal of love and appreciation for a very special lady who cared enough for the Munday family to share such a precious, treasured piece from her past. Mom (Gerald's mother) and I went to see her after the wedding to express my appreciation. She was frail and in a wheelchair, but she was perfectly delightful. I left our brief encounter acutely aware that I had been greatly favored with this opportunity to visit with so loving and sensitive a lady. Her gift of a linen handkerchief with a lace border, though yellowed and a bit stained, has come to occupy a very special place in my heart.

Dennis Mitchell, a friend of Lynn and Craig's, came from Laurel Hill, Florida, to play the piano. He earlier researched the Internet to find what music was popular in the 1950s, so he arrived at our party well informed and prepared. He brought such a beautiful gift as he sat at the piano for two solid hours playing "our songs." He was not bound by printed music, for he brought none. He had not even made a list to jog his memory. He just sat and played, and the music flowed without a single break. What a gracious and talented young man he is! His graceful demeanor created the perfect romantic atmosphere for our special day of remembering and celebrating.

In retrospect, I do not believe that Gerald and I had ever thought much about, nor had we looked forward to, this day—our fiftieth wedding anniversary. Our lives always seemed filled with whatever we were working to accomplish at the moment. The full impact of "today's being a gift" became undeniably evident as we recognized our family, our friends, and this special celebration of joy, achievement, and uniqueness. This celebration was not something that we had taken for granted; in fact I suppose that we had never in our wildest imaginations expected this day to become a reality. Gerald's health has been so tenuous for so many years, and I think that we subconsciously understood that the odds were against our celebrating fifty years of marriage. We returned to Gulf Breeze in 1992 to be near our children when he was in the final stages of liver disease. His health grew progressively worse, and it appeared that death would come soon.

God, in His mercy, continued to faithfully provide life and strength for each day. Somewhere during that time, we began to recognize each day as truly a gift. In preparing for our party that was to celebrate fifty years of life together, I was suddenly overwhelmed by the fact that this day was not only a gift of God, but today had come to us as a true and generous gift made possible by a very special young man and his family. Had it not been for the gift of life made possible in the form of a liver transplant, there would have been no joyous occasion of such magnitude to celebrate. I quickly found the enlargement of a snapshot of the donor sent to us in 1995 by his grief-stricken parents. The picture had been on our refrigerator door since it came to us. I put the picture into a gold frame and placed it in an obvious place in the fellowship hall. Beside the picture was the beautiful greeting card from our donor's parents. Gerald, the children, and I made a special effort to share our story with every guest as we intentionally guided them to the picture that has become so precious to us.

Fifty years is a long time, but from this side of it, it appears to have

Gerald and Sara Munday's fiftieth anniversary

gone so quickly. Lots of good times; lots of joys; many challenges; lots of failures; wonderful achievements; some disappointments; our share of tears: each in their own way have helped to mold us into who we are. I loved the man I married fifty years ago, but I have discovered that I love even more the man he has become. Perhaps given another fifty years of marriage and the opportunity of working on each other, we will attain that much sought-after state of perfection!

When the Iron Is Hot

Most of our days are adequately filled, but some days are filled beyond what twenty-four hours can accommodate—not to mention the limitations that our personal lack of physical energy and stamina bring to the formula. This past Monday was just such a day. In fact, we began planning on Sunday, the day before, just how we were going to survive its demands. Lest I mislead anyone, I must explain that it really wasn't the large number of chores that overwhelmed us; it was the largeness of each chore.

Atmospheric pressure from recent hurricanes Ivan and Dennis had broken the seals on our double-paned windows, and they were becoming more and more fogged. After much waiting, the men from the window company were scheduled to replace every window in our house on Monday. They came as scheduled, worked the entire day until after dark, and completed the job in one day—with the exception of one broken sash. I admit it! I am naive about things that other people seem to instinctively know. I had no idea there would be plaster and concrete dust on everything in the house. Nothing was exempt. I am convinced that I shall be removing and cleaning this powdery dust for many days into the future. The important thing is that replacing the windows is now a completed job and is checked off our list.

Since we moved into this house almost two years ago, there has been an ongoing battle between us and the crabgrass in our lawn. I made a valiant effort last year to dig it out; however, I have learned that this plague is not easily discouraged. This year's crop was more green and lush than ever. I worked again in late winter/early spring this year at the removal of this unwanted intruder, and I created large bare spots in the lawn in the process. Gerald checked with several sod companies only to learn that it might not be easy to obtain the small amount of sod we required. He finally learned that one pallet would be available on Monday in Milton, so he planned to drive there to pick it up. On Sunday afternoon, he borrowed a trailer from our good neighbor, Joe Lyvers. They hitched it to the car that same afternoon so Gerald could make an early trip and return. We hoped that we could begin the project before the grass dried out. Gerald anticipated that it would take us several days to get it all down. To make things go a bit more smoothly, Joe agreed that we could keep his trailer in our yard until all the sod had been worked off it.

Upon his return, Gerald set about getting the sod into the bare spots. It became obvious that he was getting really tired, and to make matters even worse, his back was beginning to bother him. We discussed the plans for the day early that morning, and decided that I would stay inside the house since we did not know the workman who would be coming to do the work, and they would be working in and out of every room.

I have never been one to be idle; and since I had neglected the ironing for several days, I decided that Monday would be a perfect day for me to get that caught up, and that chore would allow me to stay inside the house. It is not as easy for me to iron as it used to be; my back hurts and my knees ache. Even though there was a lot of ironing to be done, it went fairly smoothly for me. In all honesty, it may well have been—and most likely was—because I took a stroll down Memory Lane with one of my favorite people: Sally.

Even though it was very early in the morning, we could still tell that the day was going to be hot. Grannie would say to one of us children, "Go out yonder and call Sally and see if she can come and iron today." We never had to be told twice to call Sally. She was the black woman who lived in the tenant house on the next hill. We had no phones, so we "hollered," and if one of us could not make Sally hear, then we all three called together. We were ecstatic when she answered that she would "be there directly."

We reported to Grannie that Sally was coming, then went immediately and took our seats on the front steps to watch for her. When we saw her coming, we ran as fast as we could to meet her so we could walk back with her. There was always a struggle as to which of us would get to hold her hands—she only had two and there were three of us. Each of us knew that we would spend every single minute that day with Sally, and I think now that she probably also knew the same thing.

Sally always spoke to Mother and Grannie when she arrived. After they exchanged a few brief remarks, Sally got right to work. She worked quickly. When clothes were washed, they were hung on the clothesline to dry; and though they smelled so good when they were taken in, they were always wrinkled. Sally brought them to a table to sprinkle them, and the whole room smelled of sunshine and fresh air. She shook each piece of clothing and methodically laid it in a smooth layer on top of the others. When all of the clothes were spread out, she dipped her long graceful hand into a bowl of water, cupped it slightly to hold water, and with precision and skill, sprinkled each item, quickly rolled it, and placed it in a stack with all of the other pieces to be ironed.

Sally McDaniel rests in her front yard

Early that morning, Sally started a fire in the backyard. She wanted it to burn down and form a bed of hot, smoldering embers that she would use to heat the "smoothing irons." Those irons were very hot, so the person ironing had to be very careful not to scorch the clothes. There were no electric irons then with built-in controls to regulate the heat; neither were there washing machines and dryers. Several years later, our washday took on a different face and required much less effort because we were able to purchase a used Maytag wringer-type washer. We drew water from the well on the kitchen porch to be used in the washer as well as for the zinc tubs used to rinse the clothes. Afterward, the rinse water was taken in buckets to the front porch to water the potted plants.

The ironing board was a piece of one- by twelve-inch board that had been shaped and padded. Sally brought two chairs from the kitchen and carefully rested each end of the board on the backs of the chairs. Weights such as pieces of firewood were placed on the seats of the chairs to keep them from tipping over under the weight of the ironing board and the ironing process. She ironed beneath the chinaberry tree's pleasant shade until late in the afternoon. The fire was nearby and convenient for her to put the cooled iron back into its embers as she reached to get another hot one. Sallie was probably the best ironer anywhere around. There were never any "cat faces" (small ironed-in wrinkles) in the clothes that she ironed. Since the iron was made completely of metal, the person ironing protected her hand by placing a heavy pad of cloths around the handle. Sally cleaned the ashes and soot off the iron by rubbing it over waxed paper that had once been the wrapper for a loaf of bread. That process gave the iron a waxy smoothness. On other days when we had no waxed paper, she used cedar boughs to do the same thing—and what a delightful aroma came as she rubbed the hot irons over the cedar!

When the day ended, there were large stacks of beautifully ironed clothes. But the really wonderful part of the day was that we children had spent the day with Sally—all day! We laughed and talked, and sometimes she let Wrenn and me practice ironing on a handkerchief or a pillowcase. As dusk began to fall, we walked home with a very tired Sally, yet she always took a bucket of water home with her for their drinking purposes. Even after we were grown and married, we never forgot this wonderful woman from our childhood. Indeed, we looked forward to seeing her when we went back home. I stopped by her house to visit one day just a little while before she died. She was sitting on the front porch in the sunshine eating her lunch: peanut butter right out of the jar. She did not recognize me at first. She thought I was my mother. I understand now why she confused the two of us. I sometimes see myself in the mirror and wonder when Mother came.

We had a good visit talking about days of long ago and about all the people who have died; her husband Ed was one of them. She told me that her heart was not too good. I had always loved Sally, and somehow I felt that this was the time that I should tell her so. I did tell her, and I added that I sometimes think I may have loved her as much as or more than I loved my mother. She was embarrassed, and quickly chided me as she said, "Miss Sara Ann, you know you didn't love me more than Miss Bessie!" Her hands were still long and graceful, and she still possessed those wonderfully charming ways that drew us to her in the first place. Before I left, I slipped a little money into her hand. Oh, how I wished that it could have been a million dollars!

So as I ironed on Monday, I chuckled to myself as I realized again that I am one of the few people who still make starch out of powdered starch—and I still sprinkle my clothes and roll them into tight rolls before I iron them. I love it when people tell me how beautiful Gerald's shirts look, and it was Sally who taught me! Thank you, my friend!

The windows are in, the sod is all laid, the clothes are all ironed, and I spent another magical, happy day in the presence of a very special lady: Sally!

Going Home Again

I went to see my sister Wrenn last week. She is a patient in the Sumter Nursing Home in York, Alabama, about eighteen miles from the house in which my mother, my siblings, and I were born and grew up. I love that part of rural Alabama. Small rolling hills stretch as far as the eye can see, interrupted occasionally by small clusters of homes, a church, or maybe even a small country store with a gasoline pump out front. As I drove along those country roads, I stepped back several decades to the days of my childhood and adolescence. I felt content and tranquil. I was wrapped in a state of reverence as I revisited the place of my birth—lost in a collage of vivid memories of my family, my forebears, and my roots.

My reverie was interrupted by the realization that though so many things presently remain just as they were then, there are many drastic and significant changes. The Methodist church where I worshipped as a child and where my husband and I were married no longer stands. Grass covers the spot where once stood the country store in which I worked as a teenager. Many of the houses where my friends lived are gone—as are many of the folks who lived inside them. House trailers have replaced tenant shacks that once were scattered about the fields and pastures. Dirt roads have been paved, and nobody thinks twice about driving fifteen miles to Livingston. When I grew up, it was a special treat to drive even five miles to Emelle, let alone fifteen to Livingston—and the trip to Emelle was certainly never made on a daily basis.

Timber has been harvested from many of the rolling hills once covered by heavy forests, and in their place stretches lush pasture land upon which cattle graze. Large lakes and ponds now replace the numerous small pools once used to hold water for livestock. A county garbage service now makes regular pickups. It is interesting that a countywide water system came into existence shortly after the largest toxic waste dump in the world moved in just north of Emelle—even though there was supposed to be no danger for residents in the area.

Aside from the above changes, as large as they are, I began to focus on what I have personally observed over the past several decades in the lives of the African Americans in the community. During my childhood, the population ratio of black to white was seven to one. It may be even more today. My family was not wealthy, but we owned nearly a thousand acres that were farmed by a number of black tenant farmers who lived in small crude houses scattered across the farm. The large two-story house in which our family lived was the center of everything that took place on the farm.

As one of the children living in the landowner's house, I heard conversations and experienced emotions that were confusing to me. I loved and respected my grandmother. We lived in her house from the time we were born until we married and moved away into our own homes. Grannie supported Mother and us children financially for as long as she could. Little by little, however, I began to realize that there were huge inconsistencies in her attitudes toward black people. She had dreadful nightmares about "a Negro man" who was inside the house and threatening to do her harm. She dreamed that he teased and toyed with her, causing her fear to become almost unbearable. And yet she trusted and relied heavily upon "Took" Mitchell and Ed McDaniel in making decisions regarding the farm, the cattle, or a new tenant who wanted to move onto the place. On many occasions she said out loud (and in front of us children) that "Negroes have no souls." Still, even more often, she called to black people who lived on our place as they walked past our house to come get something to eat. She was concerned when any of them were sick. She loaned them money that she kept recorded in a journal until the debt was paid. I do not believe that she ever cheated any of "her" farmers out of a single penny.

The few remaining shacks along the way brought back memories of white men who sexually took advantage of black women, often resulting in births of children who would never be recognized or claimed by their father; nor would they be considered eligible for any of his wealth. As I rode I recalled the day that my father and a neighbor went to the field where a black man was working. I do not know what he had done to draw their wrath, but after dragging him from the field, they beat him brutally with an ax handle. Daddy later showed us the spot along the shoulder of the road where they had beaten the man. A large area in the shoulder-high Johnson grass growing in the ditch and along the road had been wallowed out from the thrashing laid on by the two men—and from the black man's efforts to avoid the blows of the ax handle. For months after hearing the account of that inhumanity, I felt anxious and uneasy as we passed the place where the grass was not standing upright. I knew what had happened there. Even today, I experience that same sick feeling in the pit of my stomach as I pass that spot. There are no marks there to remind me now, but I know the spot, and the memories still hurt.

Other vivid scenes began unfolding! A quarrel between a black man who had "come back home from the North" and a young white man from Emelle ended with the black man's being shot. As the black man ran, he fell onto the back porch of the country store where I was working. He lay there in the cold night air, wounded and unattended. After the local merchants closed their businesses, Mr. Fred Stegall, who was often referred to as a "Nigger lover," went home, hitched his trailer to the back of his car, and returned. He loaded the man onto his trailer, covered him with a worn tarpaulin and hauled him to Hill Hospital in York, Alabama. No words can describe the fear, the anger, the sick feeling that settled over the community that night.

July 4, 1930, just before I was born in November, was the date of a race riot that took place in Emelle. A black man who had moved away to the North had returned to visit relatives still living in the community. One of the local white men thought his attitude was "mighty uppity." Things deteriorated to a place where the white man was shot dead. The men of the community, with the exception of one or two, formed a posse that night and headed west of Emelle to the area known as the Flat Woods. My father was one of those men. White women and children locked themselves inside their homes for safety. Black people did the same. Some of the Black folks even fled their homes and hid in the woods. A black man was murdered that night. He was hanged, and then shot numerous times. I heard the men talk of that event many times. They laughingly said that the sheriff reported that a black man was running through the woods when his tie caught on the branch of a tree—and he was hanged! Then a bull with long horns gored the poor man to death.

These memories brought me no comfort—they never have. My

earlier contentment as I drove through that lovely countryside was replaced by the realization that much of the same seething hatred still lives in the hearts of some Emelle people—but it is not limited to Emelle. Sumter County's government rests today in the hands of African Americans, and white landowners are now at their mercy. It's true; many of the black people in their newly elected offices with their new responsibilities are most likely inept when compared to the earlier county leaders who had governed for generations. But there are enough black voters now to elect the candidate of their choice. Quite legitimately, I think, the black folks must have asked, "How long must we endure the inhumanities that we have experienced for so many years, and all because we are black? How many more worn clothes and old food must we accept as a day's pay for taking care of children, ironing, cooking, and cleaning?" I am convinced that the acceptance of one race by another cannot be legislated—not now, not ever! I do not offer a solution to this thorny issue, for I have none. What I do know is that there are great disparities between the world's peoples, and there will likely always come some form of reformation when any people reach the place that they believe themselves to be superior to others.

Yes, I revisited home, and I was pained at how much I miss the days of my childhood. Things were simple then—at least for me. I understand now that life was good for some of us, and I grieve for others whose lives were not. I have been privileged, from early in my life to the present, to know some very dear people who just happened to be born inside black skins—and I loved them. I cherish my memories of them, even though I was too naïve and far too protected to know or comprehend their pain.

On Passions or being Passionate

I have had many passions through the years—many of which have been adjusted, compromised, and/or replaced. Each of these passions demanded my best, as they in turn became the new and compelling drive in my life. Lines from a popular song some years ago seem to describe this waxing and waning process as my passions came and went: "When I'm not near the one I love, I love the one I'm near." I might well be regarded as a chameleon as my dedication and attention shifted from passion to passion.

As a new Christian, I became passionate about my faith. I committed all that I knew of myself to God, and I made every effort to live in such a manner that friends would see Him reflected in my life. I purposed to be a faithful child of God.

Upon entering college, I was passionate about my preparation for a life in Christian service. I worked hard to be a good student. My educational passion ended with graduation as I completed my BA degree in Christian Education. I recognized a pattern that was becoming more and more evident because I continued my struggle to be the best, or at least among the best, in whatever place I found myself.

Then came the passion of my life: my husband. He was committed to a lifetime of Christian ministry. Since studying was not his favorite endeavor, he quickly found himself in danger of being asked to leave school because of unsatisfactory grades. At that point I discovered another passion: that of keeping this wonderful man in school and focused on his goal. I went to Asbury College's Dean Kenyon and President Johnson to ask a special dispensation of grace in the form of a probationary period for Gerald. My grades were good, and I promised to do everything in my power to help Gerald get serious regarding his preparation for a life in ministry. I am not yet certain why those two men granted a second chance, but they did, and Gerald and I proved their decision to be a good one.

Asbury's social rules worked in our favor. Couples who were dating were not permitted to be together anywhere on campus before dinner. However, there was one exception to that rule, and it was exactly what we needed—we were allowed to study together all day in the library. As the library opened each morning, Gerald and Sara were there, and that is where we were every moment except when we were in class. Many long, loving glances were exchanged, but there was still time for concentrating on studies. Grades came up, and the young man who became my husband two years later was finally on the road to becoming a remarkable and unforgettable minister. My passion has probably taken on varied characteristics through these fifty years, but my passion for Gerald Munday and his wellbeing remains intense.

There are many areas in which I could have been a better mother, but this never compromised my passion for our children. I worked hard to create and maintain stability, nurturance, and standards that would undergird their very foundations as they grew into stalwart, productive people. What a joy to watch, in turn, their passions for each of their children and grandchildren!

Gerald and I together created a shared passion: that of having him become the best minister he could be. We agreed that he must complete his seminary studies of three years' postgraduate work, although we understood that this would require far more money than we had. It had been two years since Gerald graduated from college, and we were the parents of two children. It was obvious that I needed to look for employment. A student pastor's salary would not provide adequately for our family—not to mention paying seminary costs.

Gerald was given a student appointment to Epworth Methodist Church in Phenix City, Alabama, and I found a job as a seventh grade math teacher. I had no qualifications for the job since my degree was in Christian Education, which did not require the first hour of math. Math was my best subject in high school, and I took all that was offered; still, my qualifications were limited. However, as glaring as my limitations were, I made a promise to myself that my students would be as academically prepared as Jamie Weathington's, the other seventh grade math teacher, who had many years of teaching experience in her favor. I sought her experienced, educated counsel frequently, and she was always helpful. I further promised myself that the children in my classes would at least be exposed to some rudimentary elements of morality, citizenship, and faith.

About that time or possibly a few years earlier, legislation and court decrees made clear that church and state would be kept separate. There would be no more Scripture reading or praying at the beginning of the school day. The half-hour allocated for homeroom was, for the most part, wasted. Wasting time was never acceptable to me, so I determined that we would implement a pleasant, positive activity during homeroom. Upon discussing the possibilities, the students decided that I should read Dale Evans' little book *Angel Unaware* each morning until we finished it. We cried our way through that very tender story, and there were wonderful opportunities for further discussions—and other equally positive programs followed.

Roy Screws, who came from a very conservative holiness background, was in my homeroom. When he learned that I was a minister's wife, he frequently stood outside the classroom door with me while students changed classes. Most of the time, he wanted to discuss matters of faith—his faith. One weekend, as he rode his small motor scooter, he was hit by an automobile and critically injured. It was not surprising that he suffered head injuries since helmets were not required then, and according to the doctors, "too many broken bones to count." I was called almost as soon as the accident happened, and I went immediately to the hospital. Roy was unconscious for weeks. I visited him every day at lunchtime. His family of faith always included me as we prayed daily for his restoration to health.

After each visit to the hospital, my students in all six sections of math wanted to know about Roy's condition. His recovery was of such lengthy duration, I intentionally began sharing any news of his fight for life at the beginning of every class. I shared what I knew of Roy's faith and that of his family. Strictly speaking, I knew that I was probably stepping over the dividing line that separated learning from religion. I attempted to be completely open and fair in those rather controversial times of reporting. Before each faith chat, I made it clear that if any student was offended or threatened in any way, then I would give that student permission to go across the street to register his or her complaint with the Superintendent of Schools, Mr. David Self. Not a single child ever asked to go. Roy lived and returned to school, where his classmates helped and encouraged him as he struggled to catch up with his studies. I was privileged some years later to encounter some of those seventh graders who were all grown up. I was delighted that they remembered me, and I was doubly thrilled by their expressions of appreciation for the time spent in my classroom. My passion for teaching seventh graders was replaced as I resigned from my position when my husband was appointed to another city, where I sought and obtained different employment.

I was first a social worker with the welfare department in Mobile, and later in Montgomery. Those skills were priceless when I worked with inner-city children as program director for the YWCA during the time when racial tensions were explosive. It only took a short time as the volunteer Executive Director of the South Mississippi AIDS Task Force in Biloxi before I learned that my heart was not in being an administrator, but in working with people requiring services. In most of my jobs, I focused on people whose needs were large—some even insurmountable! It was my privilege to become agent/advocate on my clients' behalf; bringing relief where it was possible; sharing joys that were few; crying when nothing more could be done. I worked at being available and listening to my clients, because I never wanted to miss an opportunity to assure them of my commitment. This passion has not dimmed.

My other passions, such as counted cross-stitch, gardening, refinishing furniture, and ironing, probably seem trite or commonplace when a word as strong as passion is used, but nonetheless, I am passionate about these also. I am learning that passions often require physical stamina; and as I grow older, I am becoming convinced that passions quietly siphon physical energy away, and that energy is not missed until it is needed. I am passionate enough about ironing that I still make my own starch, sprinkle the items with water, and roll them into tight rolls before ironing them—and my ironing is usually "caught up." Gardening and cleaning and refinishing old and dear pieces of furniture could easily demand all of my time if I were physically up to it, but I find now that I must content myself with smaller doses of these activities on a less regular basis.

Perhaps my real passion was summed up long ago, before I was born or even thought about—when Jesus talked about loving God and loving our neighbors. Those things about which I have really been passionate seem to fall easily around my faith or in opportunities to serve my neighbors, God's children. These ongoing passions are consuming, demanding both hard work and commitment. My faith, my devotion to my husband, my love for our children, and my service to my fellow man have always required the best that I have to offer—*may it ever be so!*

Where Is He?
My Christmas Quest

Christmas morning, like any other winter morning, was dark and cold at our big plantation house in rural Alabama. We children stirred earlier than usual beneath the heavy quilts that held us almost motionless beneath their weight. We turned as best we could in our warm cocoon, all the while asking, "Is it time to get up yet?" or "How much longer do we have to stay in bed?" After what felt to us like an eternity, Mother and Grannie got out of bed, went to the fireplace, and removed the ashes covering hot, smoldering embers from the previous day's fire. After adding crumpled newspaper, kindling, and firewood that had been brought in the night before, they sat quietly in rocking chairs near the hearth, stretching their open palms toward the flames as they waited for the fire to bring warmth and light into the room. Only as they began to feel some semblance of warmth from the fireplace was it time for us to get out of bed.

It never took long for us to dress on winter mornings because it was always cold! Our clothes had been carefully laid out the night before—and even though the fire blazed brightly, the room was far from being warm. While we dressed, we placed our shoes and socks as close to the fire as was safe so the cold that had penetrated them throughout the long, dark night would melt away. It felt good beyond description to slip our cold feet into the warmth of our shoes and socks.

While we got dressed, Mother lighted a kerosene lamp and went to the living room, which was across the wide hall from the bedroom. Wood brought in the day before was carefully laid for a fire, so all Mother had to do was ignite the crumpled paper and kindling underneath the wood. When she felt that the fire was "catching up," she returned to the bedroom to wait with us until some of the winter chill had been chased from the living room.

Finally, we went across the hall to where the Christmas tree stood. We had waited so long in eager anticipation of this day. Much of the night had been spent in sleepless expectation as we listened for the chiming of the clock that announced the slow passage of every half-hour. Mother went ahead of us to the living room. Maybe it was because she held the kerosene lamp that provided light for us to find our way though our dark house; or perhaps it was because she wanted a ringside seat to observe our genuine pleasure and sheer delight as we discovered one by one the gifts so carefully chosen for each of us and lovingly tucked beneath the boughs of the cedar tree brought in from our farm.

Many hours had been spent in preparation for this glorious day. The house was cleaned and decorated, mostly by us children. I wonder now why Mother and Grannie did not at least direct this task, or maybe even lend some assistance—but they did not. It was usually my brother Burton and I who walked the fields looking for the perfect Christmas tree. We forgot from one year to the next that a tree always appeared much smaller in the open field under the vast winter sky than inside our living room. Dragging the tree from where it had grown in the fields back to our house was a big job for a young boy and a teenage girl, and both of us were exhausted when we got home.

My sister Wrenn and I tied fresh cedar boughs along the stair rail in the front hall, up the first flight of steps, across the landing, and up the second flight of stairs—all the way to the top. We tipped the ends of the cedar needles with snow made from Ivory Soap flakes. This snow was made by adding a small amount of water to the Ivory flakes, then painstakingly whipping it with a hand-turned egg beater until stiff peaks were formed. Its snow-white beauty was not only gorgeous, but it lasted as long as the decorations were in place. The aromatic fragrance of evergreen filled every corner of every room in our house. It was wonderful.

As Burton got older and became more accurate with his gun, he shot bunches of mistletoe out of the tops of some of the tall trees on our farm. Oh, yes, we knew the tradition. We hung sprigs in obvious places, but I do not remember that anyone ever kissed or got kissed by standing underneath it. Public demonstrations of affection by lovers were frowned upon; therefore, we just dreamed and giggled!

But somehow during this season of joy, there always seemed to be something missing for me. I was possessed by a strange sadness, a longing that I could not explain. Was it because I knew that Mother struggled every single day to meet her financial responsibilities? And was I feeling that she had really worked much too hard to provide as generous a Christmas for us as she could? Was she giving when she could little afford it? Was it because I wanted to give to every member of our family until the emptiness that I was feeling would be filled?

Grannie returned to her bed on Christmas morning, and I took her gifts to her. There she sat, still clad in her flannel nightgown, with her long, frail hands folded in her lap. Her hair was caught away from her face in a long braid that hung down her back. She did not appear eager to open the gifts that I had placed before her. Instead she said in a voice heavy with tears, "And just think—that precious Baby was born in a barn!" Her observation and vocal commentary of this special day only added to my empty longing!

Later in the morning, when daylight had fully dawned, one by one the tenant farmers living on our place came to the back door. They rapped loudly on the wooden doorsteps while calling out in a loud voice, "Christmas gift, Miss Sallie! Christmas gift!" Grannie invited them to come inside by the fire where it was warm. They removed their hats, stood politely beside the fireplace, and talked briefly. As their visit drew to a close, Grannie instructed one of us children to bring a large bag filled with apples, oranges, raisins (with seeds and still on the vine), and maybe some English walnuts as a Christmas gift for each farmer and his family. Each in turn expressed gratitude for the fruit, and returned to their homes.

Years passed. Even though I was married to a wonderful man, and had a family of my own, those same haunting feelings prevailed. In talking with family members and friends about this holy season I frequently declared, "Someday I am going to become brave enough to celebrate Christmas the way I believe it should be celebrated." However, even as I spoke, I had no plan as to the "how" to celebrate because I still did not know what was missing. Still I continued my search for that significantly special nugget that had eluded me for most of my lifetime.

Could it be that I had been asking the same question that the Wise Men from the East asked on the first Christmas? "Where is He that is born King of the Jews?" And could it be that the simple explanation of their visit, "We have come to worship Him!" expressed and continues to express my own longing to worship Him?

Perhaps I looked in all the wrong places. Mangers remind us of the place where Jesus came to dwell among men, but the baby is lifeless. He is not there! The star atop the tree speaks of the star that led the Wise Men to the birthplace of the Prince of Peace, but the star on the tree is fixed—there is no movement, and it does not bid me to follow! Angels attached to lampposts that line our city streets stir memories of the Heavenly Choir, and though I pause to listen, I do not hear the lovely melody of "Glory to God in the highest, and on earth peace, goodwill to men!"

The trappings are here, but I have failed to find Him in the obvious places. Could it be that the ache within my soul is the result of a deeply embedded fear that I, like King Herod, might be sending others to find this One Who has been born among us? Perhaps I need to hear the voice of another angel—that heavenly being who guarded the empty tomb, greeted the grief-stricken women who came to prepare His body for burial, and announced to them, "The One Whom you seek is not here! He grew to manhood! He became your risen Savior! He has gone before you with the clear directive to follow Him!"

Did Jesus not charge us with the care of widows, orphans, and those who are sick, naked, hungry, or in prison? He said that when we take care of the least of these, we are caring for Him. Did He not always relate to and spend time with those who were downtrodden, dispossessed, and cast out? Could it be that I will come upon Him where people suffer—among those made homeless along the Mississippi Gulf Coast by Hurricane Katrina? Or in Pakistan among the thousands of people still in shock following the earthquake and grieving the loss of family and friends? Or is He among the frightened people of Africa who face certain death from HIV/AIDS, or their orphaned children who struggle to survive as well as to raise their younger brothers and sisters because there is no one to assume the responsible role as parents? Or can I find Him among the lonely men and women who are far from families this Christmas because they have been deployed by the military to the battlefields of Iraq or Afganistan? Or is He in the Intensive Care Unit with parents shattered by overwhelming grief since learning that their child faces certain death unless a viable organ becomes available for a transplant? I think it is becoming evident that the Son of God can always be found at the point of mankind's pain, suffering, and need.

Is it possible that my journey is nearing completion? Am I beginning to glimpse my destination? This year, I want to remember my countless blessings and be thankful! I want to share what I have with those who have so little! I shall listen intently to hear the angels sing of "peace on earth!" I shall pray that the One Who came as the Prince of Peace will dwell in me—leading, directing as I seek Christmas and the Child who brought it! I shall search diligently for my clear revelation as to exactly *where he is—for I have come to worship him!*

Perseverance Wins Out

What causes a person to stick to a task until it is done, regardless of how difficult or distasteful it becomes? One of the basic values learned early on from my parents and grandmother was that *responsible* people can always be *trusted* to accomplish the work that has either been assigned to them or that they have agreed or volunteered to do. This philosophy suggests that completed work and finished products should be a normal expectation from jobs and projects that have been started.

This thinking seems to be at cross-purposes with what many people are doing today, for I often hear admissions that a task was begun years ago, and the same task remains incomplete—even to this day. Sometimes numerous projects have been started, and none of them have yet become a finished product. I am not certain why such behavior disturbs me, but it does. I personally have few, if any, jobs waiting for their finishing touches. Perhaps I am one of those people born with a built-in compulsion to just "get it done." Sometimes I am so driven to complete a task that I press on, maybe even rush through, just to get it behind me. I am not trying to make the case that one of these positions has any virtue over the other. Who can say?

Miss Eltie Haynie directed our high school senior play, in which I was cast as Demopolis Demijohn, the black maid. After we had done our "amateur" best, and the play was history, I asked Miss Haynie if she would sign my playbook along with the cast. I don't remember everything that she wrote, but there were some particular words that caught my imagination back then. They still do. She wrote: "Perseverance wins out!" My grandmother would never have said it so properly and succinctly. She more likely would have said, "Constant dripping wears away stone!" But however it was said, in my idealistic and adolescent thinking, I was certain those words meant that anything I wanted could be mine with enough effort, persistence, perseverance, and hard work.

Passage of time has brought even more reality to such thinking. The youthful idealism that I embraced so long ago tends to dim in the light of those things that life's lessons have taught. St. Francis of Assisi talked about "things I cannot change" as well as "wisdom to know the difference" between things that I can change and things that I cannot. I could and should have learned lessons along that line long ago—on my own—if I had only paid attention.

When I started to school, I never considered what a huge improvement riding to school in a school bus was over riding to school in a buggy or on horseback. That improvement became even more spectacular in cold or rainy weather. That giant leap forward occurred in one generation. My mother rode a horse or traveled by buggy to school. Though riding a school bus was evidence of real progress, it still was not a solution without flaws. Our route consisted of miles of dirt roads, and when the winter rains came, travel became very difficult, if not impossible. Parts of the route were not driven at all in bad weather. Even though the worst of the roads were avoided, the bus did sometimes slip from the road into one of the ditches that ran along both sides for drainage purposes.

Once in the ditch, the driver made every effort to get back onto the road. He carefully and patiently shifted the gears from forward to reverse, rocking the bus back and forth, each time spinning the wheels in an effort to get the vehicle back onto the road. It only took one time for us to learn that we could not push the bus—for when we went to the back to push, the spinning of the tires threw mud and water, muddying anyone behind the bus from head to toe. No amount of persistence or perseverance on our part was able to move that bus from the ditch to the road. The only way to right the bus was if one of the few local tractors or a team of mules or horses pulled it from the mire. The lesson that I failed to learn on those days was that *some things need help from the outside!* There are times when no amount of perseverance will change the situation!

The route to school turned south after leaving Sumterville. The Vaughan children were picked up just outside Sumterville, then the Killingsworths, then on to the Nixons' house, where Breezy, Carolyn, and Annette came on board. There were still several miles of dirt road between the Nixons and the paved road. Acres of pasture land stretched on each side as we continued toward school. Just after crossing the wooden bridge that spanned a large creek, we came quickly to a ninety-degree turn to the left. After slowing to make that very sharp turn, and downshifting to low gear, we began the immediate climb up Shiloh Hill. The hill was both long and steep, and we always held our breath in hopes that the bus might *not* make it to the top. And some days, sure enough, it didn't! After getting partway up, the bus would sputter, then choke, and finally die. When that happened, everybody began to cheer and start for the aisle to get off the bus. Mother was our school bus driver, and she calmly instructed us to return to our seats. When everything quieted down, she carefully let the bus roll back to the bottom of the hill. A narrow pasture road turned right at the corner where we had turned left, which made it possible for Mother to roll the bus a bit further away from the hill. She started the bus again, revved up the motor, put the bus in low gear, and made another run for it, only to meet with the same results: sputter, choke, and die! After several more runs at the hill with the same results, the school bus came to rest at the bottom of the hill.

On cold rainy days we stayed inside the bus huddled together to keep warm, but on nice sunny days, Mother flung the bus door open and we all clamored outside. In the springtime, we looked for violets, blackberries, or wild plums. Sometimes we just threw clods of dirt into the water flowing underneath the old wooden bridge. There were persimmons in the fall, but we knew to eat them only after there had been a frost; otherwise they were so sour they "would make a pig squeal."

Those outings were fun while they lasted, but we knew our holiday would be short-lived. When our bus was late getting to school, Joe Alexander, mechanic for the County Board of Education, would soon come looking—always with extra gasoline. All buses were fueled on a regular basis, but our school bus was different from the others: it had a square, flat gas tank. As the gas level lowered with usage and the tank neared empty, there sometimes was not enough gasoline to flow to the motor as we headed up the steep, steep hill at the Shiloh church. The gasoline ran to the back of the tank instead of to the motor, which caused the bus to react as though it were out of gas. Thank goodness, Mr. Alexander understood this eccentricity, and his gas can was kept in readiness. As soon as he poured the precious liquid into the tank, we knew our holiday was ended. We reluctantly climbed back aboard the bus, feeling a bit deprived because we knew that momentarily we would be leaving our brief escape from accountability. Mother pumped the accelerator a few times, the bus motor roared to life and relentlessly made its way to the top of the hill and turned right, and very soon, we were checking into school. No amount of perseverance could get that bus up the hill—only Mr. Alexander and his gas can.

"Perseverance wins out!" I suppose I believed that when I was seventeen. Now I am not so sure. It has been said that the beauty of youth is that they do not know that some things cannot be done, so they go ahead and do them anyway. It seems to me that the flipside of that premise is the tragedy of old age, when old folks do not believe that some things can be accomplished; therefore, worthwhile tasks go undone.

I am confused as to why I am besieged by these scrambled thoughts. Why do they plague me? Am I feeling guilty because I have failed to assume more responsible roles? Have I left too much undone? Do I need to be doing something that I am not? Are my thoughts drifting into these areas because I am well into the autumn of my life, and almost daily I hear statements like "Do Not Resuscitate" and "giving permission to die"? When should we quit? When is it time to stop? Each day the war in Iraq worsens and the American people continue to ask, "Is 'staying the course' what we should do?" On the other hand, should there not be time constraints when it comes to keeping our young men and women in that dangerous spot where life appears to be dirt cheap? Am I searching for new perspectives? Am I discovering and reestablishing personal priorities? I know beyond any doubt that I am not content to live within "the status quo"—never have been; therefore, I continue to work toward that time when God is in charge and men cease to behave as wild animals. So I work and wait for that better day! In the meantime, I struggle, as did Saint Francis when he talked about *changing the things he could, accepting the things he could not change, and the wisdom to know the difference.*

In conclusion, therefore, I prayerfully request:
Wisdom that I shall understand when I am winning;
Strength to press on and persevere; and
Grace to obediently stop at the appropriate time.

Time to Go Home

Some of the happiest days from my early childhood ended with the instructions: "Let's get ready. It's time to go home." Those words, without fail, evoked deep and earnest pleading from us children as we begged, "Do we [or you] have to go now? Can't we play just a little longer? Aw, please, please! Don't make us go home!"

Growing up in the country without close neighbors was often very lonely. We longed to live near to a friend, or anybody for that matter, with whom we could visit and share happy times—someone other than family members. It wasn't that we disliked each other, for we often played board games together, and we occasionally shared in doing our assigned chores, but sometimes we got lonely to "visit" with "other people."

I remember one very special dark winter day when I was eight or nine years old. Much of that day is a blur now, but I am able to recreate some of it with great clarity. I am not certain whether we were at home because school had been cancelled due to such cold, stormy weather, or whether it was during the Christmas holiday, but for whatever reason, we were at home. Grannie, Wrenn, Burton, and I were in Grannie's big bedroom located on the front of the house. A roaring fire blazed in the huge fireplace, bringing warmth and light into the room. We huddled near the friendly, welcoming hearth as we tried to think of some fun activity to fill the long, dreary hours stretching between us and another bedtime. I don't know which of us saw the answer first, but I do know that our discovery thrilled us beyond anything that words could describe.

As we looked from Grannie's bedroom window, we could not have been more shocked or delighted if we had been looking at Santa Claus and his eight tiny reindeer. We watched transfixed as a heavily laden horse slowly made its way up the rise beside the mailbox at the road and approached our front porch. It did not take long to recognize the riders: Aunt Lally, Jane, Drew, and Lawrence—all on the same horse. We ran to the front porch to greet them as they dismounted. We children quickly rushed back inside to gather about the warmth of the fireplace. Mother and Aunt Lally went to put the horse inside the barn where there would be some protection against the cold, damp day.

Mother and Aunt Lally had been childhood friends. Their adult lives had paralleled in weddings, children, and families—even having children who were approximately the same ages. Grannie and Mrs. Fulton, Aunt Lally's mother, had been friends for many years, so the bond of love and friendship existing between the families was one of long standing. Once inside the house, Aunt Lally explained as she removed her heavy wraps that they were tired of staying inside because of the bad weather, so she and the children decided to come spend the day with us.

Her announcement of such good news dispelled any gloom that had so recently hung heavy in that same room. We had company, and they were going to spend the day! There was no time to waste. Preparations began for the day that had earlier seemed so bleak. We lighted the fire laid days before in the living room fireplace. It ignited quickly because the wood was dry. Flames soon danced and crackled up the chimney. The living room was never heated unless we had company. It took extra work and firewood to heat rooms that were not used, so the living room, dining room, and upstairs bedrooms were usually cold. Practicing for my piano lessons was never one of my favorite things, but practicing in our cold living room made matters even worse. Sometimes my fingers felt so cold that I thought they could just freeze and drop off. Lighting was another problem when we practiced at night. We did not have electricity, so in order to have enough light to see the pages of our music book, we placed a hymnbook on the treble end of the keyboard and set a kerosene lamp on it. On very cold evenings, just the small amount of heat from the kerosene lamp was most welcomed.

The six of us children were thrilled to be together. We began to play while Mother, Grannie, and Aunt Lally went to the kitchen to find what was available for our midday meal. Jars of vegetables and fruits that had been canned the summer before were pulled from the pantry shelves and cooked with salt pork brought from the smokehouse. We had hot cornbread and butter at every meal, but on special days, we might also have biscuits with molasses or fig preserves or jelly.

When the dishes were washed and dried and the food put away, the women came into the living room. They talked quietly as they sat by the fire that had finally begun to warm the spacious living room. The fire had burned for several hours and hot ashes filled with live embers glowed along the floor of the fireplace. An unmistakable peace and serenity hovered 'round the hearth. Each of us within its warm glow realized again the bond of love that had held our families so close for several generations. We were caught briefly in a suspended sense of security and wellbeing, all the while dreading the inevitable conclusion of this perfect time.

The days of midwinter are short, and night comes quickly. Not long after we had eaten, we heard again those words that would end our time together: "Get ready, children. It's time to go home." Despite our wails and pleas for just a little more time, the horse was saddled. Coats were donned and fastened securely upon all three children. Aunt Lally mounted into the saddle, Lawrence in front of her, Drew just behind her, and Jane on the very back. With so many bodies wrapped in so much clothing on one horse, it probably would have been easy for the one nearest the back to slip off the tail of the horse, but they each held tightly to the one in front. How empty we felt as we watched the horse carrying that precious cargo carefully place each foot onto the soaked, muddy earth while making its way along the treacherous road that would lead them home. We huddled together with our faces pressed against the windowpanes until they were out of sight; and though we felt a huge emptiness, we each held treasured memories of a wonderful day.

In reliving that day, I am reminded that like children, we still feel the pain of loneliness when we are separated from those we love. Even as adults, if we are fortunate enough to share precious, special days, we still begrudgingly let them go; and our hearts still beg, "Can't you stay a little longer? Do you have to go?"

I'm a lot older now. Am I any wiser? A little, perhaps. Though many things have changed, others have remained constant. Long ago, I childishly thought that when I grew up I would go where I chose, stay as long as I desired, and never again hear and be expected to obey the instructions: "Get ready! It's time to go home!" I mistakenly believed that I would be "in charge." Too often I again feel the piercing pain of imminent separations; and too often my heart cries: "Please don't go! Can't you stay just a little longer? We are not through playing yet!"

Time has a way of coming full circle. When our son Mike was dying, I cried yet again, "Do you have to go now? Can't you stay a little longer? There are still things that we didn't get to do!" And though my heart begged Mike to stay, my mind knew beyond any doubt that it was time for him to "get ready and go Home". So I blessed his departure as much as my heart could bear, and we sent him on his way—our faces still pressed against the window as we watched him go.

As time continues its swift flight, I think of so many worthwhile jobs and projects that I need to begin and complete. Most likely these things are not important to anyone but me, and I know that they assuredly are not vital in the grand scheme of things, but I personally need to know that they are done. How sobering to realize that, like a child, I still spend my days living, loving, playing about so many things—and still like that child, I find myself waiting to hear those same instructions I dreaded to hear so many years ago: "Get ready, children! It's time to go home!"

I Believe

> This life is not righteousness, but growth in righteous;
> Not health, but healing;
> Not being, but becoming;
> Not rest, but exercise.
> We are not yet what we shall be, but we are growing toward it;
> The process is not yet finished, but it is going on;
> This is not the end, but it is the goal.
>
> Martin Luther